The Burma Cookbook

Recipes from the Land
of a Million Pagodas

From Rangoon Burma
to Yangon Myanmar

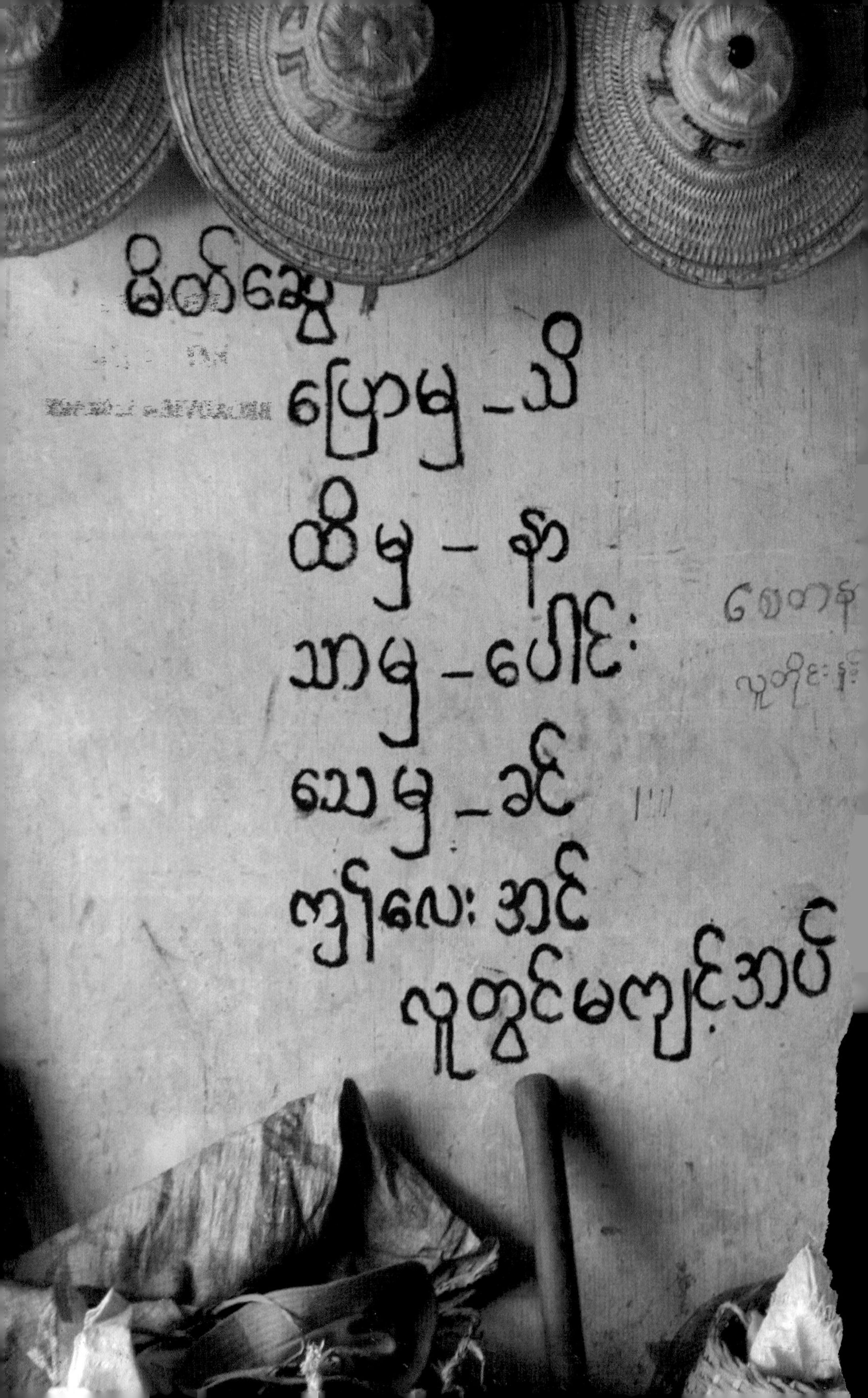

မိတ်ဆွေ

ပြောမှ _ သိ

ထိမှ _ နာ

သာမှ _ ပေါင်း

သေမှ _ ခင်

ကျွန်လေး အာင်

လူတွင်မကျှင်အပ်

ဝေတန
လူတိုင်း

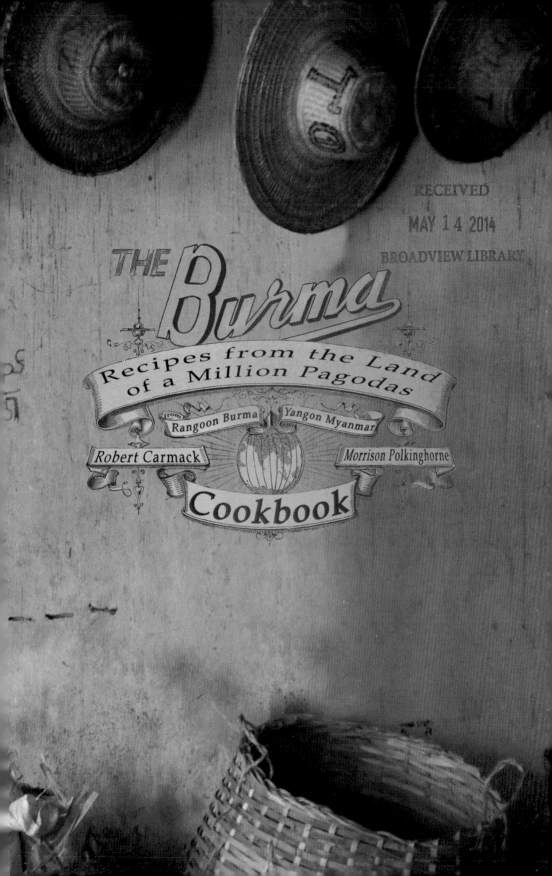

THE *Burma*

Recipes from the Land of a Million Pagodas

from Rangoon Burma to Yangon Myanmar

Robert Carmack · Morrison Polkinghorne

Cookbook

Foreword
by Anne Willan

BURMA is a magical country, brilliantly captured in the words and images of The Burma Cookbook. "If British India was the jewel in the empire's crown, then Burma was its treasury," writes Robert Carmack, and he clearly loves every kilometer of its mountains and rivers, its glimmering temples and the peaceful, welcoming smiles of its people.

I've only been once to Burma (or its modern name Myanmar), a dozen years ago, just long enough to be captivated by the place. How I wish I had had Robert's book in hand. The text weaves in and out of stunning illustrations, many of them historic photographs that must have taken years to compile. Robert's co-author Morrison Polkinghorne is both photographer and the book designer and he leads the eye irresistibly from fishing boats moored peacefully in the setting sun to dinner menus from as recently as 1972 that include long-forgotten favorites such as lobster Thermidor and minute steak.

The historic Strand Hotel on the waterfront of Yangon sums up the essence of the lingering colonial past. Everyone visits The Strand, myself included, and I was transported back to my English girlhood with the ritual of teatime. For more than 100 years, British afternoon tea has been served in that high white salon or on the shaded veranda, the tables set with snow-white cloths. The scones, delicate sandwiches, little cupcakes and fruit slices are arranged variously on classic shiny silver tiers, and shimmering jet black lacquer work tiffin boxes. "Tiffin" is another colonial fixture, that lingers on, both at The Strand, and by school children and workers who daily carry stainless- or enamelware models of this timeless "lunch box." Burma may be a link to the past, but the array of British colonial dishes ~ the mulligatawny, Scotch eggs, and blancmange ~ is misleading. Burma has one of the richest culinary heritages in the world, and Robert and Morrison have been exploring its intricacies for the last fifteen years. Today's Burmese cooking is delicate, with seasoned oil from cooking onion, garlic and ginger the primary flavor, and rarely seasoned with dried spice (as in

India). Dishes embrace half a dozen other traditions, including ethnic Burmese with some regional Shan, Mon and Rakhine specialties. Spices from India are used, but considered rare and Burmese masala is simple compared to the layered flavors of the Indian versions. The fiery salads of Thailand become less assertive in Burma; Chinese inspiration is evident particularly near the border, while a Bangladeshi influence, rich in seafood, comes across the Bay of Bengal.

The Burma Cookbook is a treasure house of recipes, and much, much more. When you simmer up a Burmese style biryani or a fisherman's stew, you will find its history and learn how it has developed into today's edition; and just possibly you might come across an image of the cook stirring it up over the fire. I was delighted to find a recipe for one of my own favorites, kedgeree. This is a country that relies on rice, though noodles creep in too, with a backup of lentils and chickpeas. Much of the cooking is done on the street, implying dishes-in-one such as mixed vegetable salads, with kebabs and other nibbles, croquettes and other deep-fried treats on little plates, chopsticks poised for action on the side. Lots of inspiration, and temptation!

The Burma Cookbook brings the cooking and the country to life. Burma is a beautiful country and this splendid book does it honor. Bravo!

Anne Willan

Founder and President La Varenne Cooking School

VIEW ON A LAKE N

RANGOON. 1824.   *Grierson: Twelve Select Views of the Seat of War.*

Table of Contents

မာတိကာ

Acknowledgments

THIS book is a project undertaking more than a decade of travel and research, over numerous journeys to the Land of a Million Pagodas. Or is it four million? Like so much of Myanmar, the sheer number of things to see and do becomes overwhelming. But it was first the architectural heritage of colonial Yangon that set us on this culinary voyage. In a way this is fitting, for some of the world's great historical chefs were originally architects.

A very special bow to The Strand, Myanmar's dowager hotel, and timeless presence along the shores of the Yangon River. On our first visit to the country so many years ago, we were introduced to its historic charm, setting in train our love for both this hotel, but especially the land and its people. And its heritage. It was Didier Belmonte, particularly, who encouraged us to study the hotel's culinary legacy, working with its chefs to compile a selection of both old and new dishes. In other words, a work of history, instead of just an ethnographic Burmese cookbook. To this we are also indebted to Sukhdeep Singh who cradled the hotel not only through its rebirth in the mid 1990s, but subsequently over the decades. Also to former executive chefs Sandro Zimmermann, who shared his post-colonial adaption for lobster Thermidor among other recipes, and especially Chris Parsons and his team in the kitchens. Long-serving assistant to the chef, Cho Aung Win, spent hours at the desk, instead of the stove, pouring over translations, helping us decipher obscure techniques, and most importantly, explaining flavor profiles. And to food and beverage director Aung Kyaw Swar, who was our liaison for this project. Cheers to the entire staff of The Strand, from rooms to tables, who we pulled in for various photo takes, making everyone a star! As befits a 5-star hotel, its personnel were ever-ready to assist by answering questions, arranging interviews, and even posing as models for so many of the photographs in the book.

We credit the librarians at the Institute of South East Asian Studies (ISEAS) in Singapore for allowing us access to their books, and particularly to Chin Kin Wah for introducing us to this invaluable collection. And to the British National Library in Yangon for opening its closed stacks for our research. Select extracts in this book are from original articles by us in the book *To Myanmar with Love* and *ANA Wingspan* magazine.

Special thanks to photographers Sher-Ali Khan for our great portrait; Nikki To for coming to our warehouse kitchen to shoot select dishes complimenting Morrison's images; and Brett Danton for all his advice on cameras, filters and cropping. Plus to Nick Loh for his design nous, teaching us the skills to personally create the book layout, and thus giving this tome our unique seal.

To Philip Cornwel-Smith for his constant encouragement and clarity of focus, and for introducing us to our publisher, River Books. Constant Reader's Peter Kirby & Martin Nunn generously offered marketing ideas, and Philippa Sandall her legal assistance. Fiona Hall gave a well-appreciated final proof read. Acknowledgments to assistant recipe testers Julio Castellano, Harriet Harcourt, Gino Lopez.

We are indebted to Ian and Liz Hempill of Australia's Herbie's Spices for helping unravel the complexities of curries. Their exceptional knowledge steered us through the multifarious paths of linguistic ambiguity, tracing many a packet of Myanmar masalas to their Indian origins. Gujariti here, Tamil there, Goan elsewhere. Fishmonger par excellence John Susman advised on how to tackle Asian-specific fish to a world-wide audience. Restaurateur Boris Granges suggested wine pairings of Western-style wines to Asian dishes.

And last, but certainly not least, to Di Parks, for editing our recipes, bringing clarity where we offered verbosity. A thankless task, with a tasteful fruition.

Robert Cornwell Morrison

BURMESE DAYS
An Introduction to Myanmar

"Pagun, in Burmah, is certainly, in a sense, the most remarkable religious city in the world. Rome, Benares, Jerusalem, Kieff -- none of these can boast so great a wealth and lavishness of fanes."
-- Pictorial Travels on Land and Sea (1909)

Burmese Days

*"The Burmese are a people infinitely attractive,
and when to-day so large a proportion of mankind
is given up to ideas altogether material and
utilitarian, it is surely something for which to
be thankful that in Burma we can still find
a country which is a garden of wonderful
beauty, and inhabited by a race entirely
in harmony with its surroundings, and who
understand what is meant by the 'joy of living'."*

-- R. Talbot Kelly, *Burma (1933)*

ADEN, Bombay, Madras, Calcutta, Rangoon, Singapore, Penang, Bangkok, Saigon, Hue, Hanoi, Hong Kong, Shanghai. "Their names roll on the tongue savourily, crowding the imagine with sunshine and strange sounds and a multi-colored activity," writes Somerset Maugham, after his travels in the 1920s. These destinations were the Asian equivalent of Europe's Grand Tour -- along the shipping routes to British and French colonies and foreign entrepots alike.

Yangon, formerly Rangoon, has had several incarnations over the ages. Although the famed Shwedagon pagoda traces back 2500 years, the town only much later appropriated the name Dagon in the 11th century, meaning "three hills" in Mon language. It was re-badged Yangon around 1755 when Mon overlords capitulated to Bamar king Alaungpaya. Literally meaning "end of strife" (or war), this was a combination of two words *yan* (enemies) + *koun* (on the run) and later mispronounced "Rangoon" by the British. The city was capital of British Lower Burma from 1862 until the taking of Upper Burma and the fall of the Mandalay throne in 1885. The following year the entire country was annexed to greater British India -- an unhappy marriage linking a Southeast Asian nation in style and spirit to a Subcontinental culture of alien religions -- and Rangoon was relegated to provincial status. Contemporary reports say the city had a backwater feel when compared to vibrant Bombay and Calcutta, and highwaymen known as dacoits terrorized the countryside.

The city regained its capital title in 1938 when Burma seceded from India and became a colony in its own right, and again in 1947 with independence. Always "Yangon" to the Myanma, the city's English name was officially rechristened Yangon in 1988. And while the country's administrative capital relocated inland to Naypyidaw in 2002, Yangon remains the country's largest city and business hub.

This was and is a lucky country, endowed in natural assets, yet stricken with a hidebound economy. Despite all, people outwardly appear content, with Cheshire-cat smiles greeting both visitors and locals alike, and a sincere desire to please and assist, leading American president Herbert Hoover to call them "the only genuinely happy people in all of Asia." Or, as James George Scott wrote in his definitive 1882 book, "The Burman is the most calm and contented of mortals." A sentiment echoed by Rudyard Kipling, when he stated, "Personally, I love the Burman with the blind favoritism born of first impression. When I die I will be a Burman..." Funnily enough, the "appeal" was reciprocated: As Scott, writing under the pen name Shway Yoe, quipped: "The best thing a Burman can wish for a good Englishman is that in some existence, as a reward of good works, he may be born a Buddhist and if possible a Burman."

Indeed, these are an incredibly polite people, who extend both arms in a gesture of etiquette to share the simplest of exchanges. Stoic in their adversity, they are our teachers in humility. Succinctly, travel writer Santha Rama Rau concurred in the mid 20th century: "Of all the countries of Southeast Asia, Burma is probably the one with the most immediate appeal."

If British India was the jewel in the empire's crown, then Burma was its treasury. The Irrawaddy delta was once the rice bowl of Asia, and the land awash in petroleum, gold and gemstones -- from star sapphires and emeralds to the world's most sought after red rubies. Colonial Rangoon was a hive of Scottish expat magnates, and the country attracted foreign entrepreneurs to make their fortunes. For literary riches, seek no further than Rudyard Kipling and George Orwell, the latter spending five years in the country towns of Upper Burma. Somerset Maugham wrote lengthily of his Burmese travels after a bout of malaria.

Today, even after decades of economic deprivation and hardship, this is truly a land of pure gold. The country's gilded shrines glisten under the sun, its pagodas encrusted with 24 karat gilt and priceless gemstones from both government and generous benefactors. Temples shine brilliantly. Shwedagon alone is gilded with some 100,000 pounds of 24-karat leaf (about 45,000 kg) plus crowned with thousands of diamonds, rubies, emeralds, sapphires, and at its apex a 76-carat diamond.

LAND OF FOUR MILLION PAGODAS

"A million." Take a moment to mentally count them. Even if you were to devote a mere second to each number, by the time you verbally calculated one million, some 17,000 thousand hours would transpire, or more than two years in time. The number is vast, and in times prior to fiscal inflation, a seeming infinity. Yet a million's vastness was the impression Burma gave to early visitors, who proclaimed it "the land of four million pagodas." Unlike tiny, landlocked Laos, which was lauded as "land of a million elephants," the Burma of old was, and is, a vast country ~ slightly smaller than Texas, but larger than France or Spain. Its territory ranges some 1200 miles/2000 km miles north to south, from the tropical waters of the Andaman Sea, up to the harrowing heights of the Himalayas. (Hkababo Razzi, towering at 20,000 feet/5119 meters is the loftiest in Southeast Asia.)

Myanmar has been called "The most Buddhist of nations" ~ no doubt because its intrinsic cultural texture appears so little affected by outside modern influences. Traditions and mores remain: Saffron-robed monks with alms bowls are a ubiquitous sight, and delightfully unexpected are the gaily pink-garbed nuns with magenta umbrellas.

> "Any morning on Rangoon's streets you will see the groups of shaven-head priests, monks and acolytes standing before shops and houses, their begging bowls held before them, waiting for whatever food (vegetarian) the devout townspeople may give them."
>
> ~Santa Rama Rau,
> *View to the Southeast* (1955)

This is a land where car license plates were long rendered in native script, and well into the 21st century even the old Imperial Standard for weights and measures remained official. People ubiquitously -- and thickly -- smear cooling *thanaka* bark paste on their face as decorative make-up (witness the Bagan watermelon vendor selling cut slices from a huge platter atop her head, and the flower seller near Mandalay); and men wear *longyi* sarongs to work and play. Or, Shan pants to the east and Naga shawls and loin cloths in the country's west; in its far north you're likely to spot yak wool felt Tibetan attire. This is a union of some 150 dispersed nationalities, although six predominate: Bamar, Shan, Karen, Kachin, Rakhine and Chin. They derive from three distinctly different origins or migrations over the past millennia: Mon-Khmer; Tibeto-Myanmar, and T'ai-Chinese. Burmese (or Bamar/Burman) represent just a 55-60% majority.

This is a country of four million pagodas and two millennia of tradition. It's ancient capital of Bagan/Pagan, sacked by the Mongols in the 13th Century, is considered the soul of Myanmar, much like Sukhothai is the heart of old Siam. Yet there were several major Myanmar kingdoms concurrently vying for power over the past millennia. To the far west in Rakhine state, the Arakan kingdom prevailed along the Bengali coast for some 2000 years, but finally succumbed to Mandalay's conquest in the late 18th century. The Mon, whose capital was based for two centuries in Bago/Pegu prevailed until the Second Burmese Empire. When they capitulated to the Burman throne in 1757, its people dispersed, and today congregate largely in and around Mawlamyine/Moulmein, the country's third largest city. (There are also Mon communities in Thailand, emigrants from both the late 18th and early 19th centuries.) Lording over all, Burma's name represents the largest ethnic majority in this hodgepodge of cultures.

GEOGRAPHY

> "The reason why Burma has grown so enormously since the British connexion is that Britain could not bear to see this no-man's land barring her from direct access to her neighbours. Therefore she prudently extended her administration to meet theirs, before they could do likewise."
>
> -- Capt F. Kingdon Ward, *Jungle-clad Basin of the Irawadi (Countries of the World series)* circa 1923

Falling at the junction where China meets India, Burma was long a geopolitical prize in the Great Game. Yet Burma adopted surprisingly little from either country. To its north mountain ridges and impenetrable jungle made both Indian and Chinese land passage treacherous. Although the famed Tea-Horse Trail of China's remote Yunnan and Sichuan provinces reached as far afield as Mandalay (and Chiang Mai in Thailand), this was passage for single file caravans adept to the terrain, not armies.

Although an historical adversary to neighboring Siam, Burma's culture, then as now, looks East, as befits a Buddhist nation. Upper Burma's cultural and political links to both Thailand's Lanna kingdom, and to Laos' northern capital of Luang Prabang are strong, and even its Shan nationals are ethnic T'ai ~ forerunners to Siam. Borders were fluid, wars frequent, and contacts plentiful.

After independence from Britain in 1947, and a later military coup in 1962, Myanmar retreated into a self-imposed isolation, and this former colony changed little outwardly. Foreign visitors' stays were restricted, first to a mere week, then a fortnight, and eventually four weeks duration. An economic embargo compounded the issue, and the country was often referred to as "a land that time forgot." Consequently nowadays, Yangon's city center is an exquisite architectural time warp, whose crumbling Victorian and Edwardian edifices clad in ivy-like vines choke the city center. In Upper Burma, imperial Bagan's two thousand temples, set amidst a desert-like landscape, date from the 11th century. Exotic-sounding Mandalay is a repository of 19th-century Burmese court traditions. Massive temple walls of the former Arakan kingdom in Mrauk-U are evocative of Medieval European fortresses, and the beauty of the whole country literally photographs itself. Visually and factually, this is a golden land, and its arts and crafts exquisite: from lacquerware to silk weaving, intricate *kalaga* tapestry and marionette carving to silversmithy.

COOKERY

Myanmar's cuisine and cooking culture embraces aspects from all neighbors, while retaining a distinct style unique to Burma alone. From India comes a predilection for dry spices, yet only turmeric and a mild paprika-like chili powder are ubiquitous. Actual curry powders and masala spice, are relatively rare ~ and used on only a scant number of typical dishes, such as the famous *khout shwe* of Shan state. Moreover, a typical Burmese masala of dried spices retains a distinct simplicity compared to the myriad layers of its Indian equivalent. To its east lies Thailand, and its chili-fiery dishes, and vibrantly tart citrus-flavored salads. Yet in Myanmar, the flavors are less assertive ~ chilies larger and milder, lime or lemon used in less quantity, and likely to be tamed or melded with chickpea flour or ground peanut. Indeed, the popularity of pulses delineates Myanmar's foodstuffs from the Southeast, linking it more firmly westward to India, or to China's Yunnan province to its northeast. To the south, along the long isthmus running down the Andaman sea and up the west coast toward Bangladesh, is a rich bounty of seafood, especially crustaceans like the massive spiny lobster, smaller scampi and plump prawns or shrimp. At markets, the fresh-water "butterfish" reigns supreme. This is a large catfish or basa, renowned for its juicy large flakes and delicate texture and taste, and the perfect complement to Burmese curry blends.

With renewed tourism popularity, ever-increasing foreign contact, and increased flights, Myanmar is no more "a forgotten land." Indeed, this is a place the Michelin Guide would rate "worth a detour."

> *"It will be noticed that purely Burmese dishes omit the use of spices, and of curry seeds, e.g. cumin, coriander, mustard, fenugreek, poppy, cullingar, etc., but invariably introduce, instead, the tender green seedlings and spouts of these same ingredients. This process modify the pungency of a dish, and gives it an enhanced fragrance, and a far more delicate flavour, besides preserving its fine light colour, so desirable in any dish, of any nationality."*

~ Olivia, *Burmese National Dishes* (1934)

A WORD ABOUT THE RECIPES

This book is a showcase of Anglo-Burmese recipes, tried and traditional, over the past century. Over some 15 years, we repeatedly traveled across the country sourcing the best cooks and their favorite recipes, plus sampled many regional ethnic specialties. We scoured through archives, researched collections, and sourced personnel for personal reflections and memories, including a taste of early colonial life. The streets of Yangon along Pansodan and Merchant, once teeming with *bouquinistes*, became our second home. Through the national troves of published and private recipes over the past century and a half, we found little kernels like this Letter to the Editor: "the candied pumpkin has dried thoroughly and well, and has also been immediately and entirely eaten up by the whole household, we appreciated it very much." Similar recipes are well worthy of rediscovery.

Classic dishes of the colonial era include Kedgeree, Mulligatawny, Colonial Goose, and even Scotch Eggs and Bombay Duck. While the names may sound familiar if somewhat exotic, those contemporary foods of lore are vibrantly different from today's ethnic fare. But newly refurbished hotels are resurrecting and adapting many such classics nowadays; or in the case of The Strand in Yangon, and The Candacraig in former Maymyo, stalwarts who held the flame over many a dark decade, and dared never to die.

Colonial era cookbooks over-represented Indian and English flavors. During British sovereignty, Myanmar's five largest cities were Indian majority, with the ethnic Bamar largely exiled to their country roots, becoming a dispossessed minority within their own land. As HRH Thai Prince Damrong Rajanubhab observed in 1936:

> "Rangoon is odd in another way because hardly any ethnic Burmese can be seen along the city streets. All the inhabitants would appear to be Indians. There are more Indians among the populace of Rangoon than any other nationality -- as many as two-thirds."

Consequently, Burmese fare has long been incorrectly considered Indian-derivative. Yet it has distinctly different flavor profiles and techniques. On top of that, there are the three historic kingdoms of Myanmar: Bamar, Arakan and Mon, plus its patchwork of some eight major national ethnic races, and some 136 secondary ethnic groups, all of which exert influence on the national cookery.

Authentic ethnic-Burmese, as well as Arakan and Mon dishes, omit Indian dried spices, yet readily incorporate tender sprouts, rhizomes and bulbs. Rarely are such curries fried with a curry powder or equivalent spices, and only a few are sprinkled -- albeit frugally -- with masala spice before serving. Thick-, dark- and light soy sauces indicate Chinese origin or influence; by contrast, Burmans traditionally use fermented fish sauce.

Yet this should not be considered solely as an historical cookbook; rather, it incorporates the timeless recipes of the past as well as the country's delicious present. While the dishes featured here are predominantly ethnic Burmese, they also include some regional Shan, Mon and Rakhine specialties, plus Eurasian, British and Indian favorites, all geared for today's palate. In other words, heritage recipes, all proudly proclaiming "Made in Myanmar."

THE STRAND

ကမ်းနားဟိုတယ်

"Half-an-hour after landing found me very comfortably installed in the Strand Hotel, a roomy bedroom with bathroom attached having been allotted to me, while its large enclosed verandah, which practically formed a sitting-room, gave me ample breathing space; and, making allowance for the latitude, the table-d'hôte was excellent and varied."
-- Burma, by R. Talbot Kelly (1905)

The Strand

O*OH la la, c'est magnifique*, purred the French tourist as she strolled through the lobby of The Strand. Her almost inaudible reflection was muttered to herself, but as an involuntary eavesdropper, I tingled with a special pride. For my partner and I are not a mere sightseers here; instead, something very special: actual houseguests.

"My hotel." The words slide so easily over my lips, an almost subliminal territorial claim.

The Gallic woman was with a small visiting group, treating the property as part of a tourist circuit to colonial Yangon. Some such visitors come for a very British afternoon tea served, variously, on classic shiny silver tiers and shimmering jet black lacquerware tiffin boxes. Others sneak in on the subterfuge of surveying the hotel's gift shops and art gallery. But how does a mere hotel warrant as a must-see stop? The Strand is not ostentatious, and its wicker furnishings less than grand. But its stately colonial Georgian facade oozes history, and The Strand is one of those hotel experiences unique to the annals of heritage travel.

"The sun never sets on the British Empire" goes the old refrain, and the late 19th and early 20th centuries were a vibrant time for entrepreneurs to the region. Colonial Burma was the gem in British India's crown, and in Rangoon, The Strand was its jewel. No property in that city was more prestigious, and it long claimed the title of "Best hostelry east of the Suez." For over a century it hosted the country's most lavish banquets and balls, while supplying lodgings to royalty, glitterati and barons alike. Today, one eerily senses the footsteps of past literary luminaries like Orwell, Maugham, Kipling and Coward traipsing its staid wainscot corridors.

The Strand was a silver-spooned scion of the Sarkies family, Armenian hoteliers who made their name up and down the Malacca Straits and Andaman Sea in an era of colonial expansion. Although Aviet Sarkies first arrived in Rangoon in 1892, it took another decade for him and his brothers to locate their hotel dream here. In the meantime, they opened two other prestigious hotels: Raffles in Singapore and the Eastern & Oriental in Penang.

Rangoon lodgings opened in 1901, the year of Queen Victoria's passing, yet at the height of Britain's Empire. The hotel's location was particularly well chosen: then, first off the dock onto the pier after a long cruise up the Irrawaddy Delta, and, nowadays, smack in the city's colonial heart, a district rich in grand Victorian and Edwardian edifices. With river frontage, the property proudly reigned as dowager over the city's widest avenue.

Through subsequent decades and wars the property sank into dilapidation, but never from memory. The Japanese requisitioned the hotel as a horse stable during their occupation, and afterwards the property went into freefall, as did cousin Raffles, before both had multi-million dollar facelifts. Oh how the mighty had fallen!

As a fitting conclusion to an eclectic century of colonialism, war, independence, then self-imposed economic isolation, this famous landmark closed in 1990 for a multi-year $15 million facelift, reopening in November '93 as the country's showcase prestige hotel. Just entering the lobby today is close to reliving the Golden Age of Travel.

Initially, only the Strand's river front three-story building underwent renovation, plus its grand ballroom across side street Seikkanthar. Adjacent to that stands the Australian Embassy, housed in the hotel's original annex and next door to the British High Commission. Latest renovations are to the 5-storey wing directly behind the original premises. To our delight when first staying here at the millennium's transit, we surreptitiously explored its then shambolic wing, with an old birdcage elevator, complete with aging sign warning against more than five passengers. This lift climbed up to the old, un-renovated Strand tower ~ a rabbit warren of crumbling rooms and decades of dust. I felt like a naughty interloper. But this unreconstructed, vacant, indeed derelict Strand gave a better idea of how low the hotel had previously sunk, and a greater appreciation of how well its original wing renovations succeeded.

The property was restored for an anticipated tourism surge after endless decades of economic stagnation. What developers did not anticipate were subsequent long years of a tourism boycott, leaving lodgings relatively empty. For literally decades afterwards, Myanmar remained dormant.

There was an indulgent, quiet comfort in all of this, and a laid-back tropical feel of yesteryear, when instantaneous communication and fast flying jets were mere sci-fi fantasy. By gentlemen's agreement each leading city hotel rotated a specific evening to entice the city's then scarce expatriates

to their bars, and most were on first name terms. Friday night was and is The Strand's draw, when half-price drinks entice expat and tourist alike to imbibe and network in equal measure. This was and is the place to relive the pleasures of classic cocktails like Pegu Club, G&T (against Malaria) or cold draft lager. The bar literally pulses. Better yet, there's scant excise tax on alcohol, and Myanmar brand beer rates as Asia's tastiest, with competition only from *Beerlao* in Laos.

Alas, we never knew the old Strand ~ neither the noble Edwardian establishment that held host to royalty, society and literary grandees, nor the post-war Strand of dilapidation. Our introduction came during our first trip to Yangon, upon winning a charity auction offering several nights at the hotel. We stood in awe. After that, all lodging alternatives proved a let down, and to this day we cannot envision a return trip to Myanmar without budgeting a night or three here.

Stepping through the front doors today is still a bit like yesteryear, but revamped for modern sensibilities: air conditioning instead of a punkawalla plying his massive fan from above; high speed internet replaces telegraph. In the lobby, a sole musician chimes soothing notes on the *pattalar*, a Burman xylophone cum harp, subtly underscoring background conversations. Potted palm fronds look straight out of an Edwardian parlor, complemented by creamy cool tiles and slightly austere wicker and teak furniture. It's much more tropical style than actual affluence, though. Looking at historic photos, one gets the feeling that old hotels such as this were not as luxe as Hollywood portrays. In the olden days you got a clean sheet and private room, only sometimes with ensuite toilet, and luck be willing, a gin and tonic with a single cube of ice. The menu was then strictly European (the Strand still offers an afternoon tea with cucumber sandwiches), with at most an Anglicized curry. Like a private club, such colonial hotels were little oases of European "civilization" in an alien environment.

". . .my bed was furnished with mattrass, pillow, and mosquito net only, no sheet or covering of any kind being provided. I imagined this to be an oversight; but the omission soon explained itself when I found that the thermometer never dropped below ninety-eight degrees all night, and in the damp heat that prevailed it would have been impossible to have endured the weight of even a silk coverlet."

~ R.Talbot Kelly, *Burma* (1905)

The Strand is a true *grande dame* of the world's hotel set, but unlike its restored contemporaries, it uniquely retains an aura of restrained gentility. Perhaps that's to do with the feeling that you are alone in its rambling premises. The original restoration allowed only for 32 rooms and a maximum of 60 guests, and that barely doubles with the new wing renovations. This probably explains why so many wannabes come to glimpse the hotel from the outside, as mere tourists and not resident guests. Yet not staying at the Strand is like visiting Hanoi without sleeping at The Metropole; touring Singapore and not drinking a Sling at The Raffles; cruising Bangkok without docking at The Oriental, or visiting Tokyo without seeing The Imperial. I wallow in such experiences, and accusations of effete snobbery be damned!

Unlike, say, former sibling Raffles' busy shopping arcade setting in Singapore, The Strand lobby is calm and subdued, with just a few mingling guests quietly chattering among themselves. Likewise, its ground floor doesn't host a veritable labyrinth of shops for new moneyed hoi polloi. No Louis Vuitton nor Shanghai Tang here. Tucked behind its signature *Grill* restaurant are just a few small shops: jewelery, antiques and a contemporary art gallery. Surprisingly, not even a bakery to tempt with the hotels' prestige tastes.

While the hotel once faced a river-front park, this was for decades fenced for security. Commercial shipping, apparently, needed to take place far from surveying eyes. That was a pity, as the hotel's former view is a feature. Next door are the colonial facades of Myanmar Airways, and the stately Australian Embassy and British High Commission. Close by lies the faded grandeur of the General Post Office. Today this district is a tourist delight, with the city's old quarter a veritable architectural museum, with Southeast Asia's largest assembly of colonial heritage buildings. The Strand today capitalizes on this

central location by giving guests a charming pen-drawn walking map printed on brown recycled paper, listing neighboring architectural treasures with a short history on each. Every repeat visit, we retrace these walks, using the maps, and we never fail to discover yet another architectural gem.

The Strand also boasts much more than pedigree and location: Guests quickly realize that this is a prestige hotel with clout! Without doubt, prices are kept high to maintain exclusivity, even during the long decades of a tourism boycott. At the airport, for example, guests can arrange to be personally escorted through customs and immigration. Butlers seamlessly attend rooms while guests are out for breakfast, then again while on a short stroll. I adore the huge bathrooms and sky-high ceilings in every room. By contemporary building standards you could fit two levels per one here. And the height allows guests to actually turn off the air conditioning, and let nature take its course by swooshing all the hot air upward. Meanwhile, leisurely ceiling fans make us feel like colonial travelers of yesteryear. All that's missing is a real punka. Then there are the very smart-looking doormen and butlers garbed in plaid *longyi* sarongs, dark jackets, and collarless white shirts, all wearing Myanmar's ubiquitous natural latex and black velvet thong sandals.

While The Strand has an aura of exclusivity, there is nothing pretentious about any of the hotel's straightforward names. They tell it like it is: *The Café, The Grill, The Bar.* They go hand-in-hand with the hotel's easy nomenclature *The Strand,* named after the thoroughfare fronting the hotel. They all reflect the hotel's honest ambiance. HRH Thai prince Damrong Rajanubhab described The Strand in his diary journeys of 1936 as the city's "largest, most spacious and most comfortable hotel." Yet after staying here, we are left with one not so simple exclamation:

What an Experience!

STRAND HOTEL   RANGOON

From Burma to Myanmar

To English-speaking perceptions, Burma was arbitrarily renamed Myanmar in 1989. But ask the locals, and they'll explain that Myanmar has been the country's name for centuries. They are confused why foreigners still use its former colonial title – a name that controversially refers to only one ethnic group. Part of the confusion arose when Burma's official name at independence in 1948 changed to "Myanmar" in its national language, but officially retained "Union of Burma" as its English name for decades afterwards. Although the term Myanmar was readily adopted by the United Nations, Germany and Japan in 1989, it failed to be accepted by most English-speaking nations.

Generally speaking, the adjective "Burmese" connotes the entire Myanmar nation, including the country's myriad nationalities; while the archaic colonial-era word "Burman" specifically applied to the Bamar or Bama ethnic majority.

Both Myanmar and Myanmarese are officially preferred adjectives for contemporary usage to connote the nation as a whole. The preferred term for a Myanmar citizen, not specifically his or her ethnic identify, is Myanma.

Myanmar *assar-asa* refers to the large, set menu served at a typical eatery. Because of transliteration, and also because British tend to place an "r" to indicate an aspirated "ah" while Americans pronounce just the opposite, spellings of assar-asa range from assarsa, asar-sa, assar-sa or simply assasa.

"Pagoda" is the Myanmar-English term for the massive symmetrical dome or tower typically built over a priceless artifact. When used in Myanmar, "pagoda" is solid, and not open to entry; "temple", by contrast, has rooms. While Westerners tend to use "pagoda" particularly for Far Eastern Oriental-style tower-like storied structures, its original definition broadly embraced any domed or pyramidal religious building.

Geographical Names

Colonial Anglicization of Burmese names rendered geographic locations unintelligible in native use. The following were re-spelled to reflect local usage in 1989, but did not change official Burmese-language names, merely English transliteration. (Current names first, former names second.)

Myanmar	Burma
Irrawaddy	Ayeyarwady
Yangon	Rangoon
Mandalay	Mandalay
Bagan	Pagan
Bago	Pegu
Pyin Oo Lwin	Maymyo
Mawlamyine	Moulemein
Pyay	Prome
Mrauk-U	Myohaung
Pathein	Bassein

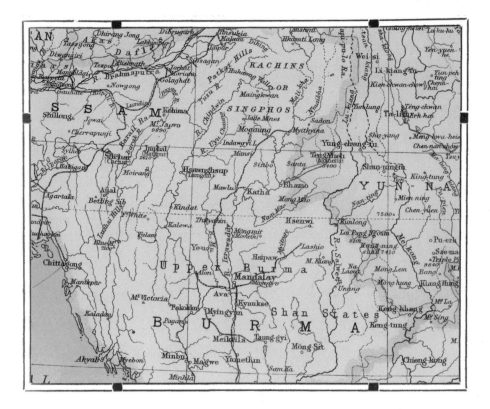

CURRY FAVOR
Curry

ဟင်းလျာ

"half the people who don't like curry are those who have never tasted it properly made."

-- M Fraser, *The Burma Guides Cookery Book* (1932)

A Curry Primer

BURMESE curries are delicately flavored with slow-fried onion, garlic and ginger. The resultant seasoned oil ubiquitously enhances local dishes with a subtle fragrance and taste. By contrast, "curry" in an English sense, evokes a dish redolent of spice. Myanmar curries are nothing of the sort, and, as well, distinctly unlike those of its neighbors. Just as importantly, curry's Myanmar translation *hin* is too broad a term for its English counterpart. *Hin* refers to any stewed recipe. Compared to Indian and Thai food, for example, curries here are veritably mild not piquant, and simply cooked without a plethora of spices. Conversely, the former excel in complex blends of dried spices, while Myanmar curries are fresh allium and rhizome based, and sweetly odorous from sliced or pounded blends of onion, garlic, ginger and the like. This is partially explained by preference, but equally as an historically political way to eschew imperialist flavors from when the country was occupied by tides of migrants ~ not only from the Subcontinent but also European overseers.

You'll find similar fresh rhizome curry paste bases (*hin a-nit*) cutting a swathe into Southeast Asia, down through Malaysia and Indonesia, but there spiced further. That is not the case in Myanmar, where the subtlety of innocuous oil impacts on the final result. Nothing overpowering, merely a blend of gentle, harmonious tastes.

Myanmar curries basically come under two banners: pounded onion and garlic (and usually ginger, as well) fried in oil, then cooked with other ingredients. Or sliced onion and garlic fried in oil, then added at the end. As a matter of course, cooks fry onion and garlic as a base, which is then reserved and re-added shortly before serving. (Locals explain this procedure keeps the oil flavorsome, but prevents the dish from becoming overwhelmed by pungent onion and garlic infusing too long.) In Rakhine State to the far west and home to the famed Arakan kingdom of lore, curries are not cooked in oil imbued with onion and garlic, and less oil is used. In ethnic T'ai dominated Shan state bordering Thailand, locals pound garlic and onions first (often with chilies) then spice the paste with chili before frying.

Specifically, there are two cooking styles here: *Hsi thut* refers to seasoning the oil by frying onion, garlic and ginger before adding meat. This is done with either thinly sliced, or preferably, pounded ingredients. In the *Lone chet* method, onion and garlic are merely boiled in the stew. This saves time when using store bought crisp fried onion and garlic, instead of starting with fresh.

Other ingredients typically include deep-hued alleppey turmeric and mild chili powder, akin to hot paprika. Fermented shrimp paste or *ngapi* is also popular, with cooks commonly adding copious quantities especially paired with tomato. (Compared to neighboring Thailand, for example, towering piles of shrimp paste sold here at the market are even taller, and in several varieties. Take pity on the vendor re-shaping the mounds daily with bare hands!)

Technically, curry powder and masala spice are different, but not in common Myanmar usage. Ethnic Burmese rarely use an Indian-style curry powder. Its local equivalent *masala hmont* is akin to a masala blend plus cumin. (Generic garum masala, although translated as "mixed spice," is actually a specific formulation made of fennel, cinnamon and caraway, plus pepper, cloves and green cardamom, and generally doesn't include cumin.) Similarly, Burmese curry powders are Indian, most comparable to standard Madras-style blends, with slight variations:

SEAFOOD MASALA
Omit fenugreek and fennel seed, add Asian chili powder.

VEGETABLE MASALA
Increase coriander seed, fennel seed and a pinch of asafetida.

BEEF & CHICKEN CHAT MASALA
Increase cassia or cinnamon, and add more cumin.

PORK TAYOTE MASALA
Mixes are equivalent to Chinese 5-spice, or simply cinnamon or cassia, cloves, cardamom and black pepper. Even then, it's frugally sprinkled atop a finished dish, such as on Shan noodles, just before serving.

Locals cook with long, finger-length chilies producing paprika more than fiery cayenne. A richer dark red pepper, slightly akin to hot paprika, it can comfortably be used by the heaped teaspoonsful before the barest glimmer of sweat hits the brow. (An even darker, coarsely chopped fried chili and whole seeds is more a condiment than an actual seasoning.) A slightly salty bright red powder *a yaung tin mote* primarily colors, and is equivalent to adding dried safflower and salt. Some cooks begin with dried whole chilies, which allows removal of all the indigestible (and fiery) seeds prior to grinding and cooking. Pinch off the top, shake out the seeds, soak pods in warm water for at least 15 minutes to soften, then pound or grind.

Richly-hued alleppey turmeric is equally essential. Unlike pale yellow Madras-style powder, this one really tastes like a fresh rhizome. Its curcumin level is twice its Indian counterpart, and as alleppey turmeric is both hard to find, and expensive, in the West, stock up cheaply when at the local market. While alleppey turmeric is specified in only certain recipes here, it is the preferred variety throughout this book.

After adding meat and or vegetables, plus a generous slop of oil, curry stews boil down into an emulsified sauce. Locals explain its ready when the oil pools atop. This simple gravy is the base for a plethora of dishes, which probably explains why some visitors find Burmese cooking "too much of the same."

Tourists may complain that Burmese cooking is unctuous, with finished recipes reminiscent of Greek dishes slathered in olive oil. And in truth, ethnic Burman or Bamar curries are made with large quantities of oil. But in fact, oil has an important role to play, especially in a region where food may stand at hot room temperatures for hours on end: it imparts a protective coating against air-borne spoilage in a country without reliable refrigeration. Such copious quantities, however, mean that oil quality is very important. (Recipes printed in this book have reduced oil quantities for modern usage; likewise, leading Myanmar hotel chefs nowadays follow this same practice.) Cold-pressed peanut oil and untoasted sesame oil are the most popular in the countryside, and usually first-pressed direct on the farm. Unfortunately, cheap soy- and palm oil are starting to replace them in the city. Use a good quality vegetable oil from your supermarket, or better yet, cold-pressed peanut- or untoasted sesame oil from a health food store. Ensure it is very fresh and not rancid. Cold pressed canola/rapeseed oil is growing in popularity over the entire region, but cheap palm oil and cottonseed oil gained ground with consumers solely because of cost, not quality. Do not use the latter two, as palm oil solidifies when cold, and is consequently a health risk (not to mention its environmental toll); likewise, the extraction process for cottonseed oil is dubious. Eschew olive oil, as it imparts the wrong flavor profile to these dishes.

Crisp Frying Shallots, Onions & Garlic

There are two distinctly different fried onions used in Myanmar cooking: the first is fried onions and/or shallots cooked until extremely wilted, soft and golden. Less oil is needed than with crisp fried, and when done the natural onion sugars start to stick on the pan bottom. (This technique also applies to puree blends.) Best done in a wide saucepan, cooking times vary from a few minutes to as long as 20, depending variously on oil and quantity fried (the more onions or puree, the longer it takes). Always reserve the frying oil, as it becomes seasoned, and is considered valuable in Myanmar cooking. (Hint: fry more oil than necessary, then store in the fridge until ready to use later in other dishes.)

Crisp fried, by contrast, is invariably produced from shallots (plus garlic and ginger), not onion, as the latter is more watery. Crisp frying is best in a wok or small saucepan, the wider the better to allow dispersal of steam and moisture, as you want the end product brittle.

Western pink and golden shallot variants are generally larger and more watery than Asian sorts, thus may not fry as crisply. One remedy is to lay them on trays in the sun briefly, or overnight in a dry environment before frying. To prevent sticking, line trays with parchment paper.

Or: lightly salt sliced shallots. Wait for 15 minutes, then wipe salt away and press firmly in a tea towel to extract excess liquid.

Or: Add a pinch of salt during final minute cooking, to help crisp.

1   Peel and thinly slice shallots and/or garlic. Keep them separate, in a single layer. Note, locals slice lengthwise, not crosswise.

2   Heat oil in wok: it should not be too hot, lest the sliced shallots burn and turn bitter. Fry at about 325°F/160°C. Cook till golden, with regular and constant stirring essential. Be vigilant, as they quickly burn. Depending on the actual heat, and thinness of slice, cooking times will vary: if very hot oil, 1-3 minutes, but safest to fry slowly for about 15 minutes.

3   Remove immediately with slotted spoon or mesh ladle, drain and spread out in a single layer to cool. If not sufficiently crisp, repeat two more times, decreasing cooking time accordingly. (This is how crisp fried shallots and garlic are commercially made.) These store up to a month, and up to 6 months when refrigerated.

All his meals were swift, passionate and enormous; they were not meals so much as orgies, debauches of curry and rice.

~ George Orwell, *Burmese Days* (1934)

Step-by-Step Myanmar Curry
a-sint sint chat pyote nee

Burmese curries are enhanced by flavoring oil, which is created prior to adding liquid, meat and/or vegetables. Flavored oil is prepared by gently and slowly frying onion, garlic and ginger. In addition, meats are rarely browned or seared prior to adding; rather, they are slowly stewed for tough cuts or quickly boiled for premium pieces.

As a general rule, Burmese home cooks slice their onion, garlic and ginger before frying, while restaurants pound these ingredients with a mortar and pestle, then fry. For convenience, you can use a blender to puree onion, garlic and ginger. But candidly, the resultant flavor of machine-blended pastes is distinctly inferior, and often slightly bitter.

Using the ingredient amounts from your chosen recipe, follow these steps to create your curry:

SEASONED OIL

1. Heat a wok, frying pan or saucepan over medium-low heat. A wok, or Indian *kadhai,* works particularly well here, as it concentrates and pools the oil, allowing for less oil and better and quicker frying. Add oil after the metal heats, not before, as this helps prevent sticking. (Some cooks like to initially season oil with dried chili flakes at this point, but this is optional. Cook these momentarily, as they burn quickly. Remove with a strainer or pass oil through a fine sieve.) Add the onions to the oil, stir periodically until lightly golden and fragrant ~ typically as long as 15-20 minutes on low to medium-low heat. Remove onions with a slotted spoon, drain and reserve. Note: onions and garlic are not fried to crispiness here for garnish; rather, they are nearly caramelized. (This is different to quick-cooked crisp fried onion, which is a typical salad garnish.)

2. Increase heat to medium high, add garlic to the same oil and gently fry until golden ~ about 3 minutes; remove and reserve. Repeat same step with wafer-thin slices of ginger, or grated ginger. You can also cook the ginger together with the garlic.

CURRY SAUCE

3. Add weak stock or water, bring to a boil and cover. Stock instead of water always improves the flavor of the final dish, especially as Western cooks, unlike locals, are unlikely to add flavor enhancer MSG. As a general rule, dilute store bought or home-made stock with 1 part stock to 2 parts or more water. Weak chicken and very diluted fish stock prove extremely versatile in these dishes, while vegetable

stock also suits most recipes, but restrict beef stock only to beef dishes, or not at all. As a rule, add minimal liquid, closer to a braise than a soup.

4 Add remaining ingredients, such as meat and vegetables, in the order listed in the recipe. (Sometimes meat is seared with dry or wet seasonings prior to adding liquid, but this is optional.) Typically, Burmese curries are cooked until sufficient liquid is absorbed to show oil rising and pools forming.

5 When the meat and/or vegetables are tender, you can choose to sprinkle with curry powder or masala. Just before serving, top with the reserved fried onions and garlic, which are then stirred into the dish at the table. If the ginger is fried in slices rather than grated, finely dice after cooking then stir into the finished dish.

HINT Stockpile Seasoned Oil and fried onion, garlic and ginger. Prepare large quantities of flavored oil using the traditional method, then strain and store. Refrigerate onion, garlic, ginger and flavored oil separately in tightly sealed containers. Flavored oil will keep for weeks, while cooked onions, garlic and ginger will keep for up to a week if refrigerated. Bring to room temperature before using.

QUICK METHOD Chop onion, garlic and ginger finely, then puree in a blender (not a food processor), drizzling in the oil while blending. As Burmese curries use a relatively large amount of oil, this is a surefire foolproof method, but best for small quantities. Large volume paste requires excessively longer frying afterwards. Fry the blended mixture for 3-5 minutes, adding additional oil as necessary.

APPROXIMATE COOKING TIMES

FISH
Cook cubed fillets uncovered over medium-high heat for up to 10 minutes. Fish on the bone may require slightly longer. Tamarind and tomato is typically added to fish curry.

CHICKEN BREAST, BEEF LOIN, PORK LOIN
Cube the meat into 1½ inch (4 cm) chunks, then simmer covered over medium-low heat until just tender -- about 15-20 minutes.

STEWING MEAT
Such as cubed (1½ inch/4 cm) beef chuck and pork neck: cover and simmer 1-1½ hours over medium-low heat. Add more water or stock, as necessary.

VEGETABLES
Carrots and potatoes require about 20minutes or until tender; okra and leafy greens such as cabbage, half that time. Coarsely chop tomatoes with skin and seeds. Green bell peppers/capsicums: seed, de-rib and cut into thick strips or rings. Add a small spoonful of fermented shrimp paste for enhanced flavor, plus garnish with dried shrimp.

Basic Curry Sauce

hin a nit

1 cup (250 ml) vegetable oil

6 small onions
 or 12 oz/350 g pink
 or golden shallots,
 peeled and thinly sliced

1 garlic bulb
 (2½ oz/75 g) cloves peeled
 and thinly sliced

2 inch (5 cm)
 knob fresh ginger,
 peeled and chopped or
 grated (about 2 oz/60 g)

2 stalks lemongrass, white
 part only, thinly sliced

2 cinnamon leaves (Indian
 bay) or bay laurel

2 tablespoons (30 ml) Asian
 chili powder or hot paprika

1 teaspoon (5ml)
 turmeric powder,
 preferably alleppey

About 1 cup (250 ml) water,
 coconut milk or stock

In a large frypan or wok, heat oil over medium-low flame. Add the onions and slowly brown until fragrant, stirring periodically ~ 15-20 minutes. Lower the heat if cooking too fast. Remove onions with slotted spoon, drain and reserve.

Increase heat to medium high, add garlic and ginger to the same oil and gently fry until golden ~ about 3 minutes; remove and reserve. Chop the cooked ginger finely. Add lemongrass, bay and spices to the same oil, fry 30 seconds.

Add meat and/or vegetables, stir to coat, then add liquid. For long-stewing meat cuts, add a cup of water, stock or coconut milk; cover, adding more liquid as necessary. Fast-cooking prime meats like chicken breast, pork or beef loin require less liquid as they cook within minutes and will not boil dry; decrease heat to low or medium low and cook. Note: most curries are cooked covered with a lid. But when coconut milk stews it should simmer without cover, as it is prone to curdling. Consequently, add coconut milk and cream at final minutes stewing. Just before serving, stir in the cooked onions, garlic and ginger.

> "The Burmese make two meals in the day, one about 9 o'clock in the morning, the other at sunset. A quantity of rice boiled hard, so that the grains do not stick, is put on a wooden plate, supported by a leg of the same material, and round this, two or three people seat themselves upon the bare ground or on simple mats, and they employ their fingers in eating. Besides the acid and sweet curry, they have commonly another sauce made of pounded napi and red pepper."

~Father Vincenzo Sangermano, *The Burmese Empire A Hundred Years Ago* (1893)

Burmese Masala Spice

This is a typical blend for contemporary Burmese dishes, ideal for both fish and meat. Sprinkle it sparingly atop a finished curry or noodle dish.

3 tablespoons (45 ml)
coriander seed

4 teaspoons (20 ml
peppercorns

4 teaspoons (20 ml)
cumin seed

1 tablespoon (15 ml) poppy
seed, preferably white

2 cinnamon leaves (Indian
bay) or 3 bay laurel

1¹/2 teaspoons (7 ml)
ground cassia or cinnamon

10 cardamom pods

5 whole cloves,
or ³/4 teaspoon (3.5 ml)
ground cloves

TOASTING SPICES Because whole spices toast at different times, heat them individually in a small frying pan over medium-high heat, stirring constantly, until they are fragrant or begin to pop. This will take anywhere from a few seconds to no more than 90 seconds. Once fragrant, remove from the heat immediately, lest it becomes acrid. Do not toast bay leaves. When cool, transfer spices into a stone mortar and grind very finely; sift through a medium coarse mesh, discarding coarse chaff. Grind once more, then sieve again. Store in a tightly sealed jar. Makes ¹/2 cup (50 g)

Simple Curry Powder

Over decades of economic hardship, imports fell drastically, and Burmese cooks resorted to simplifying Indian masala blends. This recipe is especially adapted for those without a mortar and pestle. Spices improve with toasting, but pre-ground spices burn easily so be especially diligent, stirring constantly in a dry skillet over a medium flame, until just fragrant ~ 30 seconds to 1 minute.

3 tablespoons (45 ml)
ground cassia or cinnamon

2 tablespoons (30 ml) ground
allspice, or star anise

3 tablespoons (45 ml)
ground cumin

2 tablespoons (30 ml)
ground fennel seeds

1 teaspoon (5 ml)
ground cardamom

2 teaspoons (10 ml)
ground cloves

Sieve ingredients together to create a fine powder. Store in an air-tight jar. Makes ¹/2 cup (50 g)

Colonial Curry Powder
dan pauk masala

Curry powder serves two goals: first to flavor food and second to mask rancidity ~ the latter essential in days prior to refrigeration. It's also claimed spices have anti-bacterial properties which ward off spoilage.

This curry powder is typical of colonial Burma when Indian influence held sway. Its basic composition is classic Madras and was a favorite to bottle and cork for long treks. At the campfire, the blended dried spice mix was "fried off" in oil before meats and vegetables were added, then the dish was finished with coconut milk or cream.

In this recipe the addition of curry leaves, garlic and salt probably means it originated as a French colonial version from Pondicherry. After all, the English long looked to France in matters of taste.

Note: there is a difference between toasting dried spices (masala) and frying spice blends (curry powder). The former is sprinkled over the dish just prior to serving to enhance flavor. Fried spice adds flavor the curry during cooking. Moreover, frying spice blends allows flavors to mellow and also removes "raw" tastes. Alas, the terms are translated interchangeably in Myanmar, leading to some confusion.

For best results use whole spices and grind them yourself; ensure they are roasted first to achieve maximum aroma. Pre-ground spices burn easily when toasted. A large stone mortar and pestle is essential; wooden mortars don't suit. A small electric coffee mill works a treat.

¹/4 cup (5 g) dried curry
  leaves, firmly packed

1 tablespoon (15 ml) rock salt

2 tablespoons (30 ml)
  fenugreek seed

2 tablespoons (30 ml)
  mustard seed

¹/4 cup (25 g) cumin seed

1 cup (100 g) coriander seed

2 teaspoons (10 ml)
  whole cloves

1 tablespoon (15 ml) Asian
  chili powder (or more to
  taste) or 2 dried long red
  chilies, seeded

¹/4 cup (50 g) dried garlic
  flakes, crushed or 2
  tablespoons (30 ml)
  garlic powder

¹/4 cup (25 g)
  turmeric powder,
  preferably alleppey

Crumble the curry leaves, combine with the salt and grind to a powder in a mortar and pestle or electric grinder. Pass through a coarse sieve to remove any chaff; reserve.

Toast whole spices separately in a small frying pan over medium-high heat, stirring constantly, until they are fragrant or begin to pop. When cool, grind very finely; sift through a medium coarse mesh, discarding any coarse chaff.

Separately, grind cloves, chili and garlic. Combine with the toasted spices, ground curry leaves/salt mix and turmeric. Sieve once more to thoroughly integrate and store in a tightly sealed jar until ready to use. Makes about 1½-2 cups/150-200 g

TO COOK Fry a tablespoon or two of spice powder in oil for a couple minutes, until fragrant. Then add meats, vegetables and liquid; simmer until ingredients are tender. Coconut-based curries are cooked uncovered, lest they curdle.

Thanaka

One of the defining visual features of Myanmar is the ubiquitous use of a thick cosmetic white powder called thanaka. Although sometimes ascribed to sandalwood, thanaka is made from the ground bark of several tree species. Used by males & especially females of all ages, it is a natural sun protection (akin to zinc cream), providing cooling properties in the heat.

FLYING FISHES PLAY
Fish & Seafood

ရေချိုရေငါးများနှင့် ပင်လယ်စာများ

"On the road to Mandalay, where the flyin' fishes play
An' the dawn comes up like thunder 'outer China crost the bay."

~ Rudyard Kipling, *Mandalay* (1890)

Fish & Seafood

FOLLOW the river and you will find the sea, goes an old proverb. In Myanmar's case, you also find a gate of fear and distrust. As in the case of coastal and island countries whose inhabitants historically migrated up-country to avoid seafaring marauders, the Burmans look to Upper Burma, Mandalay, Saigang and Bagan for identity and nation building. That, and perhaps the origins of its Myanmar nationality which largely traces itself inland to Tibet and Yunnan, may in part explain the limited use of salt water seafood in northern Burmese cuisine. Conversely, fresh water fish are preferred in the former Mon kingdom lands of Lower Burma and along the coasts. Here, recipes take on a slightly different character and flavor, as so many dishes center around seafood. But one particular culinary delicacy favored in all parts of the nation is the thick, plump and delicious "butterfish," which is actually a freshwater catfish. It's renowned in curry, and leading chefs today hot-smoke it Western style.

As befits a Buddhist land, locals eschew killing a living thing for food, yet they are far from vegetarian when it comes to eating fish. Although fisherman were traditionally looked on with disdain, locals used the justifiable excuse that fish willingly swim into a net, and thus take their own life.

Touring Yangon's vast fish market at dawn is riveting, but not for the faint hearted, what with its orchestrated chaos and pungent smells. However, if you really want to experience it all, travel down the isthmus, south along the coastline, or better yet, go to one of Yangon's Rakhine restaurants, where the foods are cooked simply but deliciously. Rakhine, to the country's far West bordering Bangladesh, was the historic home of the Arakan kingdom, and locals strongly maintain their historic nationalism. Its capital Sitwe's teeming fish market is arguably the country's best.

"Always fry my belly brown before you turn my back down" goes an old cooking adage. This is a good rule to prevent fish from breaking into pieces during cooking.

FISH VARIETIES & SUBSTITUTES

Geography rules over what freshwater fish and ocean seafood are available in local markets, although air freight and freezing have countered this somewhat. Indeed, even names are wont to change regionally. Freshwater fish and ocean seafood are very localized markets. Don't be so specific that it limits your opportunity to use local bounty. Substitutions should reflect first on the cooking method ⁓ e.g. fried, grilled, steamed, &c. Start with the dish first and what you want to deliver from a flavor and texture perspective. Then ask your fishmonger to nominate a style of fish that suits. Here's some generic examples:

WHITE FLESHED TENDER FISH
Sole, halibut, snapper, turbot, ling, flathead, gurnard, gummy shark, red emperor, gold band, tropical cod, blue eye cod, NZ blue cod, tilapia, basa (cat fish)

ROBUST OR OILY FLAVORED FISH
Salmon, bluefish, Spanish mackerel, tommy ruff, herring, warehou, gemfish

FIRM TEXTURED OCEAN FISH
Tuna, swordfish, mahi, marlin, wahoo, sailfish

Fried Trout with Turmeric & Mint

nga gyaw

Rubbing turmeric on seafood removes fish smells and is a popular treatment from the coastline of Myanmar down through Thailand, the Malay Peninsula and across the East Indies. Also try this recipe with salmon or sea trout.

4-6 whole trout (1 1/2 lb/ 750 g each) or fish cutlets/ steaks

1 tablespoon (15 ml) salt

1 tablespoon (15 ml) soy sauce

2 teaspoons (10 ml) turmeric powder

1/2 bunch (50 g) fresh mint leaves finely sliced/ chiffonade (page 262)

About 2 cups (500 ml) vegetable oil

About 1 cup (150 g) combined rice flours (optional; see below)

Lemon or lime wedges, to garnish

If using whole trout, gut the fish, optionally removing head but retaining tail. Or cut fish into steaks or cutlets if it fits better in the frying pan. Clean by rinsing out the bitter black stomach lining (the back of your thumb nail works perfectly, or use a soft brush). Don gloves and rub fish skin and especially gut cavity with salt, soy and turmeric and allow to marinate for at least 15 minutes. (Wearing gloves is essential, lest the turmeric dye your skin.)

Roll mint leaves into a tight cylinder and cut into fine shreds; reserve.

Heat a frying pan over medium-high heat, add just enough oil to cover the bottom to 1/4 inch/6 mm depth. When hot, fry the fish one or two at a time, until they are golden brown; turn over just once. It should take 7-10 minutes total. Remove and drain; keep warm. Cook remaining fish, adding more oil as necessary. Scatter mint atop and accompany with lemon wedges. Serve 1 whole trout or piece per person

VARIATION: CRISPY FRIED
For a crisper texture, dust the fish skin in a mixture of 3 parts plain rice flour with 1 part sticky rice flour just before frying and proceed as above.

Pickled Shad

nga thalout hin

Local shad or *hilsa*, like its foreign counterparts, are full of tiny bones, and prone to causing disaster unless carefully and painstakingly filleted. The advantage of this recipe (as in canned sardines, tuna or salmon) is that very long cooking in acidic liquid renders the tiny pin bones tender. Use a non-reactive pot here (page 365), as some metals react to acidic vinegar or lemon. Use only very fresh but oily fish for this recipe.

4-6 stalks lemongrass, cut into 6 inch/20 cm lengths (or the width of your cooking pot)

About 2 lb (1 kg) whole piece shad, bonito or albacore tuna, gutted or 4 x 7 oz/ 200 g fish cutlets/steaks

1 tablespoon (15 ml) salt

1 teaspoon (5 ml) turmeric powder

1/2 cup (125 ml) white vinegar or fresh lemon juice

1/2 cup (125 ml) vegetable oil

1 tablespoon (15 ml) thick sweet soy sauce

1 tablespoon (15 ml) fish sauce

About 8 cups (2 liters) water

Use the entire stalk of the lemongrass, not just the white portion. Take a very sharp knife to cut them into lengths the size of your cooking pot, then line the pan bottom with the stalks.

If using whole fish, remove head and tail; reserve for stock. Scale if applicable (albacore, bonito and sturgeon, for example, have no scales). Cut the body crosswise through the bone into cutlets or steaks.

Don gloves and rub fish skin and especially gut cavity with salt and turmeric. Lay fish pieces atop the lemongrass and marinate for at least 15 minutes. Add remaining ingredients and water to fully cover, plus reserved fish head and tails for additional stock flavor.

Cover pan loosely and simmer over moderate heat for about 4 hours. The liquid will evaporate, with oil remaining. Add more boiling water if necessary, lest it cook dry and scorch. Allow to cool to room temperature, then carefully remove from the pot; remove skin and serve warm from the pot or chilled in refrigerator. Accompany with rice and assorted salads. Serves 4-6

VARIATION: PRESSURE COOKER
For faster results, use a pressure cooker ~ about 1 hour on low pressure. Decrease water quantity to 3 cups/750 ml total.

Slow Boiled Fish

nga gyaw hnut

Long cooking here ensures crumbly, brittle ~ sometimes even edible ~ pin bones in shad, carp, large sardines, even mackerel and salmon. The safflower powder called for in this recipe is largely for coloring, although it is sold as a cheap imitation of saffron; it provides minimal flavor.

2 lb (1 kg) whole shad or equivalent, gutted and scaled or 4 x 6 oz/200 g fish cutlets/steaks

3 tablespoons (45 ml) white vinegar

2 tablespoons (30 ml) salt

1 teaspoon (5 ml) safflower powder, or a pinch saffron

1½ cups (375 ml) vegetable oil

4 large onions, thinly sliced

10 fresh green long finger chilies, seeded and cut into strips

1½ inch (3.5 cm) knob fresh ginger, grated

½ bulb (35 g) garlic, cloves peeled and left whole

1 tablespoon (15 ml) tomato paste or puree

If using whole large fish, remove head and tail. Cut the body crosswise through the bone into 1 inch/2.5 cm cutlets or steaks.

Rub the fish pieces with vinegar, salt and safflower or saffron and marinate for at least 15 minutes. Remove pieces from the marinade and pat fish dry; reserve marinade.

Meanwhile, heat the oil in a fry pan over medium-high flame. Fry the onions till light brown, then remove immediately with a slotted spoon to drain; reserve. Do not overcook, lest they turn bitter.

Return the pan to medium-high heat and fry the fish pieces in the same oil until golden brown ~ about 3 minutes on each side. Place the fish in an 8 cup/2 liter deep ceramic bowl or pudding basin, spooning the reserved fried onion between layers, interspersed with the green chilies.

Blend the ginger and garlic, or mash in a mortar and pestle, or in an electric blender with strained oil from frying. (It does not have to be a uniform mash.) Add this plus tomato paste and any remaining oil from the pan to the reserved marinade; pour atop the fish. Cap with grease-proof or parchment paper, then foil to secure. (Foil should not directly touch or come into contact with the ingredients lest the acid react.)

Fit a deep pan with a small trivet at the bottom and set the basin with fish on the trivet. Add water up to mid level of the basin, cover pot tightly and steam at a high boil initially for 1 hour. Add more boiling water as required. Lower heat to simmer and steam an additional 3 hours. Check periodically to ensure there is water in the pot, adding boiling water straight from the kettle.

To serve, allow to cool a bit, then carefully remove from its basin. Take to the table hot or cold and spoon large potions onto plates. Serves 4-6

Tangy Fish Salad

nga thoke

Tart with the fresh flavor of lemon and lime, this dish is a great way to use tender thin white-fleshed fillets, such as sole or flounder. The secret is lemon basil. And make certain to source young lemongrass; older stalks may prove too fibrous.

1/4 teaspoon (1 ml) turmeric powder

1 teaspoon (5 ml) Asian chili powder or hot paprika

2 fish fillets, such as sole, dory or tilapia (about 6 oz/180 g each)

2 teaspoons (10 ml) salt

3 tablespoons (45 ml) Seasoned Oil (page 42)

1/3 cup (40 g) finely sliced pink or golden shallot

2 fresh green small chilies, seeded and cut into strips

Pinch white sugar

1-2 limes, freshly squeezed

1/2 stalk lemongrass, white part only, very finely chopped

1 teaspoon (5 ml) fish sauce

1/2 bunch (50 g) lemon basil, leaves only, coarsely chopped

1 cup (125 g) coarsely chopped Chinese celery

Don gloves and rub dry spices onto the fish fillets, using just 1 teaspoon (5 ml) of the salt. Fry in the seasoned oil over medium-high heat, preferably in a non-stick pan. Turn once, cooking about 3-4 minutes in total. Remove from heat, cool and break fish into large chunks.

Meanwhile, briefly soak the shallots and fresh chilies in lime and remaining 1 teaspoon/5 ml salt plus sugar. At the last minute before serving, stir in lemon grass, and fish sauce. Gently toss the fish with basil and serve on a small bed of Chinese celery. Serves 4

VARIATION: SOUR FISH

Locals pickle fish for longer preservation by fermenting it with salt and sticky rice tightly covered with banana leaves or in plastic wrap. This generally takes 3 days at room temperature, before refrigeration. The result gets progressively more sour. If you can source prepared sour fish locally, rinse, pat dry and gently fry in seasoned oil, then proceed as above, but halve the citrus quantity and omit salt.

Crispy Fish Salad

nga thalout kyut gyaw thoke

Dried anchovy-like whitebait are commonly sold overseas under the Malaysian name *ikan bilis* (page 356). Look for them on grocery shelves, and not chilled. Some cooks prefer to quickly rinse (not soak) prior to using, or fry in oil. This recipe originates from Rakhine state to the far west and makes a great accompanying salad ~ more like a condiment than a stand-alone recipe. Do not substitute salt-cured anchovies or sardines, as the taste and texture is totally different.

1 cup (75 g) dried anchovy/
   whitebait (ikan bilis)
1/4 cup (60 ml) vegetable oil
1/4 cup (30 g) thinly sliced
   pink or golden shallots
1 lime, freshly squeezed
Pinch sugar

Pinch salt
2 teaspoons (10 ml) chili
   flakes in oil (Chili Fry,
   page 292) or to taste
4 sprigs fresh coriander
   (cilantro) very coarsely
   chopped

Heat oil in a wok over medium-low heat and, when temperature reaches 275°F/140°C, fry fish till crispy for 2-3 minutes. Caution, lest high temperature scorch or overcook the fish. Drain and cool.

Meanwhile, briefly toss shallots in lime juice, sugar and salt. Lightly mix with the fried fish, and drizzle chili oil atop, finally garnishing with fresh coriander/cilantro. Serves 4

VARIATION: SPICY FISH
Fry dried chili flakes in the oil prior to cooking fish (Chili Fry, page 292), drain. Sprinkle sparingly over finished salad.

Tuna Tartare

nga a-sane

A modern classic created at The Strand using the fresh bounty of the Andaman Sea. This version boasts a local combination of slightly tart-sweet passionfruit puree, mint and chives. If fresh passionfruit is unavailable, don't use canned, as it tends to be sweet; better yet, use frozen pulp. You can strain the pulp to remove seeds, but aficionados prefer the crunch. Black sesame seeds are available at health food shops and Asian groceries. Use very cold, very fresh sashimi-quality fish. The best variety of tuna to use here is red-hued yellow fin. Avoid pricey bluefin tuna because of its endangered status, or substitute kingfish and swordfish. For a crispy alternative, swap crisp fried shallots for the fresh, adding at the last minute.

1/4 cup (60 g) thinly sliced pink or golden shallots

2 small garlic cloves, very finely minced

2 tablespoons (30 ml) freshly squeezed lime juice

1 1/2 teaspoons (7 ml) salt, or to taste

10 mint leaves, thinly sliced

1 lb (500 g) fresh tuna fillet, skin off

2 tablespoons (30 ml) vegetable oil

2 tablespoons (30 ml) chopped chives

1 fresh red small chili, seeded and finely diced

2 fresh passionfruits, or 3 tablespoons (45 ml) passionfruit puree

Generous pinch white pepper

3 tablespoons (45 ml) coconut cream

2 teaspoons (10 ml) sesame seeds, preferably black

Sprigs fresh coriander (cilantro) or mint, to garnish

Briefly soak shallots and garlic with lime and salt. Meanwhile, roll mint leaves together into a tight cylinder and cut into fine shreds. (see page 262).

Cut the fish variously into thin slices, or 3/4 inch/2 cm cubes. In a mixing bowl, toss the fish with oil, followed by shallots and lime, then all remaining ingredients except coconut cream and herb sprigs. Allow the flavors to mix for a few minutes before serving. Adjust seasoning, drizzle with coconut cream and black sesame, and garnish with fresh sprigs of coriander/cilantro or mint. Serves 6

Dried Fish Salad

nga thoke

Myanmar markets abound with dried fish, some sun-dried, others salted, and occasionally smoked. Overseas equivalents include salt cod, or equally tasty, smoked trout. Hot-smoked fish differs from cold-smoked fish (such as classic smoked salmon), with the former fully cooked, while the later is merely cured to retain a fleshy raw texture. Eat tiny bits, as depending on the cured fish chosen (especially salt fish) it can prove very salty. For less salty versions, soak in cold water prior to cooking. Treat this dish as an accompanying salad or condiment to rice, or even as a finger snack with beer.

3 oz (100 g) hot-smoked trout, or salt fish

1 tablespoon thinly sliced pink or golden shallot

1/3 cup (90 ml) vegetable oil

1 small tomato, seeded and coarsely chopped

1 fresh small chili, seeded and coarsely chopped

1 lime, freshly squeezed

1 sprig fresh coriander (cilantro) coarsely chopped

Smoked Trout: Remove skin and bones from the fish, then break the fish into coarse pieces. Salt Cod: Optionally soak in cold water for several hours, pat dry, and slice into thin bits.

In a wok, fry the shallots in oil over medium low heat until soft ~ about 3 minutes; remove with a slotted spoon and reserve. Increase heat slightly and fry fish in the same oil for a couple minutes, or until just crisp; drain away most of the oil. Add tomato to the same pan and cook over medium flame for 1 minute; remove from heat. Stir in the chili, cooked shallot and lime, and garnish with fresh coriander/cilantro. Makes about 1/2 cup (125 ml), or more if soaked

Fish Cakes

nga soe lone

Not meant as a stand-alone recipe, Burmese fish cakes are incorporated into other dishes, whether in a stew such as Mohinga or a salad. Unlike the crab and shrimp cake recipes following, these fish cakes are stiff and chewy, made to withstand room temperature for a day or so. (But for safety it's best to keep them refrigerated. Chilling also stiffens texture.) Traditionally these are made with featherback (*nga pe*), as it is not too sticky when pounded unlike barramundi, and not too watery like catfish or carp. Flat, white-fleshed fish suit well, but press to extract all excess moisture, especially if the fish has been frozen. Adding flour is optional, resulting in a lighter, slightly leavened ball. These fish cakes are popular eaten simply with chili flakes in oil (Chili Fry, page 292).

1¹/₂ lb (750 g) skinless fish fillets, such as flounder, sole, or sea bass

1 teaspoon (5 ml) salt

¹/₄ teaspoon (1 ml) turmeric powder

¹/₂ stalk lemongrass, white part only, peeled and very finely chopped

¹/₂ inch (1.2 cm) knob fresh ginger, grated

¹/₂ small onion, finely chopped (about 3 tablespoons/20 g)

1 garlic clove, minced

1 fresh green long finger chili, seeded and finely diced

¹/₂ teaspoon (2 ml) shrimp paste, toasted (optional)

3 tablespoons (30 g) tapioca starch, or corn starch/cornflour

Oil for shallow pan frying (optional)

Rub the fish with salt and turmeric; don gloves to prevent dying hands. Marinate for at least 15 minutes and, when ready to use, press firmly in absorbent paper to extract any excess moisture.

Meanwhile, in a mortar and pestle pound together the lemongrass, ginger, onion and garlic until pulverized. (In this case, a blender renders it too liquid.) Alternatively, use the blunt end of a rolling pin in a bowl. Press through a fine mesh strainer to extract and discard any liquid, or squeeze with your palm.

Coarsely chop the fish fillets. Place in a food processor with the pureed blend, diced chili, and optional shrimp paste. Puree in quick on and off bursts, then add tapioca- or corn starch. Process until fully blended ~ a good 3 minutes, until it starts to pull away from the sides.

Lightly oil or moisten hands to prevent sticking and form small 2 x ½ inch/5 x 1.2 cm thick mounds. (Alternatively, form into 1 inch/2.5 cm balls ~ this is especially popular in soup.) Steam for about 10 minutes, or fry over medium heat until lightly golden ~ about 5 minutes on each side. Slice cakes and toss into a salad, add to fried rice or soup; serve small balls whole. Makes about 15 small cakes or 30 balls

VARIATION: STEAMED FISH CAKES IN BANANA LEAF

Make fish paste as above, without flour. Add ¼ cup/60 ml chilled thick coconut cream while processing (do not add any thin liquid). Cut banana leaves into about 10 inch/25 cm squares, shiny side down. Lay a cabbage leaf atop, then spoon about 3 tablespoons/45 ml/25 g of the fish mixture onto the cabbage. (Locally, *yai yo* leaves are used, a slightly bitter, round leaf about 6 inches/15 cm in size, similar to the leaf used in Cambodian *Amok* steamed fish custard). Gently roll over sides of banana leaf, overlapping them to make a small sausage, then fold or pull over 2 opposite ends of the second strip to its center and secure with a toothpick. Repeat with remaining fish paste and leaves. Steam parcels covered over rapidly boiling water for 15 minutes. Let cool slightly, then open parcels and serve.

HINT Laying a banana leaf in the sun for a couple of hours softens it slightly and makes it easier to fold. Alternatively, run it briefly over a gas flame until it becomes waxy and very pliable. Very fresh leaves, especially young tender ones, are best. Alternatively, use aluminum foil.

Fish Cakes Salad

nga phel thoke

A popular roadside treat, simply seasoned and eaten as a salad; or tossed with thin rice noodles. Store bought chili oils and roasted chili flakes in oil vary markedly in strength; best to add small quantities first, until achieving the desired taste. If substituting raw fish cakes commercially from Asian grocers, steam or fry prior to using.

8 oz (250 g) Fish Cakes (Recipe preceding; 2 cups/500 ml loosely packed)

1-2 limes or lemons, freshly squeezed

1 tablespoon (15 ml) fish sauce (optional)

about 1 tablespoon (30 ml) roasted chili oil, or Chili Fry (page 292)

1/2 bunch (50 g) fresh coriander sprigs (cilantro) coarsely chopped

2 fresh long finger chilies, seeded and cut into strips

1 leaf Chinese (Napa) cabbage, shredded

1/2 cup (40 g) crisp fried shallots and/or garlic (page 41, or store bought)

Slice or halve the fish cakes or balls. Toss together with the remaining ingredients, and serve immediately, while the onions are still crisp. Serves 4

VARIATION Use finely sliced fresh pink or golden shallots instead of fried onion. Soak fresh shallots with lemon or lime juice plus salt. Proceed as above. Optionally add Chinese celery sprigs cut about 2 inches/5 cm long.

"Elsewhere we see shelves laden with fish of different kinds, obtained from the streams and estuaries in their neighbourhood. Their local names are peculiar, and therefore a few may be enumerated, -- including, as they do, carp, hilsa, prawns, dog fish, cat fish, butter fish, mud fish, cock up, sable, and so on."

Charles Alexander Gordon, Our Trip to Burmah, With Notes on that Country (1875)

Fish & Mushroom Soufflé

hmo nga baung gyaw

Not a classic soufflé, more like a flan, this recipe incorporates local ingredients with English taste sensibilities. In a period of non-refrigeration, canning and preserves were the colonial norm. So feel free to use premium canned red salmon in this recipe, especially if fresh is not available.

8 oz (250 g) button mushrooms

4 oz (½ cup/125 g) butter or ghee

1 tablespoon (15 ml) minced onion

1 teaspoon (5 ml) curry powder

¼ teaspoon (1 ml) turmeric powder

1 garlic clove, minced

14 oz (400 g) canned salmon or tuna, drained, or cooked fish fillets

1 teaspoon (5 ml) soy sauce

½ teaspoon (2 ml) freshly ground pepper

½ teaspoon (2 ml) Asian chili powder or hot paprika

Pinch turmeric powder

1 teaspoon (5 ml) salt

¼ cup (30 g) chopped Chinese celery or parsley

4 eggs, separated

2 tablespoons (30 ml) cream

Rinse the mushrooms, and slice or quarter.

Melt half the butter or ghee in a wok or saucepan over medium flame and saute the onion with curry powder and turmeric for a minute. Throw in mushrooms and garlic, increase heat to fry quickly ~ about 2 minutes. Add flaked fish, soy, pepper, chili powder, turmeric and salt; remove from heat, stir in parsley or celery, cover and keep warm.

Use fingers to evenly smear remaining butter inside a 6 cup/1.5 liter soufflé mold. Beat egg white until lightly mounted but not stiff. Beat the egg yolks separately, then carefully fold into the whites. Spoon half of the mounted egg into the mold and gently spread to cover the bottom. Arrange the mushrooms and fish evenly atop, drizzle with cream, then cover with the remaining beaten eggs. Pop into a preheated 2 x ½ inch/5 x 1.2 cm 400°F/200°C hot oven and bake for about 15-20 minutes until set and lightly golden. Serves 6-8

"Fish, as I have said, can be obtained almost everywhere. They are caught in great quantities in the river, and are sold in most bazaars, either fresh or salted. It is one of the staple foods of the Burmese."

-- Harold Fielding Hall, The Soul of a People (1898)

Fish Molee

molee

Molee or moolie is a fish and coconut curry originating from southern India. Migrants adapted this recipe in Burma, where it quickly became established in the local culinary repertoire, sometimes substituting shelled and de-veined raw prawns for the fish. Optionally, roll thin delicate fish fillets to help retain shape and prevent them from falling apart during cooking.

1 lb (500 g) thick fish fillets, such as ling, cod or butterfish

1 teaspoon (5 ml) salt

1/4 teaspoon (1 ml) turmeric powder

3 tablespoons (45 ml) vegetable oil

2 small onions, thinly sliced (2/3 cup/90 g)

2-3 garlic cloves, minced

2 fresh green medium chilies, seeded and sliced lengthwise

1/2 teaspoon (2 ml) freshly grated ginger

2 bay leaves

About 1 cup (250 ml) stock or water

1/2 cup (125 ml) coconut milk

1 tablespoon (15 ml) freshly squeezed lime or lemon juice, or vinegar

Marinate fish briefly with salt and turmeric ~ at least 15 minutes.

Heat oil in a wide-bottomed saucepan over medium heat and fry onions plus garlic until golden and slightly crisp ~ 5-10 minutes. Remove with a slotted spoon. Increase heat to medium-high, and add fish fillets, searing on both sides. Quickly add chilies, ginger and bay leaves, cover with stock or water. Reduce heat and simmer for about 20 minutes, or until flaky to touch. (Thin fillets will take about 10 minutes, thicker up to 30 minutes.) Add more liquid if it boils dry. Carefully remove fish to a serving platter and keep warm. Add coconut milk to the sauce and simmer uncovered for another 5-7 minutes, or until slightly thick. Stir in citrus juice or vinegar to finish, then pour sauce atop cooked fish and top with reserved fried onion and garlic. Serves 4-6 with rice

Chili Squid

pyi gyi ngar gyaw a-sat

Whole baby squids are perfect for this recipe, although large cleaned tubes also suit, if cut into thin rings. The final fried dish is more like the concentrated flavors of a condiment complimenting rice. The quality of oil in this dish is especially important to its flavor, so ideally source a cold-pressed sesame- or peanut oil from a health food store.

1 lb (500 g) cleaned squid (page 75)

3 tablespoons (45 ml) rice wine

1 tablespoon (15 ml) fish sauce

Pinch white sugar

1 small onion, minced (1/3 cup/45g)

1 large garlic clove, minced

1 tablespoon (15 ml) freshly grated ginger

1/3 cup (90 ml) vegetable oil

2 teaspoons (10 ml) chili flakes, or to taste

2 tablespoons (30 ml) tomato puree

1 tablespoon (15 ml) grated palm sugar or brown sugar

If the squid is not cleaned, pull the head from the tube-like body. Use scissors or knife to cut away and discard the black ink sac below the head. Use your finger to clean inside the tubes; rinse well and pat dry. Marinate the squid in the rice wine, fish sauce and sugar for at least 15 minutes.

Combine the onion, garlic and ginger in a blender and puree, adding oil as needed. Fry in a medium saucepan over moderate flame with any remaining oil, stirring often until barely golden ~ 5-10 minutes. Increase heat to medium high, drain squid and add to the saucepan with chili flakes and the tomato puree, cooking 10-15 minutes until very dry; stir regularly. Lower heat in the final minutes when adding palm sugar, and scrape any caramelized sugars from pan bottom to add to finished dish. (It should not be scorched.) Offer hot or at room temperature. Serves 4-6 as a side dish

Rakhine Fish Curry

rakhine nga paung

In the far west state of Rakhine, this dish is a rainy- and cold season favorite, with char-grilling bringing out the best fish flavors in this soupy curry. This recipe is lightly soured with tamarind, but a local substitute is sweeter dried loquat paste or pulp. Alternatively, use lemon or white vinegar.

2 teaspoons (10 ml) salt

1 teaspoon (5 ml) turmeric powder

Oil (optional)

2 lb (1 kg) thick fish steaks or cutlets, such as barramundi

8 oz (250 g) canned bamboo shoots

3 large garlic cloves, minced or crushed

2 medium onions, coarsely chopped (1¹/₃ cup/175 g)

2 cups (500 ml) water

2 teaspoons (10 ml) freshly ground pepper

1 fresh green long finger chili, seeded and thinly sliced into long strips

1 tablespoon (15 ml) shrimp paste

3 tablespoons (45 ml) tamarind puree, or 2 tablespoons (30 ml) vinegar or lemon juice

1 tablespoon (15 ml) fish sauce

¹/₂ bunch (50 g) fresh coriander (cilantro) sprigs, or sawtooth coriander (eryngo) coarsely chopped

Wear gloves to rub salt and turmeric into the fish flesh and skin, and leave for at least 15 minutes. If cooking on a barbecue, place the fish pieces in a fish-shaped hinged grill basket; brush oil on the wires to prevent sticking. Alternatively, broil under the grill, set 6 inches/15 cm from heat; cook 10-15 minutes turning once.

Bring the bamboo shoots to a boil in a large saucepan of water; drain and begin again with fresh cold water. Bring to the boil, lower heat slightly, and cook 20-30 minutes; drain and rinse. If whole, cut the shoots into thin strips.

Meanwhile, make the stock: crush garlic and onion, adding to water in a pot over medium-high flame. Add prepared bamboo, pepper, chili, shrimp paste and tamarind or vinegar. Rapidly boil uncovered for 15 minutes, remove from heat, add fish sauce and fresh coriander/cilantro.

To serve, break the cooked fish into large chunks along with bones. Place in a small tureen and top with the hot stock. Accompany with additional sprigs of fresh herb. Accompany at table with a small plate, to collect bones. Serves 4

VARIATION Fish bones create a more flavorsome curry, but are a bother at the table. Substitute fish fillets, but instead of water use store bought fish stock. Grill the fillets for a much shorter time, no more than 5 minutes, and if underdone, finish cooking in stock.

HINT 10 minutes per 1 inch/2.5 cm thickness is a good gauge for fish cookery.

Rakhine Fisherman's Stew

ta ngar thae hin cho rakhine

This dish can be made simply with fish fillets as below, but better to turn it into a virtual Bouillabaisse laced with clams, prawns, squid and octopus. Authentically, Rakhine cooks prefer a more pungent form of fermented fish (*ngapi sensa*), over the bottled fish sauce used here.

1 lb (500 g) basa or catfish fillets, or meaty white fish like ling or cod, cut into chunks

2 teaspoons (10 ml) salt

1 teaspoon (5 ml) turmeric powder

10 cups (2.5 liters) fish stock

6 large garlic cloves, minced

2 medium onions, finely sliced

1 inch (2.5 cm) knob fresh ginger, grated

3 stalks lemongrass, white portion only, cut into 2 inch (5 cm) lengths.

6 kaffir lime leaves, crumbled

3 tablespoons (45 ml) vegetable oil

2 teaspoons (10 ml) shrimp paste

2 tablespoons (30 ml) red chili paste (sambal olek)

2 tablespoons (30 ml) plain rice flour, roasted

10 leaves sawtooth coriander (eryngo) coarsely chopped (optional)

$^1/_4$ cup (60 ml) tamarind puree, or 3 tablespoons (45 ml) vinegar or fresh lemon juice

2 fresh green long finger chilies, seeded and thinly sliced into strips

$^1/_4$ cup (15 g) lemon basil leaves

2 teaspoons (10 ml) freshly ground pepper

1 tablespoon (15 ml) fish sauce

Fresh coriander (cilantro) sprigs and/or mint leaves, to garnish

Rub the fish with salt and turmeric; use gloves so as not to discolor your hands.

Flavor the fish stock by boiling with half the garlic and onion, all the ginger, lemongrass and kaffir lime leaf in large pot over high flame. Cook uncovered for 15 minutes; remove from heat

In a large saucepan or pot, heat oil over medium-high flame and fry the remaining onion and garlic until soft; fry with shrimp paste and chili paste for a few more minutes.

Take a little of the stock and blend with the rice flour. Reheat the stock with sauteed onions and garlic, and stir in the rice flour paste to slightly thicken. Add seafood of choice (see below) and bring to the boil. Lower heat and add fish fillets, simmering gently for 5-15 minutes. (Tender fish will break up during long cooking, firmer pieces will not.) Add sawtooth coriander now, if using, and tamarind or vinegar (if using lemon juice add later).

At the very end of cooking, add chili strips, and lemon basil if using, and fresh lemon juice. Season with pepper, fish sauce and garnish with fresh coriander/cilantro leaves and freshly chopped mint. Serves 6

CLEANING OCTOPUS
Octopus require both cleaning, and tenderizing. Stringy looking specimens have not been tenderized, which is commonly done in a cement mixer upon docking. Alternatively soak in milk for a couple hours, or hit with a mallet. Taut curly looking specimens have been pre-tenderized, but not cooked.

Make a deep cut above the eyes and legs. With fingers, peel body by separating skin and flesh. Open up the head by inverting, and rinse away guts and black ink sack. Optionally, score with diagonal cuts on the inside of the head. Use a paring knife to pry away the tough beak in the center of legs portion. Cut the octopus legs into bite-sized pieces.

CLEANING SQUID
Pre-cleaned squid tubes are readily available. But whole squid require cleaning. Use a sharp knife to separate tentacles from head, just above the eye. Use finger to pry away the brittle beak. Some squid varieties have crunchy suction cups along their legs, which are easily removed by scraping with a fingernail. Scoop out and pull away the guts in the tube, including its plastic-like cartilage or backbone. If desired, pull away the skin, first by scraping with fingernail; retain the back fins.

CLEANING CLAMS & MUSSELS
Rinse shells briskly in cold water, pulling away any clinging or hanging strings,

especially with mussels. Discard any opened shells, but this rule only applies to fresh bivalves. Some varieties, such as New Zealand green lip mussels, are commonly exported pre-cooked and open.

COOKING A LIVE CRAB

Orange colored bones generally indicates that the crab is pre-cooked and will not require further boiling. Freshly shelled cooked crab works best, as canned crab retains a tinny, undesirable flavor and dry texture. Blue Swimmer and Dungeness crab meats also taste delicious here, but Alaska King will have a more pronounced flavor. Mud Crabs cook best when steamed or pan fried as opposed to boiled. This is because they take on excess water during cooking, rendering the flesh soggy.

Place a large pot of water on high heat; add salt generously. Bring to a rapid boil, and drop the raw crabs directly into the water and cook for about 10 minutes for smaller crabs, and up to 20 minutes for larger ones. Alternatively, place the crabs on a steamer rack, directly over the water and cover tightly; steam for 15 minutes. Remove from heat and cool, then pry apart the crab and remove its flesh.

TO SHELL CRAB

First remove its "apron" tail flap, located on its underside. Use your fingers to pry it up and off. (Large triangular flaps indicate a female, while thinner long phallic-shaped aprons indicate male.) In Asia she-crab fetches a premium for its roe.

Turn the crab over and gently pry off its top shell. Discard the shell (or retain for garnish or as a serving plate), and remove and discard the feathery gray gills from both sides of the body. The yellowish "fat" above the stomach is a delicacy, and should be retained for added flavor. Break off the crab claws where they join the body, and pull out and discard the spongy sand bags. Snap the body in half to help extract the meat. A small fork, or better yet the crab's claw tip, helps extract the meat. Use a nutcracker or mallet to crack the legs and claws to extract meat.

Soft-Shell Crab Masala

ganan pyaw masala

With modern processing, soft-shell crab has become a perennial favorite, no longer restricted to a single moulting season. At their best when purchased alive, soft-shell crabs are more commonly available frozen and thawed. (And often prepared, with no need for further cleaning.) Their size varies markedly, with frozen Myanmar exports about 3 oz/85 g each, but larger Chesapeake blue crabs twice that size at 6 oz/170 g. Store live crabs at bottom of fridge nestled between sheets of wet newspaper, for no more than one day.

About ¹/₂ cup (125 ml) vegetable oil, or ghee

2 medium onions, thinly sliced (about 1¹/₃ cups/ 175 g)

2 large garlic cloves, thinly sliced

1 teaspoon (5 ml) freshly grated ginger

4-8 soft-shelled crabs, cleaned

1 egg white (optional)

¹/₄ teaspoon (1 ml) turmeric powder

Salt and pepper, to taste

About ¹/₄ cup (35 g) plain rice flour or wheat flour

¹/₂-1 teaspoon (2-5 ml) masala spice, dry ginger powder or curry powder

¹/₂ bunch lemon basil, leaves coarsely chopped (about ¹/₃ cup/20g)

In a large saucepan, heat the oil over medium-low flame. Add the onions, stir periodically and cook until lightly golden ~ typically as long as 20 minutes. Remove onions with slotted spoon, drain and reserve. Note: onions are not fried for a crisp garnish; rather, they are slowly wilted and golden brown to create a fragrant oil. Increase heat to medium high, add garlic and ginger to the same oil and gently fry until golden ~ about 2-3 minutes. Remove with a slotted spoon and keep warm along with the onion; use the resulting oil for frying the crab.

Clean the crab: thaw if frozen and pat dry, as they can be excessively watery. Use scissors to cut off the front of the crab about ¹/₄ inch/6 mm behind the eyes and mouth. Unlike hard shelled crab, do not pull away the top shell, merely lift up and scrape under to pull away the gills. Turn over, and lift and remove the apron flap. If especially large, cut the crab in half or quarters; or retain whole. Pat dry, then toss with the optinal egg white. Season with turmeric, salt and pepper, then dust with flour. Add to the hot oil and fry over medium high heat for 2-3 minutes on each side; remove with tongs to a serving platter and keep warm. (You may need to cook in two or three batches, to avoid crowding.) Drain excess oil, then add reserved fried onion, garlic and ginger to the pan, dusting with masala spice and wilting basil at finish. Spoon this atop the cooked crabs. Serves 4 to 6 with rice

VARIATION: TEMPURA Coat the crab with Tempura Batter (page 191) and pan- or deep fry fry till done ~ about 2 minutes. Drain on paper towel. In this case, add seasoning and basil to the cooked onions just before finishing, and fry the crab in a large quantity of plain oil, not seasoned.

Deviled Crab

ganan a-sat

Hardtack, sea biscuits, pilot bread, ship's biscuit, water crackers ~ all are innocuously savory, favored for long storage. While soda crackers/saltines are most vulnerable to turning stale, these other flour-and-water "hard breads" were former favorites, still available to this day. Here, they are coarsely crushed with a rolling pin to bind the crab ingredients. Breadcrumbs can substitute. Zest is the colored outer layer of citrus fruit. Pare and use only the colored portion, as its white pith is bitter.

½ cup (35 g) cracker crumbs (see above)

½ teaspoon (2ml) finely ground pepper

½ teaspoon (2 ml) Asian chili powder or hot paprika

¼ teaspoon (1 ml) freshly grated nutmeg

1 lime or lemon, zest only, finely grated

1 lb (500 g) shelled crab meat

1½ cups (375 ml) cream or milk

2 teaspoons (10 ml) soy sauce

2 tablespoons (30 ml) melted butter, plus extra for preparing molds

2 eggs, lightly beaten

1 teaspoon (5 ml) salt, or to taste

Combine all the dry ingredients; stir in the wet ingredients to bind. Lightly spoon onto 6 crab shells or into lightly buttered individual ramekins and bake in a moderate 325°F/160°C oven for 15 minutes. Serve in shell or turn out. Serves 6

HINT Crab shells make an attractive serving dish for this recipe. Bake the mixture in the shell then bring immediately to table. Otherwise, any oven-proof dish or ramekin suits.

Fish & Crab Cakes

nga ganan lone gyaw

As these delicate croquettes are made without egg or flour binding, boil potatoes in skin/jacket, so they don't become waterlogged; peel afterwards. Potato consistency varies considerably, so if you find the croquettes crumble too easily while forming, mixing in some of the rice flour and egg to bind. But the cakes are much more tender without.

2 large potatoes (1 lb/500 g)
1 lb (500 g) mixed cooked
   fish and crab meat
2 teaspoons (10 ml) salt
1/2 teaspoon (3 ml) finely
   ground white pepper
Pinch freshly grated nutmeg

1/2 teaspoon Asian chili
   powder or hot paprika
1-2 eggs, beaten
About 1/4 cup (35 g) plain
   rice flour
8 oz (1 cup/250 g) lard, beef
   dripping or ghee
Fried parsley, to garnish

Boil potatoes in their jackets, until done ～ about 20 minutes; prick with a sharp knife or fork to test if done. Drain in a colander and when just hot enough to peel, use a cloth or tea towel to pull the skin off the cooked potatoes. Mash through a potato ricer; cool.

Stir together the cooked seafood and potatoes, and adjust for seasoning with salt, pepper, nutmeg and chili powder. Lightly oil hands, then firmly form into small oval cakes, about 1 x 2 inch/2.5 x 5 cm. If the croquettes crumble too easily, stir in some of the flour and egg. Coat with egg and flour and fry over medium heat in fat until lightly golden. Turn over and cook all sides. Garnish with fried parsley, and accompany with Mint Relish and/or Raita (pages 281, 282) or ketchup. Makes about 12 croquettes

TECHNIQUE: FRIED PARSLEY
Rinse and dry small clumps of curly parsley. Lightly dust with wheat- or rice flour and plunge into hot oil for 30 seconds or until crisp.

Crab Rangoon

ganan yangon

Basically a fancy name for "crab puffs" this recipe traces back to the mid-1950s, when it was popularized by the Polynesian-motif restaurant, Trader Vic's in the US. There's debate about the original Burmese recipe that this evolved from, but it is likely a creation of the Chinese chef working in the colonial capital, re-adapted in America using mild "jack" cheese ~ hence another name "Rangoon Crab à la Jack," ~ a fuddle of French, American and Burmese miscegenation.

In Burma blue swimmer-, fiddler- and hairy crabs are collected amongst the mangroves, but overseas common Dungeness, spider- and spanner crab meat all suit; early versions equally used canned crab. No matter what sort you procure, squeeze well to remove excess moisture. You can also substitute similar quantities of diced or shredded prawns or shrimp, lobster or mussels, all squeezed well and patted dry. If using delicate scallops, merely pat dry.

4 oz (1/2 cup/125 g) cream cheese, or shredded bland cheese like Mozzarella or Monterey Jack

1/2 lb (250 g) crab meat, flaked

3 green onions (scallions/ spring onions) trimmed and thinly chopped

1 tablespoon (15 g) all-purpose (plain) flour

1/2 teaspoon (2 ml) soy sauce

1/2 teaspoon (2 ml) Asian chili powder or hot paprika

12 oz (350 g) packet store bought wonton wrappers (about 35) square or round, or recipe following

1 egg, lightly beaten

About 3-4 cups (750 ml- 1 liter) vegetable oil, for deep frying

Beat the cream cheese until fluffy and soft. (Jack cheese merely needs fine shredding.) Add crab, onion, flour, soy and chili, stirring together vigorously, but do not whip.

Lay a wonton wrapper flat and use a small spoon to mound filling in the center. Brush beaten egg along the edges, fold over and squeeze or crimp edges together. Repeat with remaining wrappers and filling, using parchment or waxed paper between layers to prevent sticking. Cover with plastic wrap and refrigerate for up to 1 hour before cooking. For longer storage, freeze.

To cook, heat oil over medium-high heat in a wok, high-sided pan or deep fryer ~ about 325°F/160°C or slightly higher. Plunge a few wontons at a time into the hot oil and cook until golden ~ about 2-3 minutes, or longer if frozen.

Accompany, variously, with Bate Chin (page 287), or store-bought plum sauce, sweet chili sauce, hot mustard dip or soy sauce. Makes about 35 dumplings

Wonton Wrappers

2 cups (240 g) all-purpose
  (plain) flour
1 egg
1/2 tsp (2 ml) salt

Pinch baking soda
  (bi-carbonate of soda)
About 1/2 cup (125 ml) cold
  water

Combine flour, egg, salt and soda, with just enough of the water to bind, then vigorously knead as with bread ~ about 30 minutes. (Easiest to do this with a dough hook in an electric mixer, adding additional water by the teaspoonful as required.) Dough should be pliable and not sticky. Cover and chill for an hour or longer.

Cut dough in half and use the heel of your hand to roll into two long 1 inch/ 2.5 cm wide cylinders about 12 inches/30 cm long. Cover tightly with plastic wrap and again chill to allow glutens to relax. (You can do this a day in advance, but not longer.) Cut the dough into pieces, about 1/3 inch/1 cm thick. Roll on a lightly floured surface to about 3 inches/7.5 cm and proceed as above.

Prawn Kebab Curry

pazun hin ah hmway

This is a re-interpretation of a classic Burmese curry, allowing for easy barbecue grilling, then saucing later. The long mild chilies called for here are not spicy hot; or use bell peppers/capsicums. If substituting cooked prawns, they require only heating through, so decrease cooking time by half.

FOR THE CURRY SAUCE

2 small onions, finely sliced (²/₃ cup/90 g)

6 garlic cloves, minced

1/2 inch (1.2 cm) knob fresh ginger, grated

1/3 cup (90 ml) vegetable oil

2 cups (500 ml) fish stock or water

1/2 teaspoon (2 ml) Asian chili powder or hot paprika

Pinch saffron (optional)

1 teaspoon (5 ml) salt

1/4 cup (15 g) coarsely chopped fresh coriander (cilantro) stems and root

FOR THE KEBABS

2 small onions, peeled and quartered

1-2 bell peppers, seeded and cut into short wide strips

1¹/₂ lb (750 g) shelled and deveined raw/green prawns

1 teaspoon (5 ml) salt

1/4 teaspoon (1 ml) turmeric powder

About 1/4 cup (60 g) ghee or vegetable oil

Fresh coriander (cilantro) leaves, to garnish

For the curry sauce: Combine onion, garlic and ginger in a blender, and process, drizzling in the oil as needed. Pour into a medium saucepan over medium flame, add any remaining oil, and cook for 15-20 minutes, stirring regularly lest it scorch. Add stock, bring to the boil, lower heat and simmer for 10-15 minutes. (If prawns have heads, remove and gently mash to extract additional flavor. Add to water or stock and strain, then add to curry sauce.) Add optional chili powder and optional saffron, first dissolving it in a spoonful of warm water. Taste for seasoning, and just before using, stir in most of the chopped fresh coriander/cilantro.

For the kebabs: If using wooden skewers, soak in water for at least 15 minutes, to help prevent charring during cooking. Break the onion into individual pieces. Briefly pour boiling water over the onion and capsicum/pepper pieces then drain. This helps soften them, especially if the prawns cook quicker than the vegetable.

Rub the prawn meat with salt and turmeric. Skewer the prawns alternately with onions, and peppers/capsicum. Cover and refrigerate until ready to cook.

Arrange shellfish on a large flat frying pan or oven pan, one large enough to hold the kebabs flat. Brush with ghee or oil, and cook under a preheated broiler/grill about 6 inches (15 cm) from heat for about 5 minutes, turning once and basting again. Alternatively, cook on a barbecue grill. Remove skewers to a warm serving dish and pour the curry sauce atop. Garnish with any remaining fresh coriander/cilantro. Serve with rice or pilaf. Serves 6

VARIATION: FISH FILLETS
As in most of Southeast Asia, fish is commonly cut into pieces then stewed or boiled in a curry, resulting in more flavor to sauce, but detrimental if wanting to present beautiful whole fish fillets at table. Use the above sauce as a model, but do not skewer. Broil or grill fish separately, then sauce at last minute. Alternatively, cube thick fillets such as tuna and swordfish ~ about 1½ inch/3 cm ~ and skewer, cooking as above.

"The River of the Lost Footsteps and the Golden Mystery upon its Banks. Shows how a Man may go to the Shway Dagon Pagoda and see it not and to the Pegu Club and hear too much."

~ Rudyard Kipling, *From Sea to Sea* (1899)

Curried Lobster Salad

pazun doke thoke

As a cost saver, source frozen and shelled lobster meat from your local fishmonger or supermarket. Alternatively, substitute chopped cooked and shelled prawns. Although head lettuce is rarely consumed in Myanmar outside of foreign hotels, serve this refreshing salad in lettuce cups. For extra crispness, prepare the lettuce cups hours prior, wrap and chill.

3 lb (1.5 kg) cooked lobster meat

1 cucumber

About 2 teaspoons (10 ml) salt

1-2 limes, freshly juiced

4 eggs, hard boiled (page 361)

1/4 teaspoon (1 ml) shrimp paste, roasted (optional)

1/2 teaspoon (2 ml) curry powder or masala spice

1 cup (250 ml) Sweet- or Buttermilk Mayonnaise (page 291) or 1/2 cup (125 ml) cream, whipped to soft peaks

3 green onions (scallions/ spring onions), trimmed and coarsely chopped

4 fresh green long finger chilies, or 1 bell pepper (capsicum), seeded and thinly sliced into strips

1/2 teaspoon (2 ml) finely ground white pepper

6 iceberg/head lettuce leaves, trimmed (optional)

Cut the lobster into medallions or chunks; refrigerate until ready to serve.

Prepare the cucumber: Peel, then score lengthwise with the tines of a fork. Cut lengthwise, and use a small spoon to scoop out and discard seeds. Cut the halves into half moon-shapes, about 1/8 inch/3 mm or thicker. Sprinkle lightly with some of the salt and leave in a colander to extract excess liquid. When ready to assemble, squeeze gently and pat dry with a cloth.

Peel the cooked eggs and sieve through a strainer directly into a mixing bowl. Crumble and add shrimp paste if using, curry powder and pepper; mix well with a fork. Fold into the mayonnaise or mounted whipped cream. Gently fold in the lobster, onions, chilies, and cucumber. Taste and adjust for salt. Spoon into individual iceberg lettuce cups, as in *san choy bao*. Serves 6

TECHNIQUE: WHIPPING CREAM
Ensure cream is very cold, plus mixing bowl, whisk or beaters chilled. In hot weather, you may need to sit your bowl atop ice while beating. Use hand whisk or electric beater on high until cream is just mounted. Do not overbeat lest it curdle and turn into butter.

TECHNIQUE: LETTUCE CUPS
Select a light weight, loose-leafed iceberg lettuce; not a heavy dense head. Hit core against the counter to loosen, then pull away. Rinse the head with cold water directly from the faucet, and drain. Carefully pull away the outer leaves, so that they retain their whole shape. Trim frilly edges with shears, then stack the leaves together. (This step helps prevent them from splitting in storage.) If the leaves are very wet, wrap gently in toweling, then secure in a large plastic bag. Chill in the bottom of refrigerator until ready to use, up to a day ahead.

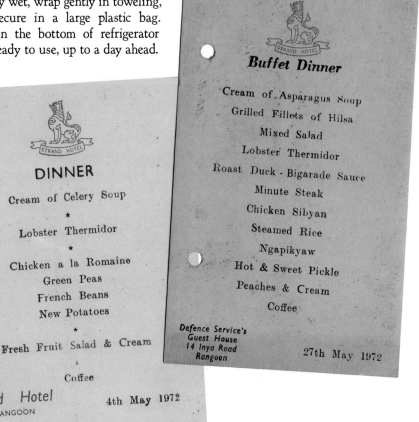

DINNER

Cream of Celery Soup

Lobster Thermidor

Chicken a la Romaine
Green Peas
French Beans
New Potatoes

Fresh Fruit Salad & Cream

Coffee

Strand Hotel
RANGOON
4th May 1972

Buffet Dinner

Cream of Asparagus Soup
Grilled Fillets of Hilsa
Mixed Salad
Lobster Thermidor
Roast Duck - Bigarade Sauce
Minute Steak
Chicken Sibyan
Steamed Rice
Ngapikyaw
Hot & Sweet Pickle
Peaches & Cream
Coffee

Defence Service's
Guest House
14 Inya Road
Rangoon
27th May 1972

Lobster Thermidor

kyuk pazun nint noe chae chese

Lobster at The Strand Hotel is an event, with living crustaceans fresh caught on the Andaman Sea arriving daily to the kitchen and stored alive in a water tank to ensure absolute freshness. The hotel was renowned for its Lobster Thermidor a century ago, and today it is surprisingly one of the rare places you can actually buy fresh Myanmar lobster in the country. During the former trade and tourism boycott, it seems that most of the country's shellfish was labeled "product of Thailand" and shipped across the world, leaving very little for the locals.

Today's classic dish is Escoffier Light ~ tasting only subliminally of the heavy white sauce of olden days, with a mere soupçon of Keen's or Coleman's mustard, and Parmesan, yet still staying loyal to its French Escoffier roots.

Of all the world's lobsters, the emerald and jade green spiny lobster of Southeast Asia wins in beauty stakes. Surprisingly, its shell does not turn bright orange-red when cooked. But most varieties of large lobster, from clawless spiny to famed Maine and North European sorts are interchangeable. All expensive definitely, but a special event!

4 cups (1 liter) fish stock or fumet

3 whole raw (green) lobsters (about 2 lb/1 kg each)

1 teaspoon (5 ml) finely chopped garlic

1 tablespoon (15 ml) tomato paste

1 tablespoon (15 ml) chopped fresh coriander (cilantro) roots, or stems

1/4 teaspoon (1 ml) saffron threads

FOR THE WHITE SAUCE

2 oz (1/4 cup/60 g) butter

1/3 cup (50 g) all-purpose (plain) flour

1/2 teaspoon (2 ml) dry mustard powder

3/4 cup (200 ml) cream

2 egg yolks

Salt and white pepper, to taste

TO FINISH:
2 1/2 oz (1/3 cup/75 g) butter, melted

2 tablespoons (30 ml) grated Parmesan

Bring fish stock to a rolling boil, then add the lobsters to the pot, cover tightly and cook for 10-15 minutes. (Smaller lobster tails will cook in half the time.) If your pot is not large enough to accommodate all at once, boil in batches. Remove from the pot and cool. (An alternative to boiling the lobster alive is to stun it by slowly immobilizing it in the freezer, prior to cooking. Another option is to set lobster in a pot of cold water, then heating quickly to anesthetize the critter.)

Use a long chef's knife to split the lobster lengthwise and through the head. Remove lobster coral and green matter from head cavity and add to the cooking broth; discard sand sacks and intestinal tubes.

Measure 3 cups/750 ml of the cooking stock, saving remainder for another use. Add garlic, tomato paste and fresh coriander/cilantro. Bring to a rapid boil uncovered, and reduce by half. When reduced, strain and add saffron.

Meanwhile, prepare the white sauce: Melt butter over medium-low heat and whisk in flour and mustard to create a paste. Continue cooking for a few minutes, without browning. (Cooking the roux removes any raw starch flavor.) Whisk in the reduced stock and cream, and simmer over very low heat until ready to serve.

To finish, gently pry the meat away from the lobster shell, and re-heat by tossing in final melted butter over medium flame for 3-5 minutes. Return to the shells, and keep warm in a large roasting pan. At the last minute remove sauce from the heat and whisk the egg yolks into the sauce; do not boil lest it curdle. Adjust for seasoning, and spoon the finished sauce atop the lobster meat in shells. Sprinkle with freshly grated Parmesan and grill for a few minutes until golden and bubbling. Accompany any left over sauce separately in a gravy boat. Serve half lobster per person. Serves 6

Piquant Lobster Tails
kyuk pazun doke lethoke

This recipe uses frozen rock lobster tails for convenience and value. Horse-shoe shaped shovel nose lobsters ("bay bugs" in Australia) work equally well, but are rarely sold raw. Adjust cooking times for raw meat. Quick frying of raw shellfish is best, as it toughens if overcooked. Conversely, cooking over too low a heat renders flesh mushy. Pre-cooked lobster merely needs re-heating.

4 rock lobster tails
(6 oz/180 g) each, or
12 shovel nose lobsters

2 teaspoons (10 ml) freshly
ground pepper

1 teaspoon (5 ml) turmeric
powder

1 teaspoon (5 ml) Asian chili
powder or hot paprika

1 teaspoon (5 ml) salt

1/4 cup (60 g) ghee or
Seasoned Oil (page 42)

1/2 teaspoon (2 ml) masala
spice or curry powder

4 fresh green and red long
finger chilies, seeded and
sliced lengthwise

Fresh coriander (cilantro)
sprigs, to garnish

Thaw lobster, if frozen. Use kitchen shears or a large chef's knife to cut the lobster tails in half lengthwise through its hard outer shell. Coat lobster meat with pepper, turmeric, chili powder and salt.

Meanwhile, in a large fry pan, heat the ghee or oil over medium-low heat. Add the lobster flesh side down, and raise heat to medium high. Cover and cook until heated throughout ~ about 3 minutes for cooked and 7 minutes for raw meat. Pry one of the lobsters from its shell to discern when done; if it is still fleshy, turn shell side down and cook a few more minutes on other side. Add masala spice or curry powder and fresh chilies at the final 30 seconds. Remove lobster with tongs to a serving platter. Top with fried chilies and fresh coriander/cilantro sprigs. Accompany with Coconut Rice (page 156). Serves 4-8

> "Kyi-Kyi also spent days extracting the red oil from the heads of about fifty crayfish or big prawns. This red stuff gives the flavouring to prawns and we therefore find prawn curries tasteless where the cooks discard the oil which the teeth and other excretions from the heads. Kyi Kyi filled jars with this rich oil and we kept it through weeks, mixing it with rice and salt."

~ Mi Mi Khaing, *Burmese Family* (1946)

photo: Sher-Ali Khan

ON THE HOOF
Beef, Lamb, Goat & Pork

အသား:

"Once a week beef can be obtained, so dinner parties are usually given on 'beef days'. Should an invitation arrive for another date, great excitement prevails as to what special delicacy has been procured."

-- Beth Ellis, An English Girl's First Impression of Burmah (1899)

Beef, Lamb, Goat & Pork

AN old Burmese adages states that of the three best tastes of the country, pork reigns over other meats. But pity the colonial butcher of olden days. Few jobs were considered more base than that of a "killer." As R. Talbot Kelly wrote in 1905, "Forbidden by their religion to take life, meat seldom forms part of their (the Burmese) diet, and to such an extreme is this principle carried that they sometimes even decline to milk their cows, who become dry in consequence." Compounding that, Hindu immigrants from the subcontinent proscribed beef, and Moslems eschewed pork, leaving omnivore Chinese to slaughter to everyone's needs. Most common today is "mutton" which in reality is goat, not sheep.

Burmese cooks by preference select tough and slow cooking cuts, not just for cost, but also flavor. Even then, a local beef fillet is unlikely to prove tender. As one local cook put it, "I prefer our stewing beef for slow cooked curries, but Western beef when I have a steak." As for that steak, it's likely to be well done. Throughout the Torrid Zone, fully cooked meat is as much a hygienic necessity as by choice. Underdone, pink and bloody flesh is prone to rapid spoilage. Consequently, rare is rare. And well done is, simply well cooked!

As fatty cuts such as belly and neck are popular, a quick way to cut fat content is to rinse cut meat with boiling water straight from the kettle. Drain and proceed as per recipe. (You can use its drained water later in stock, but then, it defeats the dietetic purpose!)

"Very few are able to afford curries of meat or fish, besides that there are not always unscrupulous people ready to disregard the law against taking life, and the material is therefore not always available."

~Shway Yoe (Sir James George Scott)
The Burman, His Life and Notions (1882)

Quick Spiced Beef

a-mae tar kin

Yogurt marinade indicates an Indian influence in this recipe, and its simplicity renders this beef dish a timeless favorite to contemporary palates. Perfect for a covered kettle barbecue or a tandoori oven. If serving at table, accompany with rice and Mint Relish (page 281). For a cocktail party variation, substitute lamb or goat rib cutlets and serve as finger food.

1¹/₂ lb (750 g) beef sirloin or eye fillet, cut into long thin strips
2 teaspoons (10 ml) curry powder or masala spice
2 teaspoons (10 ml) salt
¹/₂ cup (125 ml) plain yogurt

If using wooden skewers soak them in water for 15 minutes prior to threading the meat. This helps prevent the wood from burning. If using metal skewers, this step is not necessary.

Toss curry power or masala and salt directly onto the meat slices, rubbing well to cover uniformly with seasoning; thread onto skewers. Brush with yogurt and marinate for 1 hour, or overnight.

To cook individual chops using an electric broiler, place about 6 inches/ 15 cm from heat and grill for 3-5 minutes on each side, or until done. Alternatively, place chops on barbecue rack about 10 inches/25 cm from flame and grill over low flame for 10 minutes total. Turn meat and baste with any remaining yogurt marinade. A whole rack should be at room temperature, roasted 30-40 minutes in a moderate 350°F/175°C oven.
Serves 6

FRYING
Add ¹/₄ cup/60 ml vegetable oil to a large fry pan, preferably a rectangular one to fit the skewers. Heat the oil over medium-high heat until nearly smoking, then fry the skewers about 1 minute on each side. Remove and drain.

BROILED/GRILLED
Space the skewers not too closely on a tray and cook about 4 inches/10 cm from the heat. Cook for about 2 minutes on the first side, and 1 minute on the second, or until desired rare, medium, or well done.

BARBECUE
Place the skewers on the rack over medium-low flame and cook for about 5 minutes total. Turn over once, and baste with any remaining marinade.

TECHNIQUE: "FRENCHED" CHOPS & RACK
Remove the meat, fat and sinew from the first couple inches (5 cm) of the rib bones. Scrape with your knife to clean; this allows for easy finger-food handling later. Marinate as above and when ready to cook, wipe marinade from the bones, then wrap bones with foil to prevent scorching.

Mutton Cutlets
thoe thar kin

"**M**utton" actually means "goat" in local terminology, and lamb is rarely served. Myanmar rib cuts are typically sold with the extended fat and meat that goes to the end of the rib. As well, the meat around the rib bones tends to be fatty. "French" them for presentation (page 99). This dish is especially tasty when slow cooked over coals and makes for easy finger food.

1/4 cup (30 g) minced pink or golden shallots

2 teaspoons (10 ml) freshly grated ginger

About 3 tablespoons (45 ml) vegetable oil

6 thin lamb cutlets (about 2 oz/60 g each) or goat

1/4 teaspoon (1 ml) turmeric powder

1 teaspoon (5 ml) salt

1/2 teaspoon (2 ml) freshly ground pepper

1 teaspoon (5 ml) Asian chili powder or hot paprika

Lemon or lime wedges

Puree shallots and ginger in a blender, drizzling in oil to create a paste. Or finely mash in a mortar and pestle. Rub dry seasonings onto the meat, followed by the wet paste; marinate for 1 hour or overnight.

Heat any remaining oil in a large, heavy frying pan over medium-high heat. (If all the oil went into the marinade, no need to add more.) Reduce heat slightly so that the seasoning does not burn. Fry cutlets for about 3 minutes on the first side and an additional 2 minutes on the second side, or until done. They should be slightly crispy. Alternatively, cook over coals, basting with any additional marinade. Accompany with wedges of fresh lemon or lime and squeeze atop at last minute. Serves 3-6

Deviled Liver

a-thae gyaw chin sat

Deviled in this context means piquantly seasoned, but to non-English sensibilities, it's tame. Some cooks contend that soaking liver in acidulated water or milk prior to cooking helps improve its texture as well as ridding it of lingering strong tastes or smell. Liver devotees are likely to recoil in horror. Pork liver is a popular addition to Asian noodle soups, but calf or veal liver is milder, especially when grilled or fried as in this recipe. Or substitute chicken livers.

750 g (1 1/2 lb) veal, calf or pork liver

2 tablespoons (30 ml) soy sauce

1 teaspoon (5 ml) shrimp paste, toasted (page 370)

1 tablespoon (15 ml) Asian chili powder or hot paprika

1/2 teaspoon (2 ml) turmeric powder

1/4 cup (60 ml) tamarind puree

About 1/2 cup (125 ml) vegetable- or Seasoned Oil (page 42)

About 1/3 cup (50 g) Seasoned Flour (page 109) or plain rice flour

Crisp fried onion/shallot, to garnish (page 41 or store bought)

Whole livers form in two lobes: begin by cutting in half, and paring away any unsightly veins. The organ also has an outer membrane that chews like a tough rubber band. It's simply a case of using your fingers to peel it away and discard, and use a paring knife where resistance is greatest.

Optionally, soak the prepared liver in just enough water to cover, with a couple of spoonsful of lemon juice or vinegar. Better yet, use tamarind puree. Refrigerate and leave soaking for a couple of hours; drain and pat dry.

Cut liver into thin slices, about 1/2 inch/1.2 cm. Pare away any membrane or visible veins. Combine the soy, shrimp paste, chili, turmeric and tamarind and mix well to blend. Toss in the liver slices and refrigerate for 15 minutes, or until ready. Dredge in flour.

For best flavor, use imbued oil that was previously used to fry onion and/or garlic. Heat oil in a frying pan over medium high heat. Cook quickly, as liver toughens and loses taste when over-done ~ about 3 minutes total. (If using an outdoor barbecue, do not dredge in flour; merely baste with seasoned oil and cook on rack above the coals.) Garnish with onion. Serves 6

Steamboat
wet thar doke htoe

At Asian fondue eateries, diners swizzle meat-laden skewers into a steaming cauldron, often with a central smoking chimney, hence its common name "steamboat". Conversely, Myanmar fondue (and equally down the Malayan peninsula) features a communal stew pot in the table center, surrounded by various meat cuts. No vegetables and noodles are included.

From midday till late into the night, this is a popular street-side eat ~ locals sitting on tiny plastic stools, hunched around a portable stew pot, paying per skewer. Alarmingly, but more likely a myth, wags claim that hawkers enhance their potions with addictive drugs to entice repeat patronage. But one thing is certain: diners are guaranteed a massive dose of flavor-enhancing MSG! Some vendors also use saccharine to create a sugary buzz without the calories.

Pork is most common, with pre-cooked or blanched portions of the entire animal ~ from nose and ear to squeal and innards ~ ready skewered. (All are parboiled first, due to non-refrigeration on the streets.)

Just heat and eat, basically. Less popular beef is restricted to offal only. Other meats miss an appearance. Because of the many ~ albeit easy ~ steps to prepare this dish, begin a day ahead, and chill cooked ingredients overnight.

FOR THE MARINADE

- 1¹/₂ lb (750 g) pork neck or boneless shank
- 1 teaspoon (5 ml) Chinese 5-spice
- 1 tablespoon (15 ml) grated palm- or white sugar
- 3 tablespoons (45 ml) thick sweet soy sauce (kecap manis)
- 3 tablespoons (45 ml) rum

FOR THE COOKING STOCK

- 12 cups (3 liters) stock
- 4 medium onions, thinly sliced (4 cups/500 g)
- 2 stalks lemongrass, halved lengthwise and crushed
- ¹/₂ bulb garlic, cloves thinly sliced
- 1 inch (2.5 cm) knob fresh ginger, grated
- 6 fresh coriander (cilantro) roots or stems, coarsely chopped
- 1 cup (100 g) coarsely chopped celery leaves or Chinese celery stalks and leaves

TABLE GARNISH

- 1 lime, freshly squeezed
- Bate Chin (page 287) or vinegar

Rub meat with 5-spice, sugar, thick soy and rum; marinate refrigerated for several hours, or until ready to cook.

Make an ersatz mirepoix by lightly crushing and combining the onion, lemongrass, garlic, ginger, fresh coriander/cilantro roots and celery. Add to stock and gently boil uncovered for about 1 hour. Gently lower meat into the stock, reduce heat, and simmer an additional 1 hour, or until meat is barely tender. Allow to cool in liquid, then remove and chill.

When ready to serve, cut the meat into small dice and skewer. Arrange on a serving platter, preferably circular, around the serving pot or on individual or shared plates. Reheat the stock at stove, then strain into a steamboat, electric saucepan, skillet, or a fondue pot. (Hint: skim the stock of fat while still cold, or remove with sheets of paper towel.) Maintain stock at a gentle boil, and reheat meats. Dip the hot pieces into sauce (page 287) or vinegar. Serve individual bowls of steamed rice, allowing the juices from the cooked meats and sauces to flavor the rice. Serves 4-6

VARIATION Instead of cooked meat, use premium tender meat cuts, such pork loin or fillet, cutting into thin strips; thread on skewers and cook at table. Add cured sausage slices and blanched variety meats/offal.

Glossy Black Pork
whet thani hin

This ebony stew is a favorite at Myanmar *assar-asa* spreads. There's also a red variation given below. Use either pork rump or belly and retain the thick rind for texture. There are three distinct sorts of Chinese soy ~ light, dark and thick sweet ~ but labels can be confusing. In essence, the last is thick jet black caramel coloring and only sometimes includes actual soy; it is especially favored in slow braises such as this.

1¹/₂ lb (750 g) boneless pork rump, leg or belly, with rind

3 tablespoon (45 ml) thick sweet soy sauce (kecap manis)

1 tablespoon (15 ml) freshly grated ginger

¹/₂ teaspoon (2 ml) salt

2 small onions, minced (²/₃ cup/90 g)

4 garlic cloves, minced

¹/₄ cup (60 ml) oil

1 teaspoon (5 ml) Asian chili powder

¹/₂ lb (250 g) pink or golden shallots or small boiling onions, peeled but left whole

3 tablespoons (45 ml) grated palm sugar or white sugar

Prick the pork rind all over with a fork or a needle. Cut the meat into 1¹/₄ inch/3 cm cubes, then rub in the soy sauce and ginger, kneading well; marinate at least 2 hours or overnight.

Puree the onion and garlic in a blender, drizzling in some of the oil to facilitate. Gently fry over moderate flame with remaining oil ~ about 5 minutes. Combine with the pork and marinade, plus 5-spice, salt and boiling water to barely cover ~ about 1 cup/250 ml. Reduce heat to low, partially cover and simmer for 1 hour, until the pork is just tender. Increase heat slightly, add the whole shallots and sugar; cook uncovered a final 30 minutes. Add more boiling water if required, but remember the finished dish should be relatively dry, not soupy wet. Serves 6

VARIATION: GLOSSY RED PORK / WHET THANI CHET
Marinate the pork with light soy sauce instead of sweet thick soy; pat dry and sear with 3 tablespoons/50 g white sugar, to make a burnt caramel. Remove pan from heat, cool slightly, then fry onion puree mixture. Add ¹/₂ teaspoon (2 ml) Chinese 5-spice instead of Asian chili powder.

Oxtail Curry

nwar mhee hin

Oxtail actually means the tail from any beef. Long stewing produces a rich stock due to its gelatinous bones. After initial searing, beef cheeks substitute deliciously in this rich curry. Both are perfect for a crock pot or slow cooker.

1 inch (2.5 cm) knob fresh
  ginger, grated
2 small onions, finely diced
  (²/₃ cup/90 g)
2 garlic cloves, minced
¹/₄ cup (60 ml) vegetable oil
1 teaspoon (5 ml) salt
2 lb (1 kg) oxtail, sectioned

2 teaspoons (10 ml) Asian
  chili powder or hot paprika
About 3 cups (750 ml) stock
  or water
1 tablespoon (15 ml)
  thick sweet soy sauce
  (kecap manis)
1 teaspoon (5 ml) shrimp
  paste
Large pinch saffron,
  dissolved in hot water

Combine ginger, onion and garlic in a blender, adding oil until it is a coarse paste. Alternatively, pound in a mortar. Rub salt onto the meat pieces, then toss with marinade for at least 15 minutes, or overnight.

Heat any remaining oil in a large oven-proof pot, Dutch oven, or heavy frying pan, over medium-high flame. (If all the oil went into the marinade, no need to add more.) Sear the meat for about 3 minutes turning often, then add dry chili and cook another minute. Add 2 cups/500 ml stock or water, or to barely cover, plus soy sauce, shrimp paste, saffron, and any remaining marinade. Cover and simmer over low heat for about 4 hours or until tender. Add additional stock or water, if necessary, although it should not be too soupy. Remove pieces with tongs to a warm serving bowl or platter, then degrease the remaining sauce in pan by quickly floating paper towels onto the top, allowing fat to absorb. Pour sauce over meat and serve. Accompany with rice or potatoes. Serves 6

VARIATION: BEEF CHEEKS
Substitute one-half cheek per guest. Season overnight, then scrape marinade away from meat and reserve. Dust beef with flour and sear in hot oil, adding marinade once meat has a slight crust. Add liquid and simmer slowly for about 4 hours, or until tender.

Osso Buco Curry
kyet thar thomahote sate thar hin

Pork shank osso buco, cross cut through the bone, is perfect for slow cooking. Colonial Burma's central location brought together the cultures of the British empire, including south to the Malaccan Straits. Coconut cream ~ popular in curries from southern Thailand and Malaysia as well as southern India ~ makes an incredibly rich addition here.

2 tablespoons (30 ml) salt

1 teaspoon (5 ml) pepper

4 lb (2 kg) pork shank, cross cut 2 inch (2.5 cm) thick (about 6 pieces with bone)

3 tablespoons (45 g) ghee, vegetable oil or a combination

1/4 cup (30g) finely sliced pink or golden shallots or onion

1 small garlic clove, minced

2 teaspoons (10 ml) freshly grated ginger

Pinch saffron

1 teaspoon (5 ml) Asian chili powder or hot paprika

About 1 cup (250 ml) stock or water

1 cup (250 ml) coconut milk

Rub salt and pepper onto the meat pieces and set aside. In a wide-bottomed fry pan, heat ghee and/or oil over medium-low heat. Add the shallots or onion and gently fry until fragrant and golden, stirring periodically, about 3 minutes. Add the garlic and ginger and cook an additional minute or two. Lower the heat if they are cooking too fast. Remove with slotted spoon, drain and reserve.

Increase heat to medium high, add dry spices and gently fry for a few seconds. Add the meat, stir to coat seasoning uniformly, then lower the heat to medium. Add stock or water; cover tightly and cook for about 20 minutes. Add the coconut milk, then over low heat simmer partially covered for 1-1¼ hours, or until the meat is just tender. Turn pieces occasionally and add more stock or water if it starts to cook dry. Just before serving, stir in the reserved fried onions and garlic. Serves 4-6

Burman Scotch Eggs
whet thar kyet au gyaw

Scottish settlers thrived in 19th century Burma, many running the country's leading commercial trading establishments. Here, they adapted their favorite egg dish with local seasonings, but the irony was that the original recipe is of Moghul descent. Perfect with a ploughman's lunch, this is timeless fare, equally popular in days of yore as it is today. And it's surprisingly easy to make. A variation for quick-pickled eggs follows; this was popular when colonials needed to preserve eggs without refrigeration.

6-8 eggs

1 lb (500 g) Colonial Pork Sausage (page 111) or store bought sausage mince, or lean ground pork

2 teaspoons (10 ml) curry powder or masala spice or Chinese 5-spice

2 teaspoons (10 ml) salt

1/2 stalk lemongrass, white part only, finely chopped or pounded (optional)

About 1/4 cup (40 g) Seasoned Flour (page 109)

1 raw egg, beaten

About 1 cup (60 g) dried or fresh breadcrumbs

About 4 cups (1 liter) oil, for deep frying

Hard boil the eggs by setting in enough tepid water to cover. Bring to rapid boil, then simmer for 10-12 minutes; drain and refresh under cold water. Periodically, use a spoon to swirl the eggs rapidly clockwise, as this helps center the yolk. Drain and refresh under cold running water for 3 minutes, crack and peel. (Alternatively, for slightly moist centers, simmer eggs for 6-7 minutes in total, cool, crack and peel.)

Meanwhile, knead the ground pork and curry powder or masala together, plus salt, and lemongrass if using.

Lightly rub each shelled egg in Seasoned Flour, and work the meat around each egg. This works best by first pinching a bit in your hand and forming into the cup of your palm, adding egg, then folding and pinching to cover. Dip each egg into crumbs and deep fry a few at a time in hot oil ∼ about 325°F/160°C until lightly golden ∼ about 6 minutes. Like a paté or hard-boiled egg, serve chilled, and if desired, accompany with Fresh Tomato Chutney and/or Cooked Tomato Sauce (pages 280, 289). Makes 6-8

VARIATION: QUAIL EGGS / WHET THAR NGOAN OO GYAW
This makes a wonderful party appetizer. Boil quail eggs until set ~ about 3-5 minutes ~ in just simmering water. Drain and cool under water; shell, and proceed as above.

VARIATION: PICKLED EGGS
Cook eggs till done, then cover with vinegar and a couple spoonsful salt, and cool for 12 hours or longer. Shell, flour and envelope with meat, then proceed as above.

Seasoned Flour

1 cup (130 g) all-purpose (plain) flour

2 teaspoons (10 ml) salt

1 teaspoon (5 ml) finely ground white pepper

¹/₂ teaspoon (2 ml) Asian chili powder or hot paprika (optional)

Whisk or sieve all the ingredients together; store tightly covered. This can be prepared weeks in advance. When re-using, sieve through a medium strainer to remove subsequent clumps.

Stuffed Potato Rissoles
arluu ket tha late

This is based on a popular tea-house snack and vaguely similar to Shan Sour Rissoles (page 154) but without rice. Here they are dusted and fried, as well. Stuff with Colonial Pork Sauce (recipe, opposite) or snip off silver dollar-sized bits of store bought fresh link sausage; but ensure cooking meat before encasing.

4 medium potatoes, scoured
  (1 lb/500 g)
1/4 cup (35 g) plain rice flour
1 teaspoon (5 ml) salt
3 oz (100 g) ground pork,
  Colonial Pork Sausage or
  store bought sausage mince
1 teaspoon (5 ml) curry
  powder or masala spice

1/2 cup (75 g) plain- or
  Seasoned Flour
  (page 109)
About 1/4 cup (60 ml)
  Seasoned Oil (page 42)
2 tablespoons (30 ml) crisp
  fried garlic (page 41
  or store bought) or dried
  garlic flakes

Boil the potatoes in their skin, until soft ~ about 20 minutes. They should prick tender. Drain and when barely cool enough to handle, peel. Use a potato masher to puree or press them through a potato ricer to ensure a uniform mealy quality. Knead in the rice flour and salt until well blended. Mixture will be very thick.

Blend the sausage meat and seasoning, then fry over medium-high heat in a skillet, adding minimal oil as necessary. Remove from heat, drain and cool.

Use your hands to form 6 balls of potato mixture. Poke a small hole in center of each and spoon in about 1 tablespoon (15 ml) of the meat. Pat the hole closed, then press to form slightly oval thick patties; dust in flour.

Heat the seasoned oil in a fry pan over medium heat. Gently add the potato patties and fry until lightly golden on all sides ~ 5-10 minutes. Drain and garnish with crisp fried garlic. Serve warm or room temperature. Makes 6

Colonial Pork Sausage
wet au chaung

Fat means flavor, and tenderness. Traditionally the blend for sausages is 3 parts meat to 1 part fat, but many butchers today offer both a coarse fatty mince, as well as a lean ground pork option. The best store bought mince for this recipe is leg, blended with a minimum of 15% pork fat; alternatively simply grind pork neck or rindless pork belly. This recipe also suits pork links, made using intestinal casing, or even easier, the caul fat variation below. Ensure casing and caul are rinsed well prior to using.

2 lb (1 kg) fatty ground pork
1 tablespoon (15 ml)
 non-iodized salt
2 teaspoons (10 ml) dried
 sage

2 teaspoons (10 ml) freshly
 ground pepper
1/4 teaspoon (1 ml) ground
 cloves
1/2 teaspoon (2 ml) freshly
 ground nutmeg
1 teaspoon (5ml) sugar

For easier meat grinding, ensure meat, fat and equipment are all chilled, rather than warm or at room temperature. Frozen fat grinds especially well. Combine all ingredients in a large bowl and knead with very clean hands or wearing gloves. Alternatively use an electric mixer with the paddle attachment and work until very sticky ~ about 2 minutes. Refrigerate until ready to use as patties. Use variously to stuff fowl, fry as patties, or in link sausages. It is also delicious in soup, dropped as small meat balls into boiling stock.

VARIATION: USING CAUL FAT
Lacy caul fat, usually salted, is available at select butchers. It lays flat as a large sheet and is perfect for making sausages without intestinal casing. While it cooks, the caul melts, basting the meat throughout. Soak caul well in several changes of water; pat dry. Form meat in the shape of link sausage or small patties. Roll tightly with the caul flat ~ it should be several layers thick, then cut. Store in refrigerator for no more than a few days, or freeze.

HINT In the past, cooks dredged link sausages with flour to help prevent splitting during frying.

Spicy Beef Savory Pudding

a-mae thar paung

An old English favorite, here the meat is seasoned with masala spice or curry powder. Long cooking means you should use a tough lean meat with sinew, as that will become especially tender, but remove all fat.

About 2 tablespoons (30 ml)
  butter or lard, for greasing
  basin

FOR THE PASTRY

4 oz (1/2 cup/125 g) lard

2 1/4 cups (335 g) self-rising
  flour

1/2 cup (125 ml) cold- or iced
  water

FOR THE FILLING

1 1/2 lb (750 g) lean braising
  beef, such as chuck, skirt,
  flank or blade, fat removed
  and meat coarsely diced

2 tablespoons (30ml) curry
  powder or masala spice

1/3 cup (50 g) Seasoned
  Flour (page 109) for
  dredging meat

2 medium onions, finely
  chopped (1 1/3 cups/175 g)

1 tablespoon (15 ml) salt

2 teaspoons (10 ml)
  pepper

1/4 cup (60 ml)
  boiling water

Generously grease a deep 6-cup/1.5 liter pudding basin with butter, lard or oil.

Prepare the filling: Cut the lard with flour, as if making pastry. When grainy, stir in just enough water to form a moderately stiff paste. On a lightly floured board, use a rolling pin to form a relatively thick circle, about 12 inch/30 cm circumference. Or pat dough out with heel of hand to same size. Use a knife to cut a quarter of the dough away in a wedge shape, from edge to center. Pat this small portion into a ball and set aside for rolling the top later.

Carefully lift up and line the pudding basin. The cut portion should allow the pastry to fit in completely. Crimp the two edges to join.

For the filling, cut the meat into small pieces and rub half the curry powder or masala directly onto the meat. Add remainder to Seasoned Flour and dredge meat pieces.

Add the meat and chopped onions to the basin in layers seasoning with salt and pepper. Finally add boiling water. Roll out remaining quarter of the pastry, cover basin, and pinch into place. Top with greaseproof or parchment baking paper then cover with foil and secure both covers with twine. A final foil cover also works to secure, in place of twine. Place into a deep pot with small trivet at bottom, add boiling water to come half way up the basin side; tightly cover with lid and steam at a high boil initially for 1 hour. Add more boiling water as required, lower heat to gentle boil and steam an additional 3 hours. Check periodically to ensure there is water in the pot, adding boiling water straight from the kettle.

To serve, carefully remove basin from water, allow to cool a bit, then remove cover. Just before serving, un-mold by inverting onto a circular serving platter and gently tap. This creates a spectacular presentation, before eventual collapse. Use a sharp knife to cut into segments, and spoon out large potions onto plates. Serves 4-6

VARIATION: STEAK & KIDNEY
Add 4 oz/125 g beef kidney, cut into small dice, white core removed. Dredge pieces and proceed as above.

"Beef and mutton, the former from cattle brought down country from Prome and Thyet Myo, the latter for the most part imported, as sheep do not appear to thrive in the country. The use of pork seems to be limited to Chinamen; but they consume large quanities of the meat, as they do in their native country."

-- Charles Alexander Gordon, Our Trip to Burmah, With Notes on that Country (1875)

Colonial "Goose"

thoe paung thar kin

Boned and stuffed lamb- or goat leg vaguely resembles goose, or at least so it seemed to nostalgic colonials. This and "Bombay Duck" (which is a fish) are seemingly illogical nomenclatures, yet reminded nostalgic Britons of "home" dishes, especially appropriate for holiday or festive fare. This recipe is cooked slowly over several hours in a covered roasting pan or better yet, Dutch oven. Here, dried fruits such as currants, raisins and apples enhance the stuffing, slightly reminiscent of an old-fashioned fruit curry. Heaven only knows what the hapless Burmese cooks of yore thought of such flavor combinations! But we find it delicious to this day.

1 butterflied lamb leg or goat leg

1/2 cup (35 g) breadcrumbs

1 medium onion, finely chopped (2/3 cups/90 g)

2 teaspoons (10 ml) masala spice or curry powder

2 tablespoons (30 ml) salt

2 teaspoons (10 ml) freshly ground pepper

1/4 cup (30 g) dried currants

1/4 cup (30 g) seedless raisins, preferably golden sultanas

1/3 cup (85 g) chopped dried apples

1 egg

About 2 cups (500 ml) stock, for basting

2 tablespoons (30 ml) flour, or gravy flour (Wondra)

If your butcher has not already done so, use fingers to peel back the parchment-like fell covering the outer layer of fat, using a small knife to free where it resists.

If leg is un-boned, and depending on the actual leg cut, you may need to first cut away its pelvic bone from the sirloin end of a leg; trim any large chunks of fat from the inner areas, but avoid cutting the flesh. Turn the leg over so the rounded side faces up, then slice lengthwise along the bone, and cut around to remove it entirely. Alternatively, ask your butcher to "tunnel bone" the joint, so that there is a hole down the meat's core, with no need to roll. However, there will be less space for stuffing.

Prepare the breadcrumb stuffing, by tossing with the onion, curry or masala and half the salt and pepper, plus dried fruits; stir in egg to lightly bind.

Cut thickest muscles horizontally so that the leg opens further. Fill with the stuffing, gently roll together lengthwise, then loop four or five pieces of twine around the roast. It will vaguely resemble a goose in shape: thin on the two ends and bulbous in the middle. Rub with remaining salt and pepper

Place the meat in a Dutch oven or covered roasting pan, fat side up, and bake in a preheated 325°F/160°C oven for 3 hours. Every 30 minutes, baste with ¼ cup/60 ml stock. At final 30 minutes, turn meat over and increase heat to 350°F/175°C and roast without lid.

Remove meat from pan, lightly cover with foil and tea towels to retain heat. Rest for at least 30 minutes, if not longer.

Meanwhile, prepare the gravy: Momentarily float a couple paper towels atop the cooking juices to absorb excess fat. Sprinkle juices lightly with flour and allow to absorb in the remaining fat and juices. Place pan on stove top and over medium heat, whisk to dissolve. Add remaining stock from basting, and gently boil for a couple minutes,

When ready to serve, snip away trussing strings. Cut the roast thickly, crosswise from top to bottom, so that you get a full slice of stuffing and meat. Serves 6-8

Roast Beef & Pineapple "Soufflé"
a-mae kin nint nar nat thee puden

Post independence, and well into the 1970s, travelers were served this time-warp dish at the famed Candacraig in Pyin Oo Lwin/Maymyo. Originally built as a rest house for bachelors of the Bombay Burma Trading Company, it boasted gardens, a tennis court and arguably the town's best victuals.

Analogous to roast pork with apple sauce, this version of beef with pineapple is shared with us by Dennis Bernard, whose grandfather Albert cooked at The Candacraig, intermittently from 1924 to 1979. Albert's recipe calls for "under cut", a portion from the backside and neck, equivalent to chuck. (Premium rib eye or Scotch fillet also suits, but the cooking times here are way too long for such lean cuts.) As for the pineapple "soufflé", it's actually a steamed pudding with fruit sauce. Dennis recollects it was invariably served on an English-origin Johnson & Brothers vintage plate, with a side of Savory Mash spuds (page 243).

As one modern traveler quipped: *"Oh no!!! Memories of tepid mulligatawny served in the crumbling conservatory by septuagenarian, white-gloved waiters... circa 2001."*

To this day, meats are still invariably cooked well done in Asia for hygiene, as was the English preference in colonial days. Decrease cooking time accordingly for medium or rare, but note that the chuck called for here requires long cooking to render it tender. Alternatively, for premium cuts, allow 30 minutes for a 3 inch/7.5 cm steak at room temperature.

"Mentally, you are still in Mandalay when the train stops at Maymyo four thousand feet above sea-level. But in stepping out of the carriage, you step into a different hemisphere. Suddenly you are breathing cool sweet air that might be that of England, and all around you are green grass, bracken, fir trees and hill-women with pink cheeks selling baskets of strawberries."

-- George Orwell, *Homage to Catalonia* (1938)

FOR THE STEAK

3 inch (7.5 cm) slice chuck steak (1¹/₂ lb/750 g)

1 teaspoon (5 ml) salt

1 teaspoon (5 ml) freshly ground pepper

1 teaspoon (5 ml) grated garlic, or garlic juice

¹/₂ inch (1.2 cm) knob fresh ginger, grated and squeezed, or 1 teaspoon ginger juice

1 tablespoon (15 ml) vegetable oil

FOR THE PUDDING/SOUFFLÉ

1 egg

¹/₂ cup (125 ml) evaporated milk

¹/₂ cup (65 g) self-rising flour

Pinch nutmeg

FOR THE PINEAPPLE SAUCE

10 oz (300 ml) can crushed pineapple in water, not syrup, or 1 small under-ripe pineapple, peeled and cored

1 clove

1-2 tablespoons (15-30 ml) white sugar, to taste

2 teaspoons (10 ml) corn starch (cornflour)

FOR THE GRAVY

¹/₂ cup (125 ml) red or white grape wine, or rice wine

1 carrot, peeled and finely diced

1 medium onion, finely diced, (²/₃ cup/90 g)

1 small fresh beet (beetroot) peeled & diced or about ¹/₃ cup (70 g) canned

1 medium potato, peeled and diced

2 tablespoons (30 ml) tomato puree or 1 small tomato, finely diced

2 cups (500 ml) water or stock

Tie twine around the meat to create a compact steak. Season with salt, pepper, garlic and ginger juice; marinate for 15 minutes at room temperature. Heat a cast iron Dutch oven or similar pot with tight fitting lid over medium-high flame. Add oil and when barely smoking, sear the meat, turning after a few minutes to sear the second side. Lower heat to medium or medium low and after a few minutes add ¹/₄ cup/60 ml water, turning meat again. Cover tightly and repeat this process every 10 minutes, for 1-1¹/₂ hours. Stop adding water if it is getting soupy; it is merely added to prevent charring and to steam and tenderize the meat, not to create a stew or soup. Tender beef cuts require much shorter cooking time.

While the meat is roasting, prepare the pudding: Beat the egg and milk until frothy. Quickly stir in the flour to create a thick paste. Pour into a lightly buttered 2 cup/500 ml oven-proof bowl. (A small pudding basin is ideal.) Sprinkle with nutmeg. Place over boiling water, cover with foil and steam for 25 minutes.

Meanwhile prepare the pineapple: If using canned pineapple, do not drain.

If using fresh pineapple, cut into chunks and lightly puree in a food processor. Heat the pineapple in a small saucepan with the clove and sugar. Dissolve the corn starch (cornflour) in 1 tablespoon (15 ml) of the reserved juice or cold water and stir into pot. Bring barely to a boil, then lower heat to simmer for 15 minutes. Add up to ½ cup/125 ml water when cooking, if sauce is too thick. Immediately before serving, add sugar to taste.

Once the meat is cooked, remove and keep warm. Add wine to deglaze the pan, by stirring to dissolve any caramelized meat bits stuck on the pan. Add carrot, onion, beet, potato and tomato. Bring to a boil, adding water or stock and cook over medium-high heat until tender ~ about 10 minutes. Mash the solids to create a thickened gravy, then strain.

To serve, slice the beef, lay on an oval dish, and drizzle gravy on top. Slice the pudding and fan out on the same platter, partially draping with pineapple sauce. Serve excess pineapple and gravy to the side in separate bowls. Accompany with mashed potatoes. Serves 4

"A traveler approaches this hill station with but one universal piece of advice: Go to the Candacraig. This monument of Maymyo's brief encounter with the British Empire is thought to be the hotel most reflective of the town's history."

~ Barbara Crossette,
The Great Hill Stations of Asia (1998)

ALL AFLUTTER
Chicken & Duck

ကြက်သား နှင့် ဘဲသား

"Living in a large town among prosperous people, I could get no flesh at all, only fish and rice and vegetables. When, after much trouble, my Indian cook would get me a few fowls, he would often be waylaid and forced to release them. An old woman, say, anxious to do some deed of merit, would come to him as he returned triumphantly home with his fowls and tender him money, and beg him to release the fowls."

--Paul Edmonds, *Peacocks and Pagodas* (1925)

Chicken & Duck

Chicken was the ubiquitous meat of English colonial fare. So much so, that contemporary accounts regularly bemoaned the lack of variety. Far from "chicken ever Sunday," colonialists had little else in their daily diet, with other meats procurable only rarely. As Beth Ellis recounts in her 1899 memoirs:

"Neither fish nor joints can be procured in the native bazaar, so the poor house-keeper is often at her wits' end to introduce variety into her evening menu. She begins cheerfully: "Well cook, what have we for dinner to-night?" Cook replies laconically, 'Chicken'."

As a general rule, organic and free-range chicken invariably results in a better final dish. Quite simply, they are well bred and don't result in dry, flavorless meat. Factory-raised and battery chickens tend to easily overcook, or become unnaturally chewy. Be choosy, and discern the difference. (Burmese recipes are geared for tougher and scrawnier ~ but not necessarily old ~ fowl which have been running around the fields.) Some recipes here are adapted using boneless cuts, instead of the entire jointed bird. Boneless meat requires even shorter cooking time.

Duck and duckling are interchangeable in these recipes. Technically speaking, ducklings are young ducks, usually under 2 months. Many ducks sold in overseas markets ~ and most in North America and the UK ~ are ducklings. Other markets prefer larger birds, at 4 to 5 months. These are not equivalent to old boiling hens, rather they become fuller flavored and generally larger in size at this age. Market sizes vary, but a standard is 4-5 lbs (about 2 kg). Size is not a good indicator of age, however, as species vary markedly from an average of 3-7 lbs (about 1.5-3kg). Likewise, Asian breeds tend to have smaller breasts and more fat than those raised for Western consumers. When cooking both whole duck and pieces, ensure that you cut away the two oil sacs or scent glands on the tail flap; there is a gland on either side. Or remove the flap entirely. (Also known as the "parson's or pope's nose.")

Although much more expensive by weight, boneless duck breasts are better value, as there is little or no wastage. (Removing skin is optional for those restricting fat in their diet.) Their standard boneless weight is about 6-8 oz/200 g per single breast.

HINT As duck is extremely oily, you may wish to remove skin prior to cooking. This relates to any stewed dish or curry, but is not applicable to roast or fried duck, as the protective layer of skin is essential to baste meat during cooking. Besides, deliciously crispy duck skin is a taste treat!

Chicken Salad
kyet thar thoke

The delicate flavors combining chickpea flour with lime and cabbage is unique to this land, and the contrast of crisp fried shallot with warm chicken is delicious. For even quicker preparation, use a store bought roast chicken, removing meat from bones; toss first with turmeric, chili, and roasted (not raw) chickpea flour or ground peanut, adding salt to taste. Then assemble as below.

2 lb (1 kg) boneless chicken meat, such as breast and/or thigh, cut into thick strips

1/2 teaspoon (2 ml) turmeric powder

1 teaspoon (5 ml) Asian chili powder or hot paprika

2 teaspoons (10 ml) salt

2 tablespoons (30 ml) chickpea flour (besan or gram) raw or roasted

1/3 cup (90 ml) Seasoned Oil (page 42) or vegetable oil

1/2 cup (60 g) thinly sliced pink or golden shallots

2 tablespoons (30 ml) freshly squeezed lime juice

Pinch white sugar

6 cherry tomatoes, halved or quartered

1 cup (100 g) shredded cabbage leaves, Napa or white

1 teaspoon (5 ml) freshly ground pepper

2 teaspoons (10 ml) sesame seed, toasted

1/2 bunch (50 g) fresh mint, leaves only, thinly sliced/ chiffonade (about 1/4 cup/15 g; pages 262, 358)

1/4 cup (20 g) crisp fried shallot (page 41 or store bought)

Marinate chicken pieces with turmeric, chili powder and 1 teaspoon (5 ml) of the salt for at least 20 minutes, while preparing the recipe. Stir to coat well. Just before cooking, dust with chickpea flour.

Heat oil in a fry pan over medium high, and sear the chicken pieces on all sides, and cook until done ~ depending on strip size ~ usually about 3 minutes. Remove from flame, and leave at room temperature to assemble later. Strain and reserve the oil to drizzle when serving.

To assemble, briefly soak the fresh shallots with lime, sugar and remaining 1 teaspoon (5 ml) salt. Slice chicken into thin pieces or shred. Toss together with all remaining ingredients, then drizzle over a tablespoon or so of seasoned oil from the cooking. If not serving immediately, save the crisp fried onion for last minute, sprinkling atop. Serves 4-6

VARIATION: PRAWNS & SHRIMP
Add ¹/₂ lb/250 g cooked prawns or shrimp, shelled and de-veined. Cut the prawns into smaller pieces, if they are too large. Mix with chicken and all other ingredients.

Rakhine Grilled Chicken Salad

rakhine kyet kin thoke

This recipe begins with raw chicken breast supremes ~ even tastier when cooked over a charcoal flame. If locally available, use sweet salad onion (page 367) as a substitute for the green onions specified here.

1¹/2 lb (750 g) boneless and skinless chicken breast

1 tablespoon (15 ml) salt

2 teaspoons (10 ml) curry powder or masala spice

¹/2 teaspoon (2 ml) turmeric powder

10 fresh long finger chilies, or 2 green bell peppers (capsicums)

¹/2 bunch (50 g) fresh coriander (cilantro) sprigs, very coarsely chopped

6 green onions (scallions/ spring onions) sliced 2 inch/5 cm long

1-2 lemon, freshly squeezed, to taste

1 teaspoon (5 ml) pepper

Make shallow cuts into the chicken flesh, then rub the salt, curry powder and turmeric into the meat. (Wear plastic gloves, lest the turmeric stain your skin.) Marinate for at least 20 minutes. Grill the chicken under a broiler or on a barbecue about 6 inches/15 cm from the flame for about 10 minutes, turning once. Cool, then roughly shred or break into chunks.

Meanwhile, cut the chilies or peppers into thick julienne strips, toss with the onions and soak in lemon juice. Combine all ingredients together. Serves 6

"Besides the quantities of poultry in the public market, we meet with jungle fowl in abundance exposed for sale, pigeons of various kinds ~ although they appear to be perhaps less plentiful than ordinary fowls and ducks. Crows also there are, evidently to be sold for purposes of food, and nice Burmese game fowls, handsome in form..."

~ Charles Alexander Gordon, *Our Trip to Burmah, With Notes on that Country* (1875)

Ginger-Marinated Deep Fried Chicken
kyet thar gyaw

Across Asia you'll find road-side vendors with bubbling woks of frying chicken ~ sometimes un-coated, other times dredged in flour or in a slurry. Surprisingly, their cooking temperatures are as low as 300°F/150°C, to allow full cooking of the meat, without over-browning the crust. Wings are usually cooked whole, but you get more into the pot by jointing into three segments. If rice flours are unavailable, use all-purpose or plain wheat flour. The result is not as crispy, but still deliciously good. Also try with drumsticks and breasts.

10 large chicken wings

FOR THE MARINADE

1 teaspoon (5 ml) turmeric powder

6 garlic cloves, minced

1 inch (2.5 cm) knob fresh ginger, grated

1 lemon, freshly squeezed (3 tablespoons/45 ml)

2 teaspoons (15 ml) salt

TO FINISH

1/4 cup (30 g) sticky (glutinous) rice flour

1/2 cup (60 g) plain rice flour

Oil, for shallow- or deep frying

Cut the chicken wings at the joints into "drumsticks," discarding the meatless tip portion. Toss with the marinade ingredients, and refrigerate several hours or overnight.

Sieve the two rice flours together, then dredge the pieces, shaking away excess flour. Pan or deep-fry in hot oil set over medium flame until done ~ 12-15 minutes, turning occasionally. Serves 4-6

VARIATION: SPICY CHICKEN WINGS Add 1 tablespoon/15 ml chili flakes to the marinade.

HINT For dredging, place chicken pieces and flour in a deep

plastic container with tight fitting lid and shake vigorously. Alternatively, use an extra large zip-lock plastic bag. Sieve any remaining flour for later use.

Chicken Wing Curry
kyet thar masala hin

This dish is traditionally oily, but with superb flavor. But be careful about the chili powder you use, as Asian chilies are much milder than Latin American equivalents. Because of the large quantity called for here, its safest to use a blend of mild and hot paprika. (Or simple paprika: it is still delicious!) You can substitute boneless chicken pieces, in which case use stock, not water, to compensate for the lack of flavoring imparted by the bones, and decrease cooking time by half.

3 lb (1.5 kg) chicken wings, jointed, or pieces

2 teaspoons (10 ml) salt

1/4 teaspoon (1 ml) turmeric powder

1/3 cup (90 ml) vegetable oil

1 medium onion, thinly sliced (2/3 cup/90 g)

6 garlic cloves, thinly sliced

2 teaspoons (10 ml) freshly grated ginger

2 tablespoons (30 ml) Asian chili powder or hot paprika

1 cinnamon leaf (Indian bay) (optional)

1/2 cup (125 ml) water or stock

2 teaspoons (10 ml) cumin seed, roasted and ground

Coat chicken with salt and turmeric, leave to marinate briefly.

Meanwhile, in a large frypan, heat the oil over medium high flame. Add the onion, stir periodically, and lightly brown until fragrant, then add garlic and ginger; saute until soft. Remove with slotted spoon, and reserve. Keep the oil in the fry pan.

Heat the oil again over medium high flame, and lightly sear chicken on all sides. Add chili powder and optional cinnamon leaf; add a little water or stock to keep the meat from scorching. Cover and cook covered slowly over medium flame ~ about 40 minutes. (Boneless cuts like breast will cook in half the time.) Shake periodically to prevent sticking, and mid way through lift lid to see if additional water or stock is needed. When nearly finished, add the reserved onion and garlic, sprinkle with cumin and stir. Serves 4-6

Bachelor Curry

kyet thar ka la thar

This watery curry is especially popular at street-side eateries late in the night and has been named after their predominant clientele, bachelors, or *balchar*. The story also goes that country lads on a lark would steal a chicken to hurriedly cook the contraband in a watery broth with basic foodstuffs. There's something almost addictive in its simplicity; indeed, some contend marijuana is essential. (This is common in neighboring Lao stews, as well.) Here, that particular ingredient is replaced with lemon basil.

1 teaspoon (5 ml) salt

1/2 teaspoon (2 ml) turmeric powder

2 lb (1 kg) chicken pieces on the bone

1/4 cup (60 ml) vegetable oil

1 medium onion, thinly sliced (2/3 cup/90 g)

3 large garlic cloves, minced

1/2 inch (1.2 cm) knob fresh ginger, grated

1/2 teaspoon (2 ml) Chinese 5-spice

3 cups (750 ml) stock or water

1 lb (500 g) winter melon or gourd, peeled, seeded and cut into small chunks

2 fresh red or green long finger chilies, seeded and cut into strips

2 teaspoons (10 ml) fish sauce

1/2 bunch (50 g) lemon basil, leaves only, coarsely chopped

Don gloves to rub salt and turmeric onto the chicken pieces; marinate for a few minutes or longer. Heat oil in a large saucepan over medium high heat. Add onions and gently fry for about 3 minutes, then add garlic and ginger and cook another couple of minutes; stir in Chinese 5-spice. Add the chicken, coating well, then stock or water. Bring to a boil, then reduce flame to low and simmer covered for 30 minutes. Stir, add gourd or winter melon, and bring back to boil. Cover and lower heat, simmering another 10 minutes, or until the pieces are tender. Add fresh chili and fish sauce, and at last minute, stir in the lemon basil. Serves 4-6

Rakhine Chicken Curry

rakhine kyet thar hin

Curries in the country's far west use much less oil than Burman counterparts, and in turn, are not distinctly flavored with fried onion and garlic. Fresh curry leaves are available at most Indian grocers, sometimes in the freezer.

2 lb (1 kg) chicken pieces on the bone

1 tablespoon (15 ml) dark soy sauce

1 teaspoon (5 ml) turmeric powder

1 tablespoon (15 ml) vegetable oil

4 small onions, thinly sliced (1⅓ cups/170 g)

2 large garlic cloves, minced

1 inch (2.5 cm) knob fresh ginger, grated

¾ cup (200 ml) stock or water

pinch saffron

6 fresh curry leaves

1 teaspoon (5 ml) shrimp paste

2 tablespoons (30 ml) coconut cream

Place the chicken pieces in a large bowl and rub them with soy sauce and turmeric. (Don gloves lest you stain fingers.) Leave to marinate at least 15 minutes.

Heat oil in a fry pan over medium heat, and gently fry the onions, garlic and ginger for a few minutes. Add the chicken, and stir to coat.

Add water or stock and saffron, and once it boils, lower heat to medium low; add curry leaves and shrimp paste. Simmer covered for about 45 minutes, or until tender. Drizzle coconut cream atop and accompany with rice. Serves 4-6

"It is wonderful what a variety of disguises a Burmese chicken can take upon itself. The quick change artist is nowhere in comparison."

~ Beth Ellis, *An English Girl's First Impression of Burmah* (1899)

Duck Curry
bae thar hin

Different duck varieties will produce greater or lesser quantities of rendered fat; Asian ducks generally extrude the most and have meagre breasts. Searing the pieces here helps render excess fat before stewing. Alternatively, remove duck skin entirely prior to cooking.

4-5 lb (about 2 kg) duck pieces

1 tablespoon (15 ml) salt

1/4 cup (45 ml) soy sauce

1/4 cup (60 ml) oil

6 curry leaves

2 bay leaves or 1 cinnamon leaf (Indian bay)

1 teaspoon (5 ml) whole peppercorns

6 small onions or 12 oz/ 350 g pink or gold shallots, sliced (2 cups/270 g)

1/2 inch (1.2 cm) knob fresh ginger, grated

1 tablespoon (15 ml) Asian chili powder or hot paprika

5 garlic cloves, thinly sliced

About 2 cups (500 ml) water or stock

Pinch saffron

Trim excess fat and some of the skin from the duck. Prick the duck skin all over with a fork, taking care to just penetrate into the skin and fat, not into the meat. Use a cleaver or large chef's knife to cut duck into 2 inch/5 cm pieces. Rub pieces with salt and soy and marinate at least 20 minutes.

Heat the oil in a fry pan over medium heat, and fry the curry and bay leaves plus peppercorns until fragrant ~ about 2 minutes; reserve. (Careful, lest it splutter.) Add the onion and ginger and fry gently for about 5 minutes; remove with a slotted spoon and reserve in a separate bowl. Increase heat to medium high. Remove duck pieces from marinade, saving that sauce to add in a few minutes. Sear the pieces in this same pan on all sides. (If your pan is small, you may need to do this in two lots.) Drain any resulting oil, then add reserved marinade and water or stock to cover. Also add the reserved fried spices to the pot plus saffron; lower heat and barely simmer for 1 hour or longer, or until tender. (Boneless breasts will take less time.) Just before serving, stir in reserved onion mixture. Serves 4-6

VARIATION: DUCK BREAST
This makes an ideal dinner party dish, with one boneless fillet for each guest. Substitute 6 to 8 boneless duck breasts, searing skin side first, then reducing cooking time to 30 minutes. Serve whole or sliced.

Roasted Duck Breasts
bae yin pone kin

An extravagant dinner main, simple yet tasty with its glazed skin. Oven-roasted meats are not traditional to ethnic Burmese cooking, rather they are Chinese or Moghul in origin. Here's an easy way to guarantee delicious results.

6-8 boneless duck breasts
1 tablespoon (15 ml) salt
2 teaspoons (10 ml) freshly
   ground pepper

2 teaspoons (10 ml) coriander
   seed, toasted and ground
About 2 tablespoons (30 ml)
   oyster sauce or hoisin sauce
   (optional)

Prick the duck skin all over, lightly with a fork. Make a dry rub spice blend of salt, pepper and coriander seed. Rub on the meat and skin and allow to marinate for at least 20 minutes or overnight.

Remove from the marinade and wipe the pieces, then lay the breasts, skin side down, on a pre-heated seasoned or non-stick fry pan (without oil) over medium-high flame. Sear for a few minutes until golden, then turn the meat over so the skin side is upward. At this point optionally baste the skin with a thin layer of oyster- or hoisin sauce.

Transfer the pan to a preheated 400°F/200°C oven, lower the heat immediately to 350°F/180°C and roast for 5-10 minutes. (Burmese prefer their meat well done, so adjust to your personal preference.) Remove from the heat, then serve whole, or cut the meat into bite-sized strips, fanning them out on the plate. Serves 6-8

*"He bought a number of ducklings, and had them fed up so
that they might be fat and succulent when the time came for
them to be served at table. They became very fine ducks,
and my friend had promised me one."*

~ Harold Fielding Hall, *The Soul of a People* (1898)

Duck & Pomelo Salad

bae thar nint kyawel gaw thee thoke

This recipe is typical of Eurasian cooking in former Burma, using local ingredients paired to European sensibilities. A delicious alternative to grapefruit, pomelo is dryer, flakier, nor as sour nor bitter. It combines beautifully with roast duck.

4 roasted duck breasts
  (preceding recipe)
1 pomelo or 2 grapefruit,
  segmented
1¹/₂ cups (375 ml) Sweet
  Mayonnaise (page 290)

Fresh mint sprigs, to garnish
Asian chili powder or hot
  paprika, to garnish

Prepare the roast duck well in advance, allow it to cool thoroughly, and cut into thick slices. Prepare Sweet Mayonnaise.

Peel the pomelo or grapefruit, and segment (page 367). Keep the pieces whole and arrange them neatly on a serving platter. Cut the duck into thick slices and intersperse, and generously dollop mayonnaise atop. (Do this at the last minute, lest it get watery if dressed in advance). Garnish with mint, and sprinkle lightly with Asian chili powder for color. Serves 6-8

Roast Duck with Sugarcane

bae kin nint kyan choung

Much easier than using fresh sugarcane, the canned version is available from Asian supermarkets. It's already peeled and ready for action.

4-5 lb (about 2 kg) whole duck

1 tablespoon (15 ml) salt

2 tablespoons (30 ml) thick sweet soy sauce (kecap manis)

¹/2 bunch (4 oz/125 g) Chinese celery

1 oz (30 g) dried shiitake or Chinese black mushrooms

7 oz (200 g) lean pork sausage mince

1 small onion, thinly sliced (¹/3 cup/45 g)

¹/3 cup (80 ml/3 fl oz) soy sauce, preferably dark

1 teaspoons (5 ml) salt

2 teaspoons (10 ml) pepper

1 bulb garlic, cloves separated but left whole with husk

15 small onions or 2 lb/1 kg pink or golden shallots, unpeeled

¹/2 cup (125 ml) vegetable oil

1 x 12 inch (30 cm) piece fresh sugar cane, peeled and cut into thin sticks, or canned sugarcane, drained

2 fresh red long finger chilies, seeded and thinly sliced, to garnish

Cut away the two oil sacs above the duck tail: make a 1¹/2 inch (about 4 cm) incision at the back of the tail and remove. Lightly prick the duck skin all over with a fork. Rub the duck cavity and skin with salt, then brush with the thick soy sauce. (This can be done from one hour to overnight in advance.)

Chop half the celery very finely, the other half coarsely. Pour boiling water atop the mushrooms and soak until soft ~ about 20 minutes. With scissors snip and discard the tough stems. Cut the mushroom caps into thin strips.

Mix together the pork sausage and the finely chopped celery, plus chopped mushrooms, soy sauce, salt and pepper. Lightly spoon this into the bird's cavity. Jab 3 of the sugar cane sticks deep into the cavity and through the meat. (If the cane sticks out, just scissor to fit. Skewer with a toothpick to close cavity.

Arrange remaining sugar cane pieces to line the bottom of a covered roasting pan and top with a bed of the coarsely chopped celery; set the duck atop; surround with garlic and whole onions or shallots. Heat the oil until smoking, then pour this atop the duck to blister the breast skin. Cover and place roasting pan, uncovered, on the lowest shelf in a preheated 400°F/200°C oven; cook for 20 minutes.

Cover duck with lid, then lower the heat to 350°F/180°C and roast a further 30 minutes, turning over once. When done, the wing or leg should wiggle freely. Remove lid, use tongs to turn duck breast side up again, then roast uncovered a final 15 minutes. Remove from the oven, lightly cover with foil, and rest before carving.

When ready to serve, spoon the stuffing from the bird and put into a serving bowl. Cut the duck into serving pieces and transfer to a platter. Use a slotted spoon to remove the cooked onion, garlic and celery, and garnish with these, topped with chili slices. Serves 6

HINT Resting at least 15 minutes allows roast to finish cooking, and results in a more tender and juicy bird. Cover with foil and several layers of tea towels; keep in a warm spot until ready to carve.

Deviled Duck

bae kin a-sat

Although the term can be traced back even further, in Victorian and Edwardian times dishes cooked in a spiced sauce were popularly referred to as "deviled." Typical ingredients were Worcestershire sauce, mustard and curry powder and chili or cayenne, sometimes paired with acidic vinegar.

4-5 lb (2 kg) duck pieces

2 tablespoons (30 ml) white vinegar

1 tablespoon (15 ml) cumin seed, toasted and ground

1 tablespoon (15 ml) mustard seed, toasted and ground

1 teaspoon (5 ml) Asian chili powder or hot paprika

1 teaspoon (5 ml) ginger powder

1 teaspoon (5 ml) pepper

2 teaspoons (10 ml) salt

6 small onions, or 12 oz/ 350 g pink or golden shallots peeled, left whole

3 garlic cloves, crushed

2 cups (500 ml) stock

1 tablespoon (15 ml) hot mango pickle, chopped

1 tablespoon (15 ml) sweet mango chutney, chopped

Trim excess fat and some of the skin from the duck. Use a cleaver to cut the duck into small 3 inch/7.5 cm pieces, then prick skin all over with a fork; rub pieces with vinegar. Grind together a dry-rub spice blend of the cumin, mustard, chili, ginger, pepper and half the salt. Rub on the pieces, and allow to marinate for at least 20 minutes or overnight.

Arrange pieces in a covered roasting pan, skin side up, and roast, uncovered, in a preheated 450°F/220°C oven for 15 minutes. Remove pan from oven, drain away any rendered fat, then pour boiling stock in the bottom of pan. Add onions and garlic, cover, and return to oven. Reduce heat to 350 F/180 C, and roast 30 minutes. At that point, turn the duck pieces over, add the mango pickle and chutney to the cooking liquid and cook a further 20 minutes, covered. Remove from the oven, and arrange pieces on a serving platter surrounded with the onions; cover and keep warm.

Pour the cooking juices into a saucepan. Remove excess fat by briefly floating a paper towel directly on the liquid surface, allowing the fat to absorb; repeat several times with new towels. Bring to the boil and reduce by one half, add remaining 1 teaspoon/5 ml salt, and pour into a gravy boat to accompany the duck. Serves 6

Buffado

With its Portuguese-Indian origins tracing to Goa, this stew is a fascinating glimpse of migration heavily influenced by the spice trade. European variations add cabbage and potato, but this Burmese version is lighter. Classic Portuguese Buffado is cooked with vinegar. In such a case, omit the coconut cream and add $^{1}/_{2}$ cup/125 ml vinegar just before serving.

2 medium cucumbers
(10 oz/300 g)

1 tablespoon (15 ml) salt

4-5 lbs (about 2 kg) duck pieces

1 lb (500 g) small onions or pink or golden shallots

3 garlic cloves, minced

$^{1}/_{4}$ cup (60 g) ghee or oil

4 cloves

4 cardamom pods

2 blades mace ($^{1}/_{2}$ inch/ 1.2 cm each) or 1 teaspoon (5 ml) freshly grated nutmeg

1 cinnamon quill (about 2 inch/5 cm long)

10 whole allspice

10 peppercorns

2 bay leaves

1 cup (250 ml) stock

$^{1}/_{2}$ cup (125 ml) coconut cream

Peel and halve the cucumbers lengthwise. Use a teaspoon to de-seed the cucumbers and cut into 2 inch/5 cm wide half moons; de-gorge with 1 teaspoon (5 ml) of the salt, briefly leaving them in a strainer to drain.

Trim excess fat and some of the skin from the duck. With a cleaver, cut the duck into small 3 inch/7.5 cm pieces and rub with remaining salt.

Finely slice 2 of the onions with the garlic. Heat the ghee or oil in a fry pan over medium heat, add the prepared onions and garlic and fry until soft ~ about 5 minutes. Remove with a slotted spoon and set aside. Fry the dry spices in the same oil until fragrant ~ about 2 minutes; remove with slotted spoon and reserve. Increase heat to medium high and sear the duck pieces on all sides in the same oil; drain and discard the oil. Pour the stock over the duck, add the remaining whole onions and reserved fried spices. Once it boils, lower heat and simmer covered for 1 hour. Remove lid to allow juices to thicken for a further 20 minutes.

Add cucumbers and reserved fried onions and garlic; simmer 5 minutes. Stir in the coconut cream, heat through and serve with rice. Serves 4-6

STAFF OF LIFE
Rice & Wheat

ထမင်းနှင့် ကောက်ပဲသီးနှံများ

"Rice is the staple of every meal, except in the dry zone. The millet and sorghum which there take the place of rice are cooked in the same way but need longer boiling."

~ Max. & Bertha Ferrars, *Burma* (1901)

Rice & Wheat

RICE, even more than bread or potatoes in the West, is considered the mainstay of a meal. Meat and vegetable dishes are mere accompaniments. Consequently, the grain is raised to a reverential status, as exemplified by this traditional nursery rhyme:

> *"Oh, Moon King of the skies,*
> *Give my child rice sprinkled with oil,*
> *and dishes on a solid gold tray."*

Colonial Burma, especially the Irrawaddy Delta region, was the rice basket to the Commonwealth and much of the world. That prized title vanished long ago, usurped by Thailand and Vietnam. But the Myanmar people's love for rice has never abated ~ they just keep more of it for themselves these days with less for export.

Locals contend Thai jasmine and Chinese long grain rice are too heavy to accompany rich Burmese dishes laden with oil. British overseers encouraged production of short- or round grain varieties, especially as that was the best sort for the then-popular rice pudding. That small grain is still most prized in Myanmar, fetching a premium at market. But medium grain white rice has long reigned as the norm, both for cost and taste. In certain regional areas like Shan state, sticky or glutinous rice is an equal staple. And for select dishes, such as Biriyani and Pilau/Pilaf, where hot rice is maintained over long periods, long grain ~ or better yet, basmati ~ is prized.

Varieties of rice are legend, and in any Myanmar rice store you are likely to encounter at least a dozen choices – not just long, medium, short and sticky, but also old versus new harvest, and regional classifications akin to France's *appellation d'origine contrôlée.* (For example, round- or short grain rice from Pathein (formerly Bassein) township fetched a premium in colonial days, and today short *fat paw san hmwe* is especially prized.) Then there's broken grain, mixed and premium unbroken. Old harvest generally fetches the highest price, but there are equally passionate epicures who prefer the relative moistness of a recent crop. The latter is especially tricky, as it's easier for it ~ with its higher moisture content ~ to turn mushy during cooking. Unfortunately, overseas supermarkets are unlikely to cater to these differences, but Asian grocers offer a wider selection to their ethnic clientele. After all, it's not dissimilar to European's penchant for various breads, from slow rise to sour dough, to wheat, whole grain and spongy sliced white.

The English language term "steamed rice" is a misnomer. In fact, most long grain varieties are boiled in a precise ratio of grain and water, absorbing the liquid, but in essence steaming from within. This is different from the Indian method for, say, basmati rice, where grain is sprinkled into a boiling pot of unmeasured water, for the grains to dance about freely while cooking, then drained later to remove excess moisture. Conversely, sticky or glutinous rice is truly steamed ~ first soaked for hours, then cooked in large baskets set above boiling water. (Confusingly, another version, black sticky rice, is sometimes cooked as a porridge in water.)

Old Burmese cookbooks specify an earthenware pot of an exact size for cooking rice, allowing grains to swell up to its undulating opening. The vessel somewhat resembles a giant spittoon, with roly-polly base. Moreover, a wood fire, with its lower heat, is preferred over coal, which has a higher heat that is likely to crack the pot. Nowadays, of course, electric rice cookers are the norm.

Use raw rice in these recipes, unless they specify "cooked rice," as when making fried rice.

HINT Rinse a wooden spoon or rice paddle prior to dishing out cooked rice; its less likely to stick that way, and is easier to wash up afterwards.

Rinsing Rice

Health authorities and nutritionists counsel not to rinse rice, as this robs essential nutrients. Conversely, un-rinsed rice cooks gluggy due to starch build up. In the post-war years of the mid 20th century there was a drive to ensure rice consumers received essential vitamins and minerals, not dissimilar to fortifying milk or breakfast cereals today. Consequently, rinsing such rice is detrimental. However, for cultural, taste and texture reasons, most East Asian countries eschew fortified rice, as rinsing is essential to achieve perfectly cooked kernels. Today few places still enrich their rice, outside of North America where it is required by law in some states, the South Pacific, and parts of impoverished Africa reliant on food charity.

HOW TO RINSE RICE To remove starch, combine rice and a cup or so of water in a bowl; use your hand to rub and create a wet slurry. Drain, and repeat with fresh water three times in total. Each step should take about 10 seconds; excessive rinsing tends to break grains. Finally, cover the rice with a large quantity of fresh water; it should appear clear, not cloudy.

Step-by-Step Cooking Plain Rice

Medium and short/round grain rice is preferred in Myanmar, but this absorption technique works equally for Thai Jasmine and Chinese long grain. An electric rice cooker is simplest, but if you do not own one, here are time-honored options:

1 Rinse medium grain rice until the water runs clear. Drain and place the rice in a deep, heavy-bottomed saucepan with a tight-fitting lid.

2 Fill with just enough water to come within 3/4 inch/2 cm over the rice level. Traditionally, cooks measured by placing their index finger on the rice, adding just enough water to touch their first joint. Do not measure from the pan's bottom, rather from the top of the rice.

3 Over high heat, bring to the boil and continue boiling until craters form on the rice's surface. Immediately cover tightly and lower the heat; simmer for about 20 minutes, or until tender. Do not lift the lid during cooking.

4 Use a rice paddle to fluff the rice up and loosen the grains. (If cooking on a non-stick surface, use a bamboo or wooden implement, lest metal scratch the surface.) Finish cooking rice over low heat, uncovered, for just a few minutes, to remove excess moisture.

Step-by-Step Cooking Sticky Rice

1 Rinse, then soak the rice in sufficient water to cover, for a minimum of 3 hours and preferably 8 hours. Drain and transfer the rice into a steamer lined with cheesecloth or muslin. Alternatively, use a conical basket, and if available, place a small round bamboo mat, about 6 inches/ 15 cm diameter, into the bottom of the basket before adding the rice. This facilitates cleaning later, and ensures the rice sits well above water.

2 Place the rice above boiling water, or place conical basket atop a tall, narrow pot partially filled with boiling water. These steamers should fit snugly deep inside the pot, but not touch the water. Place a lid over the rice and steam over briskly boiling water for about 20 minutes, or until tender. (You may need to lay strips of thin cloth between cracks, to prevent steam from escaping.) Mid way through the cooking, toss the rice so that it is upended. It should form into a cohesive ball at this point.

3 Transfer the rice to a wooden, porous surface and quickly work with a wooden paddle to cool slightly. Turn the rice over several times to remove excess moisture while cooling. This ensures the sticky rice will be relatively light and not seize into a tough lump. Cover and keep warm, or in individual sandwich-sized plastic bags, as it hardens quickly when exposed to air.

VARIATION: BLACK STICKY RICE
Because of its outer hull, this requires longer cooking: double the time compared to white sticky rice. Boil well-rinsed grains: 1 part rice to 2 parts water, for about 30 minutes, stirring occasionally at the beginning, and frequently toward the end. It will turn quite gluey. This is especially prized as a savory gruel or enriched with coconut cream and sugar at the end.

Step-by-Step Cooking Basmati Rice

No Indian biriyani or pilaf is complete without this small grain. Termed the queen of rice, its flavor is further enhanced by lightly frying in seasoned oil, prior to adding liquid. Over the decades in Myanmar basmati became increasingly replaced by other domestic varieties, especially those holding up to long periods of heating after initial cooking.

Basmati rice can be cooked in a large pot of unlimited water, allowing the grains to float freely during cooking; drain and use. Alternatively, cook in a measured quantity of liquid: 1 cup/200 g rice to 1½ cup/375 ml liquid.

1 Fill a large pot with water and bring to a rolling boil over medium to high heat. Gradually sprinkle in the rice, so that the water continues boiling and the grains dance around without sticking. Stir minimally, as you do not want the starch to turn gluey. Boil uncovered for about 12-15 minutes, then strain.

2 Turn the rice out onto a lightly oiled or buttered baking dish; cover and keep warm in a low oven for about 15 minutes, until it is completely tender and dry. Serve as is, or use as a base for other ingredients.

HINT This cooking method equally works for long grain varieties, but increase water quantity to 2½-3 parts liquid per 1 part rice, drain excess water after cooking; cover and return to very low heat, allowing kernels to dry slightly and fluff up.

"Under the wayside palms and under the eaves of the trim cottages, the unhusked rice lies in great encircling bins of mat, a ruddy yellow in the sun. Prosperity is in their contour, and in the faces of the people there is an ample reflection."

~V. C. Scott O'Connor, *Mandalay and Other Cities of the Past in Burma* (1907)

Step-by-Step Fried Rice

Ideal for left overs, fried rice starts with cold dry grain, as your aim is for individual granules versus clumps. In other words, don't steam a fresh batch if intended for fried rice; use yesterday's. Indeed, it's best when the rice is cold and dry, not freshly made. Proceed with all possible speed once you start frying, so ensure ingredients are prepared and measured in advance, ready for addition at each step. A wok is preferred when preparing this dish as the quantities are likely to overflow and spill out of a conventional frying pan. That being said, ensure you do not overcrowd your wok when searing; cook several batches if need be, adding more oil as needed. A metal wok shovel or spatula is essential, as wooden- and plastic spatulas do not adequately scrape sticking rice. Even in the best-seasoned pan, expect rice to adhere ~ which is not a bad thing, as the coagulated crispy rice at bottom is especially prized.

1   Heat the wok over medium heat and when just smoking, increase to high. Add oil and swirl around the pan to coat all sides. (Well-prepared fried rice calls for more oil than expected ~ typically 1/4 cup/60 ml or more per 3 cups/400 g cooked rice.)

2   Season the oil by frying with thinly sliced onion, garlic and ginger first, then removing with a slotted spoon to add at the end. Add more oil if necessary.

3   Add cooked rice, stirring at all times. The rice should be almost crisp, so keep scraping the pan to loosen any already crisp pieces to blend into the moister grains. (This is different from scorched rice, which gives an unpleasant taste.) Top with fried onion, garlic and ginger; or stir into rice to combine.

4   Optional ingredients such as fried egg, blanched vegetables and cooked meats can be added at the end and heated through.

5   Garnish with chopped herbs such as fresh coriander/cilantro leaf, basil, chervil, or garlic chives, plus chopped chilies. Accompany with sauce of finely chopped green onion and sprouts, blended with salt and freshly squeezed lime.

VARIATION Cut dried Chinese sausage into thin slices, then fry briefly in oil prior to other meats. Burmese ubiquitously add sprouts from fresh pigeon- or field peas in their fried rice. Various sprouts are available from greengrocers and health food stores, but as they are more delicate than standard mung bean sprouts, add at last minute.

Fried Rice

hta min gyaw

A breakfast favorite, this dish was introduced by the Chinese and adopted ~ and adapted ~ by almost every Southeast Asian nationality, as well as Eurasians and British colonialists alike. For a special treat, use thick-diced prosciutto here. Mandalay market vendors sell a similar ham from neighboring Yunnan.

2 oz (¹/₄ cup/60 g) lard or vegetable oil

2 medium onions, finely sliced (²/₃ cup/90 g)

2 tablespoons (30 ml) ghee or clarified butter

1 cup (150 g) cooked shelled crab meat or diced prawns

1 cup (150 g) diced ham or prosciutto

1 rib celery, coarsely diced

2 fresh red or green long finger chilies, seeded and diced

3 eggs

3 cups (400 g) cooked cold rice

1 teaspoon (5 ml) salt

1 teaspoon (5 ml) freshly ground pepper or chili flakes

To GARNISH

Fresh coriander (cilantro) sprigs

Fresh mint

Green onions (scallions/ spring onions)

Melt the lard or oil in a wok or large saucepan over medium-high heat and fry onions to golden color; drain and reserve. Add butter, then throw in cooked chopped meats and heat through. Add celery and chilies for 1 minute, then break eggs directly into mixture and cook till eggs are dry, stirring regularly. Add rice, tossing constantly, plus salt and pepper. Heat through and mound onto a hot dish with reserved fried onions atop. Garnish with freshly chopped coriander/ cilantro sprigs, mint and green onions/scallions. Serves 4-6

"Breakfast for many people in Burma is fried rice. Usually it is a mixture of cooked rice and other leftovers from the evening before, vegetables, meat or shrimps; sometimes an egg or two is stirred into it; sometimes there might be a sprinkling of thinly sliced Chinese pork sausage; sometimes a variety of steamed beans sold by vendors in the early hours of the morning might be added. It is a fairly substantial and tasty meal."

~ Aung San Suu Kyi, Letters from Burma (1995)

Rice Salad
htamine lethoke

Roadside stands showcase various salad ingredients, which are then combined all together with one's hands at the last minute. At home or in up-market restaurants, rice is heaped onto on individual plates, garnishes surrounding and dressing spooned atop each mouthful. Use freshly cooked and cooled medium grain rice, although other varieties also suit. Cold, refrigerated rice will prove too hard textured. Southeast Asian butchers and fishmongers stock fresh fish cakes or balls (page 64). These are sometimes pre-cooked; if not, steam, boil or fry prior to using.

1 cup (100 g) bean sprouts, blanched

1 cup (100 g) sliced fish cakes (page 64) or 1 cooked fish fillet (7 oz/ 200 g)

2 tablespoons (30 ml) fish sauce

1/4 cup (60 ml) tamarind puree

1 teaspoon (5 ml) sugar

3 cups (400 g) cooked rice

2-3 green onions (scallions/ spring onions) trimmed and coarsely chopped

2 tablespoons (30 ml) chickpea flour (besan or gram) roasted

1/4 green papaya, peeled and grated (optional)

1-2 tablespoons (15-30 ml) chili flakes in oil (Chili Fry, page 292)

To GARNISH

1/2 cup (35 g) crisp fried onion/shallot (page 41 or store bought)

Crisp fried noodles (page 213 or store bought)

1/2 cup (60 g) dried shrimp, pounded or floss (optional)

Trim bean sprouts of tail and germ, as these are bitter. If the beans are very fresh, they benefit from quick blanching: immerse in a large pot of rapidly boiling water, wait 5 seconds, then drain immediately and refresh in ice water. Older sprouts wilt, and are not suitable for this step. Slice the fish cakes into strips.

To make the dressing, whisk together the fish sauce, tamarind and sugar. Toss together the cooled rice, sprouts, green onions, fish, chickpea flour, and papaya if using; drizzle chili oil to taste. Arrange in a bowl or platter, and top with crispy fried shallots and noodles, plus optional shrimp. Serves 6

Quenching Rice in Iced Water

htamine thingyian

THE hottest months of the year mark the change in climate from dry season to Monsoon. Annually from April 12-15, but continuing even longer in some regions, Southeast Asia celebrates its real New Year. This celebration is known as *Thingyan* in Myanmar. Revelers dance in the street under cannon bursts of water and locals return to their hometowns to celebrate with family. It's a time of utter abandon and frolic, yet conversely, a spiritual time to return to the temple and sacrificially wash one's sins away.

A most interesting dish made to accompany the celebration is *Yae thin yae nant* in Mon language, or Thingyan Rice. It is a bowl of cooked rice served in fragrant iced water, and accompanied by myriad sweet and savoury dishes such as fried sweetened shrimp paste and minced fish, green mango salad and fried chili flakes. A very similar dish in Thailand is called *khao chae*; indeed, the Thai dish is believed to have been introduced by Mon settlers there.

Rare sandalwood has long been a prized in Myanmar's forests for its fragrance, but this culinary use is unusual, and expensive! To scent this rice dish's fragrant water, originally sandalwood sawdust was burned with wax in a horseshoe-shaped candle, to imbue a distinct flavor and aroma. Nowadays, it's more common to find such candles scented with exotic botanicals, but rarely actual sandalwood. Equally, coconut milk is scented by burning these same candles to imbue its milky extract. This is especially popular in fine desserts.

To achieve, light a candle in a small bowl and set or float this in a larger bowl containing liquid; once blown out, the candle is designed to smoke. The larger bowl is securely covered to contain the smoke as it imbues the liquid.

Shan Sour Rissoles

shan htamine chin

The mild sourness of this dish derives entirely from tomato. Popular Shan hawker fare, from Myanmar's rich agricultural lands along the border of Thailand, these rissoles are served plain with cooked tomato sauce on the side as a ready-to-eat snack ~ akin to a sandwich, really. Locally, these patties are made with dried or smoked snakehead fish, or as here, with smoked trout or other hot-smoked fish; fresh catfish or basa also suit (see variation). For best results, use freshly cooked rice, as it is more tender than leftover rice.

½ cup (100 g) sticky (glutinous) rice

2 cups (400 g) short- or medium grain rice

4 medium potatoes (about 1 lb/500 g)

About 1½ cups (400 ml) vegetable oil

3 large garlic cloves, thinly sliced

1 cup (125 g) thinly sliced pink or golden shallots

4 thin slices fresh ginger, minced

½ teaspoon (2 ml) turmeric powder

1 smoked trout, skin and bones removed, or 1 lb (500 g) cooked fish fillet

¼ cup (60 ml) tomato puree

2 teaspoons (10 ml) salt

OPTIONAL GARNISHES

Fresh coriander (cilantro) sprigs freshly chopped

Chives

Green onions (scallions, spring onions)

Peanuts

Soak the sticky rice for at least an hour. Rinse the two rices well, and cook together as you would plain rice. In other words, use the absorption method (page 146) or in an electric rice cooker with pre-measured water.

Boil potatoes in their jackets till tender, cool slightly, then peel. Mash, or pass through a potato ricer; cover and reserve.

Heat oil in a large pan over medium heat, then fry garlic until golden and crisp ~ about 3 minutes; remove with a slotted spoon and reserve. Add shallots, ginger and turmeric to the same oil; gently fry until soft and golden ~ about 10 minutes. Drain most of the oil and save for other use, then add fish and onions to same pan and fry briefly; cool.

In a mixing bowl, combine the rice, fish, potato, onion and tomato, kneading well with hands. Gradually add a couple spoonsful of the reserved seasoned oil plus salt to taste. Lightly oil your hands with more of this oil and form the patties into the size of a half tennis ball, then pat gently to create a thick patty or rissole ~ about 3 x 3/4 inch/8 x 2 cm. Press the reserved crisp garlic atop, drizzle with additional seasoned oil, and garnish variously with freshly chopped cilantro/coriander leaf, chives, green onions/scallions and fried peanuts. Serve at room temperature, or gently reheat in the oven. Makes about 16 rissoles

VARIATION: FRESH FISH

Coarsely chop fish fillets, then marinate in fish sauce and ginger for 30 minutes, or overnight. Remove with a slotted spoon, reserving the ginger to fry with shallots. Place fillets in a saucepan with stock or water and remaining marinade. Bring just to the boil, then immediately remove from heat, cover, and allow to cool. The fish should be just cooked, flaking to touch. Drain, then add some reserved seasoned oil to fry briefly before combining with rice, potatoes and other ingredients.

WRAPPED IN BANANA LEAVES

Lay out 2 leaves as a cross, about 10 x 8 inch/25 cm x 20 cm and place rissole in center. Spoon 1-2 tablespoons/15-30 ml pureed tomato or Cooked Tomato Sauce (page 289) atop each prepared rissole. Top with fried garlic slivers (page 41) and wrap securely with the leaves. Fold edges into the middle and wrap as a parcel, securing with toothpick at top. Steam until warm throughout ~ about 5-10 minutes. (These can also successfully re-heated in a warm oven.)

HINT Cut leftover rissoles into 1/2 inch/1.2 cm thick slices and dry fry over medium heat in a non-stick pan, or shallow fry in seasoned oil till lightly golden. For delicious finger food, put the slices on a lettuce leaf with myriad fresh herbs and chopped peanuts. Wrap with the lettuce and pop into mouth.

Coconut Rice

ohn htamine

In Myanmar this is classic wedding fare. Ethnic Indian in origin, it's equally known down the Malay Peninsula, where it is usually accompanied by a sambal of dried miniature whitebait/anchovy (page 285). Note that coconut rice tends to scorch: a heat diffuser is essential for stove top cooking. Hence, alternative instructions for oven cooking are also given. This dish is made variously with round/short-, medium- or long grain rice. For special presentation, wrap cooked rice portions in fresh banana leaves to keep warm.

2 cups (400 g) short- or round grain rice

2 tablespoons (30 g) ghee or butter

3¹/₂ cups (850 ml) thin coconut milk (or blended with water)

1 teaspoon (5 ml) salt

Pinch saffron

3 cardamom pods

3 whole cloves

2 cinnamon quills (2 inch/ 5 cm each)

1 pandan leaf, scrunched (optional)

Banana leaves for wrapping (optional)

ACCOMPANIMENTS

Hard boiled eggs (page 361)

Balachaung (page 293)

Crispy Fish Salad (page 61)

Rinse rice until the water runs clear; drain. Melt ghee in a wide-bottomed saucepan or frying pan over medium flame. Add rice and fry for a few minutes, but do not brown. Add remaining ingredients. Bring just to a boil heat, stirring occasionally lest it scorch. Immediately lower heat to simmer, cover tightly and cook for 20-30 minutes. (Ideally, use a simmer diffuser for the stove top.) Stir and return to low heat and finish cooking until tender. Alternatively, transfer partially cooked rice to a buttered covered pan and continue cooking in a moderate 350°F/180°C oven.

If desired, fold into banana leaf parcels (page 356) for re-heating later in a steamer. Serve with accompaniments of choice and barbecued meats. We're especially partial to it with Deviled Liver (page 101). Serves 4-6

VARIATION: BUTTER RICE / HTAW BUTT HTAMINE
Substitute water or stock instead of coconut milk and during final minutes of cooking add raisins or sultanas, roasted cashews and green peas.

Table Etiquette

Burmese eat with their hands. "It tastes much better that way," locals contend. Yet unlike India and Bangladesh where the full palm comes to play, Burmese delicately clutch their food with finger tips. (Naturally, there are exceptions.) The trick is not letting the rice come un-clumped in the process. Indeed, you may observe diners quickly scooping several bites at once, trying to get a sizeable portion, followed by the actual gravy and meat. Thankfully, with its proximity to Thailand, these days forks and spoons are just as likely proffered, or chopsticks for noodles. But whatever the utensil of preference, foodies are certain to relish one of Asia's least known cuisines.

Meals are served communal, or family style, with rice as the centerpiece. Dishes are served all at once, not in courses, with a range of two curries or *hin*, a couple soups (either clear sour or lentil puree), salad (*a-thoke*). Small portions ～ no more than a few bites worth ～ are scooped onto a plate, then eaten before taking another portion. To do otherwise indicates gluttony, and bad manners.

Most important ～ and hardest to find overseas ～ is fermented decayed fish and chili sambal. (On formal occasions meals are accompanied with a dry crumbly Balachaung of dried fish and chilies (page 293) as this is not as pungent as putrefied fish sauce.) Also accompanying is Bate Chin "dipping sauce" variously made of soy sauce or fish sauce, or weak lime-based vinegar. The latter is used to season at table. Condiments like chili sauce accompany specific dishes, especially deep-fried snacks, and are not served as a generic relish.

These dishes are eaten off individual plates ～ or better yet, on large and exquisite, partitioned lacquerware *daung lann* platters; not small rice bowls as in China. Conversation is discouraged at mealtime, and the eldest (usually father) is served first, by the youngest child as a sign of respect.

"The commonest lacquer goods are platters (byat and daunglan), which are turned of teak or yamanè wood and given two or three coats of thissi."

～ Max. & Bertha Ferrars, *Burma* (1901)

Anglo-Indian Pilaf

sate thar hin in di yan sa tile

This is a very adaptable rice-with-meat recipe, made using slow-cooked lamb, or more authentically, goat. Also suitable for tough cuts of beef or even chicken, so adjust cooking times accordingly (see below). If using premium meat cuts, decrease cooking time markedly. For best flavor, cook meat pieces on the bone, such as ribs, but diced boneless meats also work.

1 1/2 lb (750 g) goat or lamb leg, or other meats (page opposite)

2 teaspoons (10 ml) salt

1 teaspoon (5 ml) pepper

1/2 cup (125 g) ghee, or a blend vegetable oil and butter

3 medium onions, thinly sliced (2 cups/250 g)

6 garlic cloves, thinly sliced

3 eggs

1 teaspoon (5 ml) ground cumin seed

1 teaspoon (5 ml) ground coriander seed

4 whole cloves

1/2 teaspoon (2 ml) turmeric powder

4 cardamom pods

1 cinnamon quill (3 inch/ 7.5 cm long)

2 bay laurel leaves or 3 cinnamon leaves (Indian bay)

1/2 teaspoon (2 ml) freshly grated nutmeg

2-4 dried chili pods, seeded

1/2 teaspoon (2 ml) salt

About 2 1/2 cups (675 ml) water or stock

1 1/2 cups (300g) rice, rinsed

Cut meat into large cubes, about 1 1/4 inch/3 cm, and rub with salt and pepper.

In a large saucepan or pot, heat ghee over medium-low heat. Add the onions and lightly brown until fragrant, stirring periodically lest they stick and scorch ~ about 15 minutes. Lower the heat if they are cooking too fast. Remove onions with slotted spoon, drain and reserve. Repeat process with garlic, but cooking time is 3-5 minutes; reserve.

Increase the heat to medium and fry the eggs flat, one at a time in the same hot oil, cracking the yolk mid cooking. Flip and cook other side ~ about 3 minutes total. Blot with paper towel, cut into thin strips, and set aside for garnish at end.

Add spices to same oil and fry till fragrant ~ 1 to 2 minutes. Increase heat to medium high and add meat, stirring well to coat ~ about 3 minutes. Add half the fried onions and all the garlic, water or stock; bring to the boil then lower heat. Cover and gently simmer ~ up to 2 hours. Tough cuts will require long stewing before adding rice; but if using premium or quick-cooking lean cuts such as loin, add rice immediately. (See cooking times below.)

Spoon rice atop the cooking meat, and barely stir in ~ just enough to ensure the rice is submerged in the stock. Float parchment paper directly atop, then cover with a lid. (Note: If your stew becomes too dry, you may require additional liquid.) Bring to a gentle boil, and immediately lower flame to simmer; and cook until the rice is almost tender and liquid absorbed ~ about 30 minutes. Toss ingredients lightly and continue cooking uncovered a further few minutes to allow any excess liquid to evaporate. Top with the remaining reserved fried onion, plus cooked egg garnish. Serves 6-8

CHICKEN Best to use an old hen or boiler, jointed and chopped into large pieces, which allows for long slow cooking, 1-2 hours total. Ensure very slow cooking throughout, lest the meat dry. Free range organic fowl cooks in about 45 minutes to 1 hour total and supermarket battery chicken in about 30 minutes on bone, or as little as 15 minutes for boneless cuts; even quicker for breast.

LAMB Diced leg cooked for an initial 30 minutes, plus an additional 30 minutes after adding rice. Fillet & Backstrap: add at same time as rice.

GOAT Diced goat leg and shoulder cooked for between 1-1½ hours, depending on cut and age.

BEEF Cut into 2 inch/5 cm pieces. Stew tough chuck for about 1 hour, or shank 2 hours or longer. Premium cuts like sirloin and blade should be cooked at the same time as the rice.

Biriyani
dan bout htamine

Biriyani is a veritable mosaic of color reflecting its myriad ingredients ~ although Burmese versions are more austere than Indian counterparts. Locals usually eschew rich additions like raisins, pistachios, saffron and rosewater. Roadside vendors in Yangon ply a huge trade with workers taking a quick bite at lunch or en route home for dinner. By local standards, its cost is relatively high. Classic biriyani is made with basmati rice, but long grain is more popular in Myanmar today, as it can be kept warm for long periods.

Technically speaking, in a biriyani, meat and rice are cooked apart in separate layers, then folded or stirred together to finish. Typically, the meat simmers underneath while raw~ or semi-cooked rice steams directly atop. Pilaf, by contrast, is cooked with the meat and rice blended together.

1¹/2 lb (750 g) chicken pieces
2 tablespoons (30 ml) curry
    powder
2 teaspoons (10 ml) salt
¹/4 cup (60 ml) yogurt
¹/3 cup (90 g) ghee or
    vegetable oil
1 medium onion, thinly sliced
    (²/3 cup/90 g)

2 cups (400 g) rice,
    preferably basmati or
    medium grain, rinsed
¹/2 inch (1.2 cm) knob fresh
    ginger, grated
3¹/2 cups (850 ml) stock or
    water
¹/2 cup (75 g) shelled green
    peas, or frozen pigeon peas
    or soy beans
Pinch saffron (optional)

Rub chicken pieces with curry powder and salt and marinate in yogurt for at least 30 minutes, or overnight.

Heat half of the ghee or oil in a large pot with a tight-fitting lid. Fry onion over medium-low heat until golden and slightly crisp ~ about 10 minutes; remove with a slotted spoon. Add remaining ghee, increase flame to medium-high and brown marinated chicken pieces, cooking on all sides ~ about 5 minutes in total.

Add rice and ginger, ensuring that the chicken pieces are at the bottom to prevent grains scorching. Top with reserved cooked onion and stock or water and bring just to a boil. Immediately lower flame to simmer. Float a piece of parchment paper atop, and cover tightly with lid; cook until the rice is almost tender and liquid absorbed ~ about 30 minutes. Add peas, and if using, dissolve saffron in a few spoonfuls of warm water; stir or toss lightly; continue cooking uncovered a further 10-15 minutes to allow any excess liquid to evaporate. Accompany with chutney or condiments (pages 279-289). Serves 6

Classic Rice Pilaf

dahm bauk in di yan sa tile

Whether called pilaf, pilau, palau, or by its Burmese name *dahm bauk*, this is the gilded lily of rice dishes, literally oozing a surfeit of ingredients. And somewhere, deep within, you may even discern some rice! During colonial days when Rangoon was largely an Indian-populated city, this dish was especially prized as the "starch" at formal dinners. This version is made without meat (albeit with some stock), although small cuts of goat or chicken can be added to create a one-pot meal. Use various sorts of white rice: basmati, medium grain or long grain. Dried fruit in pilaf is popular with ethnic Indians, but decidedly less so among ethnic Burmese.

½ cup (125 g) ghee or clarified butter

3 medium onions, thinly sliced (2 cups/250 g)

½ inch (1.2 cm) knob fresh ginger, grated

3 cups (600 g) rice, preferably basmati, rinsed

5 cups (1.2 liters) rich stock

4 cardamom pods

4 whole cloves

3 cinnamon quills (3 inch/ 7.5 cm each)

2 bay laurel leaves or cinnamon leaves (Indian bay)

½ teaspoon (2 ml) salt

3 tablespoons (45 ml) raisins or sultanas

6 prunes, pitted and coarsely chopped

6 dried apricots, pitted and coarsely chopped.

2 tablespoons (30 ml/15 g) sliced almonds, toasted

2 tablespoons (30 ml/15 g) coarsely chopped pistachios

Large pinch saffron strands

2 eggs, hard boiled and quartered (page 361)

2 tablespoons (30 ml) rosewater (optional)

Heat half the ghee or clarified butter in a large pot with tight fitting lid. Fry onions uncovered over medium-low heat until golden and slightly crisp ~ about 15 minutes; reserve. Cook ginger for a few minutes in same oil, then reserve with onion. Add remaining ghee or butter to pot, increase flame to medium-high and fry rice for a couple minutes until barely golden. Add stock and spices (cardamom, cloves, cinnamon, bay and salt) and bring just to the boil. Stir once to ensure it is not sticking, and immediately lower heat to simmer. Float a piece of baking- or parchment paper directly atop the rice, cover tightly with lid, and cook until the rice is almost tender, and all liquid absorbed ~ about 20 minutes. (You may require a heat diffuser to avoid scorching.)

Use a fork to gently toss in dried fruit and nuts, as you want the rice to be fluffy, and not mashed. Dissolve saffron in a spoonful of warm water and drizzle atop; add eggs carefully so as not to break, and top the rice with reserved fried onion. Cover with just paper, but not lid, and cook for a final 10 minutes over low heat. Gently toss again to blend ingredients and sprinkle with optional rosewater immediately prior to serving. Serves 8-10

Kedgerree

A classic Anglo-Indian recipe, kedgeree progressively deviated from the original *khichri*, which was a meat-less combination of cooked rice and split peas. Its British counterpart stipulates smoked haddock, although kippers, smoked salmon and smoked trout all suit. Anchovy paste comes in tubes, available in the deli section of select supermarkets; alternatively use fish sauce. The amount of salt used will depend on the fish.

2 oz (1/4 cup/60 g) ghee or clarified butter

1/2 cup (125 ml) minced onion, or pink or golden shallots

2 teaspoons (10 ml) turmeric powder

5 oz (150 g) cooked fish, skin and bones removed, flaked (1 cup/250 ml)

2 cups (270 g) cooked rice

4 eggs, hard boiled and chopped (page 361)

1 tablespoon (15 ml) anchovy paste or fish sauce

2 teaspoons (10 ml) freshly ground pepper

1 teaspoon (5 ml) salt, or to taste

TO GARNISH
Slices of tomato
Wedges of lemon or lime
Chopped parsley or dill

Melt the butter in a fry pan or wok over medium heat, add onion and turmeric, and fry until soft ~ about 3 minutes. Increase flame to high, add fish, rice, eggs, anchovy paste and seasoning. Stir vigorously to heat through and garnish with tomato, lemon or lime, and parsley or dill.
Serves 6

VARIATION Stir cooked cracked wheat (recipe following) into the dish.

Wheat Khichri
dalia

As a variant to rice, Burmese Indian markets proffer untreated cracked wheat they call *dalia* (generically named after the porridge of the same name). As it is not commonly available overseas, substitute bulgur wheat/burghul. The latter is parched and cracked, with the advantage of cooking in a fraction of the time. Serve this recipe as a rice substitute, or blended with cooked rice for extra goodness, as in Beans & Rice (page 178).

2 tablespoons (30 ml) ghee
  or oil

2 cinnamon quills (about
  2 inch/5 cm long)

5 cardamom pods

2 bay laurel leaves or
  cinnamon leaves (Indian
  bay)

1 cup (175 g) cracked bulgur
  wheat (burghul)

About 2 cups (500 ml) water
  or stock

Season the ghee by frying the spices gently over medium heat for a couple minutes; remove with slotted spoon and reserve. Add the bulgur wheat and continuing frying gently until it cooks golden ~ 5-7 minutes. Add water or stock plus fried spices; bring to the boil, then lower heat to simmer. Float a parchment paper cover directly atop the wheat, and gently cook for 15 minutes, or until just tender and all moisture is absorbed. Stir often with a wooden spatula to prevent sticking, adding more liquid as required. Remove from heat, cover, and rest for at least 10 minutes. Serve as a substitute to rice, accompanying other dishes. Makes about 2 cups/500 ml

Rice & Lentil Khichri

khichri

This recipe is truer to its simple Indian origins than most Burmese adaptations from the colonial period. Rinse and sort through dried lentils or beans to remove any grit or stones.

1/2 cup (125 g) ghee or clarified butter

3 medium onions, thinly sliced lengthwise (2 cups/250 g)

2 teaspoons (10 ml) freshly grated ginger

1/2 teaspoon (2 ml) turmeric powder

1 teaspoon (5 ml) peppercorns

5 cardamom pods

2 cinnamon quills, 3 inch/7.5cm each

2 bay laurel leaves or cinnamon leaves (Indian bay)

2 cups (400 g) medium grain rice

1 1/2 cups (275 g) pink lentils or hulled mung beans, rinsed

5 cups (1.2 liters) stock or water

1-2 teaspoons (5-10 ml) salt, to taste

Heat ghee over medium heat in a large saucepan. Add onions and cook over medium low flame, uncovered until golden ~ about 15 minutes.

Increase heat and fry spices in the same oil for 1 minute Add rice and lentils or mung beans and cook for several minutes, stirring often. Pour in stock or water, add salt, and increase heat to high and bring just to the boil; reduce heat to low. Float a piece of parchment or wax paper directly atop the grains and cover pan tightly; cook until all the liquid is absorbed ~ about 20 minutes. To finish, scrape bottom of the pan with a wooden spatula to lift and toss the grains. If still slightly moist, cook for a few minutes longer, uncovered. Garnish with the reserved fried onions. Accompany with curried stew, grilled meats, and condiments. Serves 8

Bread Pillows

poori

Strong, high gluten wheat is essential to create this billowy fried bread ~ that, and minimal water and fat. Indian atta flour is ground from whole durum wheat and is best, as it allows for especially thin rolling. Otherwise, use a specific bread flour adding gluten or dough enhancers ~ typically 1 tablespoon per 6 cups (900 g) flour. These airy balls can be eaten as is, or in Burmese tea shops are usually accompanied with a watery potato curry of Indian origin (see facing page). Serve immediately, as they deflate quickly.

1 cup (150 g) atta flour or
   bread flour
1 tablespoon (15 ml) ghee
1/4 teaspoon (1 ml) salt

About 1/3 cup (90 ml) water
About 2 cups (500 ml)
   vegetable oil, for frying

Sift flour, then use your fingers to crumble in the ghee and salt, as if making pastry. Add water by the spoonful, working quickly to combine; once the grains cling together, knead with your palms until it sticks together as a ball ~ about 10 minutes. At this point it is easiest to transfer to an electric mixer with a dough hook and knead for another 30 minutes on slow speed. (You can also do this by hand.) Add more water 1 teaspoon (5 ml) at a time, to bind, as required. It should not be sticky. Brush very thinly with oil to prevent drying out, and cover with a tea towel; rest 30 minutes, or longer.

Transfer the dough to a smooth surface, very lightly oiled. Oil hands minimally, as needed, to prevent sticking. Divide dough in half, and with your palms roll to about 1 foot long (30 cm). Use a knife or pastry cutter to cut into about 8-10 equal pieces, and form into 1 oz/30 g balls ~ about the size of large walnuts. Keep covered with tea towel.

On a lightly oiled smooth surface, press with the palm of hand to form into a flat disk about 3 inch/7.5 cm across, and use a rolling pin to thinly roll from center outward, expanding to about 8 inch/20 cm diameter. Roll and cook one at a time.

Heat oil in a wok over medium high heat. Fry one at a time for about 60 seconds, using a spatula or spoon to carefully splash the Poori top with hot oil while frying. Tapping gently with the back of a spoon helps it to fill with steam and puff out. Turn over; cook for another half minute until golden and puffy; drain and repeat with remaining dough. Replenish wok with additional oil as needed; there should be about 3 inches (7.5 cm) depth in the pan. Serve immediately, as the bread quickly deflates. Accompany with a light curry sauce or Thin Potato Curry, and cooked pulses or dal. Or serve as is, sprinkled with sugar. Makes 16 "pillows"

Thin Potato Curry
arluu hin

This is the traditional Indian-inspired accompaniment to Poori, more like a runny sauce to sop up bread, rather than a thick stew. Yet, its flavor is tantalizingly different from the simple Potato Curry in Three Ways (page 242).

1 lb (500 g) potatoes
2 tablespoons (30 ml) vegetable oil
1 teaspoon (5 ml) cumin seed
2 teaspoons (10 ml) turmeric powder

2 teaspoons (10 ml) Asian chili powder or hot paprika
3 cups (750 ml) water
1-2 teaspoons (5-10 ml) salt

Boil the potatoes in their jackets ~ about 15 minutes or until they prick barely tender; do not overcook. (Boiling in skin retains additional potato flavor.) Drain in a colander; allow to cool slightly, then peel while still warm. Use a tea towel to protect your hand, using a small paring knife to help pull away the papery skin, as opposed to thick peeling. (Or, gently rub potatoes with the cloth; the skin often peels away.) Cut into large chunks about 1 inch/2.5 cm.

Meanwhile, heat the oil in a saucepan set over medium flame. Add the cumin, turmeric and chili and fry for 30 seconds. Immediately add water and bring to the boil. Lower heat to simmer and add potato chunks. Cook covered for 30 minutes or until the sauce thickens slightly; taste for salt. Serves 4-6, as only a small portion accompanies the bread.

VARIATION Add 1/2 teaspoon/2 ml toasted brown mustard seed at the beginning when frying spices and 1 stem (about 8 leaves) fresh curry leaf plus 1/2 teaspoon/2 ml safflower powder when adding water. Proceed as above.

JOLLY OLD BEAN
Pulses & Dried Beans

ပဲနှင့်အစေ့များ

"Use several varieties of lentils or grams to increase protein, sprouted ones, raw, being especially high in Vitamin C."

--Rangoon International Cook Book (1954)

Pulses & Dried Beans

Surprisingly, 19th century colonials never mention beans, lentils and peas as a Burmese marketplace feature. Noodles, rice, fruits, fowl and meat, yes, but pulses were out of sight. By contrast, today Myanmar positively excels in dried bean or pulse dishes, and its famed fritters seem ubiquitous. These are influences from both its Indian neighbor to the west, and to a slightly lesser extent, China's Yunnan to the northeast where fresh pulses are the norm.

Technically speaking, oval legumes are beans, while peas are round, and lentils come oval lens-shaped (as in spectacles or reading glasses). "Pulse" is used especially for dried forms, but there is some overlap with fresh. Fresh beans are seasonal: shell and boil for 20-30 minutes, or until tender. Some fresh varieties, such as fava/broad beans, benefit from shorter cooking, and toughen when overcooked.

Dried beans require pre-soaking, so as to ensure even cooking later. Soak beans overnight, or use the Quick Soak method, following page. Always drain, and cook in fresh water. Lentils and peas can be cooked straight from the packet. Generally, most pulses are boiled in an unlimited quantity of water, then drained. Lentils, like rice and other grains, can also be cooked in pre-measured water ratio (1 part pulse to $2^{1/2}$ parts liquid), with all or most liquid absorbed during cooking.

Preparing Dried Pulses

Rinse and pick over to remove any grit or stones. Lentils and cracked dried peas do not require pre-soaking. For larger pulses plus whole chickpeas and beans, soak in water overnight, and drain. (If it's very warm, refrigerate while soaking, as occasionally beans sour.) Bring a large pot of fresh water to boil over high heat and cook beans for 1 minute or until froth raises to the top. Skim and drain. In fresh water bring the beans to the boil, reduce heat and cook uncovered until just tender ~ about 45 minutes. Simmer means very gentle boil ~ you need the beans fully cooked as undercooked beans can cause extreme gas; and likewise, over-cooked beans disintegrate. Unlike cooking fresh beans, do not add salt to boiling water until final 15 minutes cooking, lest the pulses harden.

QUICK SOAK Instead of overnight soaking, plunge dried pulses in a large pot of cold water and over high heat bring to a rolling boil; cook for exactly 1 minute. Remove from heat and cover immediately; stand for 1 hour. Drain, then cover with fresh water and cook as above.

CAUTION Beans, whether dried or fresh, need boiling to destroy lectin that can cause cramps and nausea. Boil for at least 10 minutes, as lesser temperatures do not destroy toxins. Peas and lentils are much lower in lectin, which explains the local practice of merely frying chickpea and lentil fritters.

Dal Croquettes

kalapae gyaw

What can be better than fried croquettes dipped into that most British of condiments, ketchup? This recipe works a treat, whether as party finger food, or sit-down starter. But as it is very delicate, take care when forming and especially while frying and turning. If you find them too fragile, blend into the dough 1/2 beaten egg, adding just enough breadcrumbs to bind; form and coat as below. For a slightly sour taste variation, add tamarind pulp to the cooking liquid.

1 cup (185 g) shelled mung beans or yellow split peas

About 4 cups (1 liter) water

1/2 teaspoon (2 ml) turmeric powder

2 tablespoons (30 ml) tamarind puree

1/4 teaspoon (1 ml) freshly ground pepper

Pinch of ground cinnamon

1 teaspoon (5 ml) salt

2 sprigs fresh coriander (cilantro) finely chopped

1 egg, beaten

About 1/2 cup (35 g) dry breadcrumbs

About 1/3 cup (90 g) ghee or Seasoned Oil (page 42)

Rinse peas, cover with fresh water and bring to a boil; skim away any froth; add turmeric and optional tamarind. Gently boil, partially covered, for at least 20 minutes or until pulses begin to disintegrate. (Mung beans will cook faster, peas up to 45 minutes.) Drain through a fine mesh discarding the liquid. Puree in a food processor, then stir in pepper, cinnamon or cassia, salt and fresh coriander/cilantro. When cool, use your palm to press firmly into small cylinder rolls ~ about 1 x 2 inch/2.5 x 5 cm. (If they prove too fragile, stir in egg and extra bread crumb.) Dip lightly into egg to coat all sides, then roll in breadcrumbs. Heat ghee or Seasoned Oil in a fry pan over medium-high heat and fry, carefully turning to crisp all sides ~ about 5 minutes. Drain and serve warm. Accompany with ketchup or Cooked Tomato Sauce (page 289). Makes 8

Beans & Rice

pe-pyoke htamine see sun

Myanmar's most popular bean is about the size of a blue boiler pea, but grey green or tan brown in color (or enhanced bright green on some packaging). Mostly sold dried overseas, they are sometimes found frozen or refrigerated at Indian grocers. It's known as pigeon pea, or on Indian packaging *toovar lilva*, but generic field bean, cow pea and royal bean suit just as nicely. When fresh it is sprouted overnight before cooking for additional nutrition. Overseas, the best substitute is chickpea, but in actuality that pulse is very different.

This simple recipe is true "comfort food" Burmese style ~ and indeed, across the Subcontinent. In its most humble form, beans are boiled with a little onion and oil, then spooned over steamed rice.

Save it for a lazy weekend morning breakfast in bed. Enhance with accompaniments of choice, such as Cooked Tomato Sauce (page 289), Chili Fry (page 292) and crisp fried shallots and onion (page 41). Or better yet, fried egg and sausage.

*1/2 cup (100g) dried pigeon
 peas, or beans of choice*
2 tablespoons (30 ml) oil
*1 small onion, finely sliced
 (1/3 cup/45 g)*

Pinch turmeric powder
1 teaspoon (5 ml) salt
*3 cups (400 g) cooked rice
 or Wheat Khichri (page
 165) or a combination*

Soak the beans overnight in water to cover.

Heat oil in a medium saucepan over moderate heat. Add the onion and turmeric and saute till just soft. Drain beans, add to the saucepan and cover with 2 cups/500 ml fresh water. Bring to the boil, skim any froth that rises and gently boil, partially covered, until beans are tender ~ at least 45 minutes to as long as 1½ hours, depending on the age of the bean. (If using packaged beans, do not soak; add direct from freezer. Cut cooking time to 20 minutes, and decrease water quantity.) Add additional water if necessary to prevent scorching, but you want this relatively dry, not soupy. Add salt and cool in the cooking water, then serve with slotted spoon.

Re-heat the rice (a microwave works well with a moist paper towel atop), then press it firmly into a lightly moistened bowl and turn out onto a plate. (You can do this in one large bowl, or several smaller individual bowls.) Top with a spoonful of cooked beans and serve with accompaniments of choice. Serves 4-6

VARIATION Blend cooked cracked wheat with rice, and proceed as above.

photo: Sher-Ali Khan

Rangoon Val

peigyee a yan hin

Of Indian extraction, these field beans were so popular in the olden days that they adopted the name of colonial Burma's capital city. If available, use ajowan seeds, instead of thyme. For a quicker version, use canned butter- or lima beans, drained.

2 cups (500 ml) dried field beans, pigeon peas, or small dried lima beans

1/4 cup (60 ml) vegetable oil

1/2 teaspoon (2 ml) dried thyme or 1/4 teaspoon (1 ml) ajowan seeds

Pinch asafetida powder

1 teaspoon (5 ml) Asian chili powder or hot paprika

1/4 teaspoon (2 ml) turmeric powder

1 tablespoon (15 ml) grated palm sugar or brown sugar

2 teaspoons (10 ml) tamarind puree

1 teaspoon (5 ml) salt

Soak the beans in water to cover overnight. Drain and cover with fresh water. Bring to the boil, skim any froth that rises and gently boil until beans are just tender -- at least 45 minutes to as long as 1½ hours, depending on age of the bean. Cool in the cooking water, then drain.

Heat the oil in a saucepan over medium flame. Add the spices and herbs and cook for just a second to flavor the oil; any longer and they burn and taste acrid. Immediately add cooked beans. Add 1/2 cup (60 ml) water (or liquid from drained canned beans), palm- or brown sugar, tamarind and salt. Bring to the boil and simmer for about 10 minutes, until it cooks almost dry. Serves 6

Burmese Butter Beans
pae htaw pat a yan hin

Canned beans suit especially well here, as reconstituted dried lima beans tend to loose their outer hull when soaked. Otherwise begin with dried beans, soaking and cooking as per previous directions.

¹/₄ cup (60 ml) vegetable oil

1 medium onion, thinly sliced (²/₃ cup/90 g)

1 teaspoons (5 ml) turmeric powder, preferably alleppey

4 garlic cloves, thinly sliced

2 x 14 oz (400 g) cans lima or butter beans, drained

¹/₄ cup (60 ml) water

2 teaspoons (10 ml) salt

Heat oil in a saucepan over medium heat. Add the onion, and cook with turmeric until golden and barely crisp; add garlic and cook an additional few minutes. Remove with a slotted spoon and separately reserve oil, plus onion and garlic. Add water, beans and reserved cooking oil. Bring to a gentle boil with salt, then simmer uncovered for a few minutes. Serves 6

VARIATION: FRESH SHELLED BEANS
Seasonal borlotti or cranberry beans are especially delicious here. Pour in just enough water to cover; add salt and seasoned oil from cooking the onions and garlic. Boil over medium high heat, uncovered, until just tender ~ 20-30 minutes. The beans should be soupy and slightly thick. At the end, garnish with fried onion and garlic.

Chickpea Curd / Burmese Tofu
to hu war

Unlike tofu made of soybean, Myanmar *to hu* derives from chickpeas. It sets naturally, or here with agar. The result is more like a dense quivering jelly than a firmly set aerated curd. Canned chickpeas are a time saver, but you can begin with dried pulses. Cheese salt is a non-iodized, fast dissolving salt available through specialist suppliers. (Iodine inhibits desired cultures and bacteria that help coagulate the mixture.) Shan *to hu*, a regional variant, is softer than standard Burmese tofu, sometimes even porridge-like in its consistency, and contains no agar. Unset *to hu* is served as a warm porridge. Serve in a salad, or with a meat sauce. Unlike classic *to hu,* this recipe sets with agar and is consequently not suitable for heating, nor frying.

3 x 14 oz (400 g) cans
 chickpeas, drained and
 rinsed
8 cups (2 liters) water
1/4 teaspoon (1 ml) turmeric
 powder

2 teaspoons (10 ml) non-
 iodized salt or cheese salt
3 tablespoons (20 g)
 agar powder
About 1 tablespoon (15 ml)
 vegetable oil

Pour chickpeas into a food processor and, with the metal blade, puree until uniformly fine textured; add minimal water as necessary. At this stage, the easiest step is to progressively pass through a rotating Mouli grater, which extracts all rough solids. (Use all three blades if not using a food processor to first blend. Or only the two fine blades if pre-blended. Locals do all this by squeezing through cloth, but it's laborious.)

Discard any rough pulp (there may be none or minimal, especially if using canned beans; dried beans will have more roughage.) Combine the fine paste -- you should have about 2 cups/550 g -- with water in a large pot or cauldron over medium heat. Add turmeric and salt. Bring just to the boil, then reduce heat to medium low and stir constantly with a long wooden spoon in one direction only. After about 10 minutes the paste should thicken slightly. Stir in agar powder and continue stirring and cooking another 5 minutes. Remove from heat and pour into a lightly oiled baking tray to set ~ at least 1 inch (2.5 cm) high (preferably high to avoid spills) and about 12 x 14 inch/30 x 35 cm. When set, brush lightly with remaining oil to prevent tough skin from forming and drying out; cut into strips or desired shapes. This will keep for several days in the refrigerator, tightly wrapped. Makes about 4 lb/1.8 kg

Grate the bean curd as shavings and use to garnish.

Cut into strips and toss into salads, both Burmese and Western.

Cut into pieces and top with curry.

Garnish atop soups

Shan Tofu with Meat Gravy

to hu nwae

This Burmese comfort food is traditionally made with soft Shan chickpea curd topped with accompanying gravy. Surprisingly, the traditional meat sauce contains no garlic nor masala spice; and is rather bland. At table, enhance with a salty condiment such as Bate Chin (page 287) or pique its flavor with roasted chilies in oil (Chili Fry, page 292).

About 1 lb (500 g) soft/ silken tofu, or 3 cups (500 g) cubed Chickpea Curd (preceding recipe)

2 medium onions, thinly sliced (1¹/₃ cups/175 g)

¹/₄ cup (60 ml) vegetable oil

1 lb (500 g) ground pork or chicken mince

1-2 teaspoons (5-10 ml) Asian chili powder or hot paprika, to taste

1 teaspoon (5 ml) salt

3 tablespoons (45 ml) tomato puree

1 tablespoon (15 ml) corn starch (cornflour)

1 cup (250 ml) stock

Fresh coriander (cilantro) sprigs, mint, or green onion (scallion/spring onion) to garnish

Prepare the Chickpea Curd, or use store bought soft tofu ~ at room temperature, not cold.

Pound or finely chop the onions until pureed; alternatively use a blender, adding some of the oil to help it blend. Heat oil in a large saucepan over low flame and cook the onions slowly ~ about 20 minutes; careful, lest they burn. Add the ground meat, stirring to brown lightly on all sides. Dissolve cornstarch in a spoonful of water. Add this to the meat, plus stock and ingredients. Simmer for 15 minutes, uncovered.

To serve, place warm curd on a platter or bowl and top with the meat gravy. Garnish with fresh herbs. Serves 6

Tofu Salad

to hu a-thoke

A delicious way to serve Burmese chickpea curds. Alternatively, soft or silken soy curd works a treat here, although it's not authentic. If using the latter, keep the curd in one large square or mound, scoring lightly; top with the dressing ingredients.

3 tablespoons (45 ml) sesame seeds, roasted

1-2 tablespoons (15-30 ml) chilies in oil (Chili Fry page 292) or store bought

2 tablespoons (30 ml) tamarind puree, or lemon- or lime juice, or white vinegar

Pinch white or grated palm sugar

$^1/_3$ cup (60 g) peanuts, finely chopped

About 3 cups (500 g) cubed chickpea curd, or soft/ silken soy tofu

$^1/_2$ cup (30 g) very coarsely chopped fresh coriander (cilantro) sprigs

2 teaspoons (10 ml) crisp fried garlic (page 41, or store bought)

If you have a mortar and pestle, lightly crush the sesame seeds, although this is optional. This is merely to bruise, not to puree. Alternatively, use the blunt end of a rolling pin. Combine with the chili oil, tamarind, sugar, and peanuts to create a dressing. (If it is too thick, add a tablespoon water.) Toss with curd, fresh coriander/cilantro, and at last minute, crisp garlic.

Serves 4-6

VARIATION Make a heartier salad by adding sliced tomato, shredded cabbage and dried shrimp; season with salt and pepper, and toss with roasted chickpea flour instead of peanuts.

Fried Bean Curd Salad

pae pyar thoke

Use firm- or hard soybean curd here, or packaged pre-fried soy tofu in cubes or triangles. In the latter case, substitute Seasoned Oil and Chili Fry (pages 42, 292) instead of starting from scratch. In Asia tofu is sold very fresh, but overseas it is packaged in water and marketed for weeks or longer. To counter the taste, blanch tofu briefly, then salt and cool to extract excess moisture; pat dry and fry. Soft- or silken soy does not fry well, unless first coated with flour.

12 oz (350 g) firm soybean curd/tofu

1 tablespoon (15ml) salt

About 1 cup (250 ml) vegetable oil

2 teaspoons (10 ml) chili flakes

3 garlic cloves, thinly sliced

1/2 teaspoon (2m) turmeric powder

1/2 cup (60 g) dried shrimp (optional)

1 tablespoon (15 ml) chickpea flour (besan or gram) roasted

1/3 cup (90 ml) freshly squeezed lemon or lime juice

2 tablespoons (30 ml) fish sauce

1 teaspoon (5 ml) freshly ground pepper

1/4 teaspoon (1 ml) white sugar, or to taste

6 leaves Chinese (Napa) cabbage, shredded

2 small tomatoes, cut into thin wedges (5 oz/150 g)

6 green onions (scallions/ spring onions) trimmed and cut into 1 inch (2.5 cm) lengths

1/2 bunch (50 g) fresh mint, leaves only, or fresh coriander/cilantro sprigs, very coarsely chopped

Blanch the whole bean curd in boiling water for no more than 1 minute. Drain and pat dry, then sprinkle with half the salt to extract excess moisture. When cool, wipe dry.

Heat the oil in a wok or fry pan over medium heat and fry the chili flakes momentarily; remove with mesh spoon and reserve. Fry garlic and turmeric together in this same oil, until lightly golden ~ about 2 minutes. Do not overcook lest the garlic turn bitter; remove with a slotted spoon and reserve.

Increase heat to medium high and fry bean curd in batches. Fry until golden on first side ~ about 2 minutes, then turn over and repeat. Remove from oil; strain and cool the oil.

Pour boiling water over the dried shrimp, if using; soak for 15 minutes and drain and reserve.

To make dressing, whisk together the chickpea flour, lemon or lime juice, fish sauce, pepper, remaining salt and sugar to taste. Just before serving, toss the cabbage with half the dressing. Arrange a bed of dressed cabbage and tomato on a serving platter or large salad bowl, and top with fried bean curd, green onion and reserved shrimp. Drizzle remaining dressing atop and sprinkle with fresh herb, reserved fried chili flakes and garlic. Serves 6

Fritters

a gyaw soan

It's precarious, if not downright dangerous: vendors lining the streets of Myanmar's cities carrying on yokes vast cauldrons of sizzling oil. There, they clamor for space with passing pedestrians, frying any manner of crispy lace-like fritters, from vegetables to dried beans and pulses. Heaven forbid tripping near one of these stands or worse yet, colliding with a hawker with hot oil hazardly hanging from his pole. But in the end, it's presumably worth the risk, for fritters are the undisputed kings of Burmese cooking. Not just a snack eaten on their own, or better yet, with strong chili and garlic table sauces (page 287), fritters crown dishes as a garnish and are crumbled like crackers and croutons in a soup. Indeed, a bowl of Mohinga stew, the country's unofficial national dish, is positively naked without myriad fritter crisps.

Unlike foods fried with a dry flour crust, fritters are bound in batter. There are two styles: most common are saucer-shaped lacy fritters, cooked thin to showcase key ingredients such as dried peas, prawns, onions and gourd or winter melon. Then there is the new kid on the block: tempura, which coats completely, and puffs pillow-like. While there is no hard and fast rule, tempura is generally more tender than traditional Myanmar fritter batters and billows when baking powder is added. Tempura batter sometimes includes wheat flour, with or without leavening (it's more crispy without), but traditional hard-crisp fritters marry best in salads. It is also worth investigating various tempura dried mixes at the supermarket, as they are often better than making your own.

Working wheat flour to develop gluten is good for bread, but poor for fritters, as it cooks tough not brittle. Consequently, minimally mix fritter batters that contain gluten. Likewise, use iced cold water to minimize gluten development. And let the batter stand after preparation. Rice flour contains no gluten, so no risk overworking rice flour batters.

Fritters and tempura are fried in hot oil, but once ingredients are added, heat is lowered slightly so as to cook uniformly. If the temperature is too high, the outside burns while inside is gooey; too low, the fritters will be soft and absorb too much oil during cooking. As a general rule, start higher at 375°F/190°C, then finish frying at 350°F/180°C. Do not cook too many fritters at once, as crowding lowers the temperature too much, as well as results in fritters sticking to each other.

HINTS Flavor batters with, variously, a generous pinch of dried ginger, onion and/or garlic powders. If you find batter not adhering, first dust ingredients with starch or flour. To reheat fritters, place in a very hot 400°F/200°C oven for a few minutes. Lower temperatures tend to render fritters soft.

HARD ROOT VEGETABLES like potato and carrot should be cut very thin to cook throughout during short frying (4 minutes is typical) while medium-soft ingredients such as gourd or winter melon cut about $1/3$ inch/1 cm, and soft foods like banana cooked whole. Just a quick dip into batter and dunk into hot oil.

SMALL INGREDIENTS such as corn kernels or diced onion, are easiest to shallow fry in a flat-bottomed skillet, as if making pancakes ~ but with lots more oil. Otherwise, fritters fried in a wok may require pre-shaping on a large spoon or saucer as it is slowly lowered into the oil to set. For example, several school prawns can be assembled together to make one fritter, in the same fashion.

SHRIMP OR PRAWNS Use small school prawns, heads and all (stringy beards are cut or pulled). Pour a little batter in pan to make a base, arrange a few prawns atop, and drizzle with more batter.

SMALL FRESH FISH & WHITEBAIT Use whole and un-gutted.

ONION Cut small to medium-sized yellow or white onions into petals: top and tail, then peel. Slice bulb in half from top to bottom; then cut each half into quarters or thirds, again from top to bottom. Separate the florets.

EGGPLANT/AUBERGINE Use any sort of purple-black skinned eggplants, from long narrow Japanese-style to standard bulbous. Cut into 2 inch/5 cm long sticks or wedges, but thin enough to cook through ~ about $1/3$ inch/1 cm.

CORN Easiest to use frozen corn kernels, thawed. Otherwise, use pre-cooked or steamed corn, then pare deeply from the cob in one stroke; separate kernels.

BANANA Use whole ladyfinger bananas; plantains are not common. If using large Cavendish bananas, cut into 2 inch/5 cm wedges.

GOURD OR WINTER MELON Cut thumb thick, like a British chip.

DRIED CHICKPEAS Soak overnight, drain and pat dry. Generally, just a few (3-5) scattered pulses per fritter. Local whole chickpeas are relatively small and fully hulled; overseas varieties such as Italian *ceci* or American garbanzo can be quite large. As you want to ensure the pulse is fully cooked during frying, use split peas if the peas are huge.

PUREED PULSES Another sort of fritter is made from pureed pulses, such as yellow beans, which are formed into a falafel-like patty or roll and fried.

Tempura Batter
a gyaw mone hnint

Use this batter for cooking vegetable pieces, fruits like banana, and even meat. It should be rather thick, to coat ingredients completely.

1 cup (150 g) plain rice flour
1/2 cup (75 g) sticky (glutinous) rice flour
1 tablespoon (15 ml) baking powder

1 teaspoon (5 ml) salt
1/2 teaspoon (2 ml) turmeric powder
1 cup (90 ml) water

Sift together the dry ingredients, then stir in water; blend well. Coat ingredients by dipping into the batter and fry.

Indian Fritter Batter
a gyaw inn di ya sa tyle

This coating batter results in a tender ~ not crisp ~ fried batter, so it should be eaten immediately.

1 cup (150 g) all-purpose (plain) flour
1/2 cup (75 g) chickpea flour (besan/gram) raw

1/2 teaspoon (2 ml) turmeric powder
1 teaspoon salt
1 cup (250 ml) water

Sift together the dry ingredients, then gently stir in water until just combined; do not over mix, as it results in tough fritters. Coat ingredients by dipping into the batter one by one, and fry in hot oil.

"Egg" Peanuts

kyet oo myay pae

A beer snack, or nibbles pre-dinner, its name derives from the egg-like shape when nuts are coated and fried. Burmese peanuts are much smaller than contemporary overseas varieties, and close to the original "Spanish peanut." Consequently, raw small peanuts cook in a short time. If using larger standard peanuts, use roasted nuts.

Oil, for shallow frying
1/2 cup (75 g) chickpea flour
 (besan/gram) raw
Pinch salt

Pinch turmeric powder
1/2 cup (85 g) shelled and
 hulled peanuts

Heat oil in a fry pan or wok until barely smoking. Meanwhile, mix flour, salt and turmeric with just enough water to create a thick slurry and use your fingers to coat the peanuts. (Wear gloves, lest the turmeric stain your skin.) Drop into the hot oil one at a time, and stir to prevent sticking. Cook until just crisp ~ about 3 minutes. Makes about 1/2 cup (125 ml)

HINT As a palate cleanser to freshen the mouth while eating oily tempura, serve a plate of small diced lime and a bowl of sugar. Dip the lime on the sugar and suck.

Chickpea Fritters

ba-yar gyaw

A very crunchy fritter batter, ideal for thin lacy crisps. This recipe uses drained canned chickpeas, but more authentic is dried chickpeas soaked overnight, then drained, battered and fried without pre-cooking.

14 oz (400 g) can chickpeas, drained

³/4 cup (50 g) plain rice flour

¹/3 cup (90 ml) water

¹/4 teaspoon (1 ml) turmeric powder

¹/2 teaspoon (2 ml) salt

About 2 cups (500 ml) vegetable oil, for deep frying

Pat dry chickpeas. Alternatively, soak dried peas overnight, or use the fast preparation method by boiling for 1 minute, then soaking exactly one hour, as this semi-cooks them (page 176). Drain and lay out on a tray to dry until ready to use.

Make a thin slurry batter of flour and water, seasoned with turmeric and salt.

Heat oil in a wok over medium-high heat until almost smoking. (Using a wok pools less oil; if using a frying pan increase oil quantity.) Spoon in just enough of the mixture to form a disk about 2-3 inch/5-7.5 cm wide. Repeat, making two or three fritters at a time; do not crowd them. Decrease heat slightly while frying. Use a spoon to splash the uncooked top, and once set ~ about 2 minutes ~ turn over. After about 4 minutes total the fritter will be crisp and golden brown. Remove with a slotted spoon and drain on absorbent paper; repeat with remaining ingredients. Serve hot or at room temperature. Makes 8-10

VARIATION Add thin slivers of garlic, onion and finely chopped fresh small green chilies.

Fritter & Lettuce Parcels

a gyaw thoke

Hawkers create a delicious snack wrapping fritters, rice and onion in lettuce leaves. Here the dish is reinterpreted, so you roll your own at the table, like *san choy bao*. Use freshly cooked chickpea fritters, juxtaposing cool crisp lettuce with hot crisp fritter; room temperature leftover fritters can also be used. Skewer with a toothpick for party finger food. Accompany with Tamarind Sauce or Bate Chin, (page 287), or simple Fish Sauce Dressing (recipe, below).

Fritters of choice

Iceberg lettuce leaf "cups", whole but trimmed

Green onions (scallions/spring onion), chopped

Cooked rice noodles or rice, at room temperature

Tamarind Sauce (page 287) or fish sauce dressing (below)

Cool, then cut or break the fritters into large bite-sized pieces. Lay out a lettuce leaf or cup and place a spoonful of rice noodles or rice in the center. Top with fritter, onion and a spoonful of sauce. Wrap to enfold, and eat.

Fish Sauce Dressing

a-chin yay

3 tablespoons (45 ml) fish sauce
2 tablespoons (30 ml) water
1 tablespoon (15 ml) freshly squeezed lime juice
1 teaspoon (5 ml) sugar

1 garlic clove, finely sliced
1 fresh small chili, finely diced
1 sprig fresh coriander (cilantro) coarsely chopped

Combine all ingredients and allow flavors to meld. Makes about 1/3 cup/90 ml

Fritter Salads

a gyaw a-thoke

The secret is last minute assembly, to ensure crunchy fritters instead of soggy sponges. Unlike a tossed salad, this is traditionally served with the shredded lettuce and fritters together in a bowl but not dressed; a small bowl of dipping sauce sits to the side. The simplest dressing is chopped garlic and chilies marinated in fish sauce. Or toss with a dipping- or table sauce (page 287). Traditionally, copious accompaniments of small green chilies are eaten plain as a refresher, and whole garlic cloves eaten raw.

8 chickpea fritters
(page 193)

6 lettuce leaves, shredded

2 leaves white cabbage,
shredded

1/4 cup (60 ml) Fish Sauce
Dressing, recipe opposite
(or sauces, page 287)

Cut the fried fritters into pieces. Arrange a bed of shredded lettuce and cabbage, top with fritters, and spoon dressing atop, or serve on the side. Serves 4-6

USE YOUR NOODLE
Noodles

ခေါက်ဆွဲနှင့်မုန့်ဖတ်များ

"*Let us note in their order the commodities that are displayed as we proceed; their variety is itself indicative of the tastes of the people. . . Next to it is vermicelli, of native and Chinese manufacture.*"

-- Charles Alexander Gordon, *Our Trip to Burmah, With Notes on that Country* (1875)

A Noodle Primer

NOODLE dishes are typically served as one-dish meals ～ from soupy broths to slurpy rich coconut sauces ～ but there are exceptions. Noodles can take the place of rice at a meal, form the base to salads, or can be fried crisp in fritters to garnish dishes.

Noodles come in myriad varieties, mainly wheat and rice, but also mung bean and yam. Fresh, sometimes fermented, and ubiquitously dried, they vary in size and flavor from delicately brittle to resiliently pliable. Because varieties were introduced from China, and as most noodles purchased outside Myanmar will be of Chinese and Japanese origin, generic equivalents are listed in recipes here. Made from an alimentary paste of flour or starch and water, rolled noodles are cut into flat strips, while extruded noodles are forced through a mesh to create round strips. Overseas, dried noodles are most common. Fresh noodles may be found on the counters of some Asian markets, but should be consumed within a day. Refrigerated varieties are also available, especially wheat varieties, but Southeast Asians typically eschew chilled rice noodles, claiming refrigeration is detrimental to their texture. Italian pasta noodles, both dried and fresh, are generally made from durum wheat and take on an entirely different character to Asian wheat noodles.

You will see noodle vendors briefly reheating parboiled or pre-cooked noodles in a small basket, by plunging into a vat of boiling water or stock briefly to re-heat. This is a time saving method, for last minute assembly. Do as the locals, and pre-cook your noodles, and when ready to use, do the same. It's more practical for single bowls, then big groups.

SUPERSTITION Long noodles symbolize long life, hence it is considered bad luck to cut them.

Noodle Varieties

Wheat- & egg noodles & ramen / khout shwe
Dried and fresh, thick and thin, Chinese-style mee/mie and ramen may or may not contain egg. Japanese-style udon, soba and somen, by contrast, are simply made from wheat flour and alkaline water, although some add egg yolk. Ramen is a thin extruded noodle; in its "instant" packaged form it comes pre-cooked and dried, for simple soaking in boiling water prior to eating. As in all of Asia, it is increasingly popular at hawker stalls.
COOKING Boil fresh noodles for 2-4 minutes, depending on thickness. (Japanese udon takes up to 15 minutes). Boil dried noodles 4-6 minutes, or until soft.

Hokkien noodles / mee ngaw
Somewhat a misnomer, as original Hokkien noodles refers to a cooking style, and not its wheat- or bean- component. Today, these wheat noodles are marketed fresh and pre-cooked, available in refrigerated store cabinets.
COOKING Soak in warm water for 1-2 minutes to separate and soften, then stir fry. Also ideal for crisp frying (but do not pre-soak in this instance).

Rice noodles / san khout shwe
DRIED & FRESH: Thin rice noodles (or vermicelli) and thicker rice sticks (*Mee Shwe*) are made from plain rice flour or starch, hot water and sometimes tapioca starch and sticky rice flour. They are brittle, but when made from glutinous or sticky rice flour/starch, noodles will have a chewy bite.
COOKING Soak dried rice noodles in hot water for 15-20 minutes prior to using. Use fresh rice noodles directly from the packet. Refrigerating fresh rice noodles makes them hard; consequently, they should be consumed on the day of purchase.

Cellophane- & glass noodles / kyar san
Also known as bean thread vermicelli. Although similar in appearance to rice vermicelli, these dried noodles are flexible and resilient if crushed and turn transparent when soaked or boiled. Their cooked consistency is much tougher than other noodles. Commonly made with mung bean, but also from sweet potato or yam.
COOKING Soak in boiling water for 1 minute, drain, then soak in cold water for 1 minute. Drain and eat as is, in a soup, or stir fry. Alternatively, soak in cool water for 15 minutes prior to cooking. Can also be stir fried. (HINT Buy pre-packaged in small skeins, as large packets of bean thread noodles are notoriously hard to separate prior to cooking. Or use scissors ~ but be aware that this may be construed as a negative omen; see *Superstition*, previous page).

Crispy fried noodles / khout shwe a quit gyaw
Made from both dry rice vermicelli, rice sticks, dried bean thread (glass noodles), and some wheat noodles. Use both as a garnish topping or as a base for gravy-laden stir fried meats and vegetables.
COOKING Do not cook, merely heat in oven or serve as is.

Specialty Noodles

"A steaming bowl of mohinga adorned with vegetable
fritters, slices of fish cake and hard-boiled eggs and
enhanced with the flavour of chopped coriander leaves,
morsels of crispy fried garlic, fish sauce, a squeeze of
lime and chilies is a wonderful way of stoking up
for the day ahead."

~ Aung San Suu Kyi, *Letters from Burma* (1995)

Mohinga

Arguably Myannar's national dish, Mohinga is a luxuriously rich and creamy fish-based soup with thin rice noodles, typically served steaming hot from massive cauldrons along the roadside. It's so rich you would be excused for presuming it contains dairy milk or coconut cream (it does not). And best of all, it's accompanied by myriad fried crisps and patties, making it closer to a one-pot feast than humble stew.

Unfortunately, one of Mohinga's main ingredients is especially difficult to source overseas: the heart of young banana stalk. Purists may forage in a kindly neighbor's garden, but alternatives equating to its texture include canned heart of palm, or alternatively, increase quantity of well-cooked onion or shallot. Candidly, just leave it out if unavailable.

DIFFERENCES

There are as many variants to this recipe as there are ethnic nationalities in Myanmar (in other words, hundreds). But suffice to say, authentic Mohinga is made from fresh-water carp or catfish (*nga gyin tha* or *nga khoo*); alternatively try with trout or pike, ocean-water snapper, cod, grouper or halibut. Generally speaking, avoid the oilier and stronger tasting varieties, but that being said, locals from the southern Dawei coastline use mackerel.

Standard practice is to cook whole gutted and scaled fish on the bone, then painstakingly pick the meat from the carcass later. It's easier to use fish fillets, but to compensate for the bones' added flavor, gently boil bones separately for stock, then strain and cook fillets in the resulting stock, instead of in water. And to finish: Some cooks gently fry the cooked fish in oil after boning and boiling.

NOODLES

Fine rice noodles or vermicelli *moute phat* are the best, although we suspect some locals blend a bit of sticky rice into their dough to give a unique chewiness. Overseas cooks may substitute thin wheat noodles such as somen, although this makes the dish quite different. Do not use thin spaghetti as the texture and color is wrong. Likewise, do not confuse rice noodles with chewy mung bean vermicelli, which turns transparent and slippery-slimy when cooked; hence its name glass noodles.

REGIONAL VARIANTS

You'll encounter a thicker stew in Mandalay with more chickpea flour; in far west Rakhine state it's spicier with dried red chili and more condiments. "Hot palate, hot tongue," goes the local expression. The Dawei version is thickened with sticky rice flour instead of besan. The final syllable Mo-Hin-Ga can mean "bitter" depending on the accent of the speaker. But this soup is not.

Mohinga

1 lb (500 g) skinless fish
fillets or 1 1/2 lb (750 g)
whole gutted fish

1 1/2 inch (4 cm) knob fresh
ginger, grated

4 garlic cloves, minced or
pounded

8 fresh coriander (cilantro)
roots, or 2 tablespoons
(30 ml) chopped stems

2 teaspoons (10 ml) turmeric
powder, preferably
alleppey

2 teaspoons (10 ml) salt

3 stalks lemongrass, halved
lengthwise

2 tablespoons (30 ml) fish
sauce, or more to taste

1/4 cup (35 g) chickpea flour
(besan or gram) raw, or
plain rice flour

1 1/2 cups (165 g) peanuts,
coarsely chopped

1/2 cup (125 ml) vegetable oil

1 tablespoon (15 ml) shrimp
paste

4 medium onions, quartered,
or 1 lb (500 g) whole peeled
pink or golden shallots

3 oz (100 g) peeled young
banana or plantain stem,
thinly sliced and pounded
(optional)

2 tablespoons (30 ml)
tamarind puree or fresh
lemon

8 oz (250 g) rice vermicelli

Toss and briefly marinate the fish with ginger, garlic, coriander roots and half the turmeric and salt. Bend or slice in half the lemongrass sticks and arrange at the bottom of the saucepan to prevent the fish scorching. Lay the marinated fish on top. Add fish sauce and just enough water to cover ~ about 2 cups (500 ml). Gently boil uncovered, until the fish meat is very soft and easily flakes from the bone ~ about 30 minutes. (Fillets need to cook equally long.) Strain and discard the lemon grass, but retain the liquid. If cooking bone-in fish, use your fingers to remove the fish meat from bone, then reserve. (HINT for added flavor, crush the bones, return to the cooking broth, and strain again.) Cool and use fingers or two forks to shred the fish meat.

In a medium saucepan over high heat, bring 4 cups/1 liter water to the boil and gradually whisk in the chickpea flour; add the peanuts. Lower heat to simmer and cook for about 20 minutes, whisking occasionally lest it clump. Transfer the solids into a blender to create a slurry, then add all the stock from cooking the fish.

Heat oil in a large saucepan over medium heat, add remaining 1 teaspoon (5 ml) turmeric and shrimp paste, and fry for 30 seconds or until fragrant, then quickly fry the shredded fish meat for a couple minutes; add remaining salt. Add the reserved slurry from the chickpea and peanuts, plus the fish broth. Add another 4 cups/1 liter water. Add the onions and, if using, banana stem. (If not using banana stem, double the quantity of whole small onions or shallots.) Cover saucepan and bring to a gentle boil, then simmer until tender ~ about 1 hour. Stir occasionally to prevent scorching. At the last minute, add tamarind and taste for seasoning with fish sauce.

To assemble, boil the vermicelli until done ~ about 3 minutes. Drain, and arrange equal portions in large individual bowls. Ladle broth atop, and garnish at the table as desired. Serves 6-8

OPTIONAL SEASONINGS & GARNISHES

> Chili flakes in oil/Chili Fry (page 292)
> Chili powder or roasted chili flakes
> Fresh lemon or lime
> Freshly chopped coriander/cilantro sprigs
> Hard-boiled egg (page 361)
> Crisp chickpea fritters (page 193)
> Fish sauce or Bate Chin (page 287)
> Chopped green onions/scallions
> Crisp fried garlic (page 41 or store bought)
> Crisp fried onion or shallots (page 41, or store bought)
> Gourd Fritters (page 245)
> Fish Cakes (page 64)

Turkey Noodles
shwe taung khout shwe

Harking from the central town of Shwe Taung near Bago/Pegu, this is a drier variant of soupier coconut noodles. (The latter is similar to the famous *khao soi* from Thailand's Lanna kingdom in the north.) Like *Mohinga*, Shwe Taung noodles are a typical morning fare. Chicken is a popular substitute.

1 lb (500 g) raw turkey breast sliced into thin strips

1 teaspoon (5 ml) salt

1 teaspoon (5 ml) Asian chili powder or hot paprika

1 teaspoon (5 ml) turmeric powder

1/2 cup (60 g) thinly sliced onions, or pink or golden shallots

4 garlic cloves, crushed

1 tablespoon (15 ml) freshly grated ginger

About 1/4 cup (60 ml) vegetable oil

1 tablespoon (15 ml) chickpea flour (besan/gram) raw

1 cup (250 ml) stock or water

1 cup (250 ml) coconut milk

1 teaspoon (5 ml) curry powder or masala spice

1-2 tablespoons (15-30 ml) fish sauce

1 lb (500 g) Hokkien noodles or 8 oz (250 g) packet dried flat wheat- or rice noodles

To GARNISH

Crisp fried noodles (page 213 or store bought)

Fresh limes or lemons, quartered

Green onions (scallions/ spring onions)

Fresh coriander (cilantro) sprigs

Fish Sauce or Bate Chin (page 287)

Hard boiled eggs, chopped

Shallots, sliced

Chili flakes in oil (Chili Fry, page 292)

Tamarind puree

Toss the turkey strips with the salt, chili and turmeric, rubbing to incorporate evenly; set aside. (Don gloves, lest the turmeric stain your fingers.)

Combine onion, garlic and ginger in an electric blender, adding oil as necessary until it is a coarse paste. Alternatively, pound in a mortar. Toss with the turkey and marinate; refrigerate for longer marination or overnight.

Heat any remaining oil in a large saucepan over medium flame and add turkey and marinade, arranging carefully so all sides touch the hot oil to crisp. (You may need to do this initial searing in two batches.) Reduce heat to low and slowly cook for 20 minutes or until slightly caramelized; turn regularly, so both the marinade and turkey cook golden.

Whisk the chickpea flour with the water or stock to dissolve. Pour stock and coconut milk into the pan, increase heat and bring just to the boil, then simmer uncovered for about 10 minutes, or until ready to serve. (If cooking for a prolonged time, remove turkey with a slotted spoon, reserve and keep warm, to re-add at finish.) At the last minute, sprinkle the curry powder or masala spice on top, and adjust seasoning with fish sauce.

Meanwhile, prepare the noodles. Plunge into boiling water and cook per package directions. (Hokkien noodles cook in 1-2 minutes, while dry wheat noodles 4-8 minutes; rice noodles take half that time.) Drain, then place in individual bowls or a large tureen. Ladle the hot turkey stew atop and garnish. Serves 6

VARIATION: WITH CRISP FRIED NOODLES
Like classic North American chow mein in days of yore, substitute crisp fried noodles, instead of boiled. Ladle the stew directly atop the dried noodles and serve. If you cannot locate ready-made crisp noodles, make your own (page 213).

Shan Noodles

shan khout shwe

This dish is a Shan specialty from the easternmost state bordering Thailand, and the country's richest agricultural area. Here, noodles are flavored and thickened with peanut powder not chickpea/besan. To the north, locals prefer medium-thick extruded *nan latt* rice noodles, while to the south thinner *nan gyi* and thinnest of all *nan thay* are preferred. Ingredients vary, with some of the more exotic being fried flour and water "glue balls" and crisp chicken skin. But the essential condiment is Salty Pickle (page 283). If you don't encounter this at a restaurant table, it indicates the restaurateur is saving money by restricting portions. Salty Pickle is always part of this dish. Ethnic Burman versions use fish sauce instead of bean paste and substitute roasted chick pea flour for the peanuts.

1 cup (250 ml) stock
1 tablespoon (15 ml) fermented/salted beans, or fish sauce
Large pinch Chinese 5-spice
1/4 cup (20 g) mixed crisp fried onion, garlic and ginger (page 41 or store bought)
1 lb (500 g) chicken or pork, finely sliced or shredded
7 oz (200 g) packet dried rice noodles

1/4 cup (60 ml) Seasoned Oil (page 42)
1/4 cup (40 g) chopped peanuts, roasted
About 1/4 - 1/2 cup (40-85 g) Salty Pickle (page 283)
1/4 cup (20 g) bean spouts
1/4 cup (15 g) coarsely chopped fresh coriander (cilantro) sprigs
About 1/2 teaspoon (2 ml) Chinese 5-spice

Have all ingredients ready for quick assembly. Ideally, prepare one or two bowls at a time, serving immediately as the noodles tend to turn gluggy.

Combine stock with fermented beans or fish sauce and 5-spice and bring to the boil; simmer with the fried onion mixture and meat until done.

Boil the noodles in a large pot of water ~ for just a few minutes, or until tender, then drain. Divide between 4 serving bowls, tossing with Seasoned Oil and peanuts. Portion meat and stock onto the noodles, plus a spoonful of Salty Pickle in each bowl. Top with bean spouts and fresh coriander/cilantro, and a pinch of 5-spice. Accompany with table dipping sauce, such as Bate Chin (page 287). Serves 4

Fried Noodles with Duck Breast

khout shwe gyaw nint bae thar

Duck makes this Chinese-inspired dish especially rich, suitable for dinner parties as well as an indulgent family meal. Equally, substitute chicken breast or pork loin, dried Chinese-style sausage or fresh prawns and dried shrimp. Traditionally, this recipe calls for rendered lard for extra flavor, but oil is a good substitute. Both standard white and Chinese (Napa) cabbages suit here.

2 roasted duck breasts (page 134)

3 packets or "nests" ramen noodles (about 3 oz/100 g each)

1 oz (30 g) dried shiitake or Chinese black mushrooms

About ¹/₄ cup (60 g) lard or vegetable oil

4 eggs, lightly beaten

2 small onions, chopped (²/₃ cups/90 g)

4 leaves cabbage, chopped

2 garlic cloves, finely sliced

1 cup (170 g) coarsely chopped Chinese celery

1 cup (75 g) bean sprouts

3 tablespoons (45 ml) soy sauce

2 teaspoons (10 ml) salt

1 teaspoon (5 ml) freshly ground pepper

Green onions (scallions/ spring onions) sliced into rings

Cook duck and slice thinly. Pour enough boiling water over the noodles and mushrooms to cover and leave to soak for 15 minutes while preparing the dish.

When ready to assemble, remove mushrooms from water, and use scissors to cut and discard the tough stems; slice caps thinly. Drain noodles.

Add half the lard or oil to a pre-heated wok over medium-high heat. Add the eggs and scramble until the curds are cooked and dry; remove with a slotted spoon and reserve. Increase heat to high, add more fat, then onion, cabbage, garlic. Saute for 1 minute then add celery and bean shoots. Stir-fry rapidly, then add drained noodles. Toss furiously until hot throughout, adding soy sauce and duck at the end. Taste for seasoning. Garnish with green onions and reserved cooked eggs; accompany with Bate Chin sauce (page 287), or soy- or fish sauce. Serves 6

Rice Noodles & Fish

nga chauk nint myee shae gyaw

Salted dried fish is added sparingly here for a crispy salty burst. Slice into small thin pieces, as large bits are overpowering. Although dried salted fish ~ often made from barramundi, sea bass or cod ~ is non-perishable, it may be sold refrigerated in small pre-sealed packets. A little goes a long way. If unavailable, substitute salt cod/bacalao, but do not pre-soak.

2 stalks lemongrass, sliced lengthwise

1 lb (500 g) skinless white fish fillets, such as cat fish/basa, redfish or cod

3 small onions, chopped (1 cup/135 g) or pink or golden shallots

3 garlic cloves, thinly sliced

1 inch (2.5 cm) knob fresh ginger, grated

1 teaspoon (5 ml) salt, or to taste

3/4 cup (200 ml) vegetable oil

1 1/2 oz (45 g) piece saltfish, thinly sliced

1 teaspoon (5 ml) turmeric powder

1 teaspoon (5 ml) shrimp paste (optional)

1 teaspoon (5 ml) white sugar

About 8 oz (250 g) dried rice sticks or noodles

1 tablespoon (15 ml) chickpea flour (besan/gram) raw

1-2 teaspoons (5-10 ml) Asian chili powder or hot paprika

1 teaspoon (5 ml) freshly ground pepper

Fresh coriander (cilantro) sprigs, coarsely chopped, to garnish

Line the bottom of a saucepan with the lemongrass, add about 5 cups/1.2 liter water and bring to the boil. Simmer covered for 30 minutes, then add the fish fillets, so that they lay atop the lemongrass and are not touching the bottom of the pan. The water should barely cover the fish. Bring just to the boil, cover and immediately remove from heat, allowing the fish to cool in its stock.

Combine onion, garlic, ginger and salt in a blender, adding about $^{1}/_{2}$ cup/ 125 ml of the oil until it is a coarse paste. Alternatively, pound in a mortar.

Heat half the remaining oil in a wok or frypan over medium-high flame, and when hot add the saltfish. This will cook quickly, under 1 minute. When crisp and golden, remove with a slotted spoon; coarsely chop and reserve. Add turmeric and optional shrimp paste to the same pan, frying for an additional minute. Add the pureed onion mix and cook slowly for about 20 minutes; stir regularly (especially in the final minutes) lest it scorch. Add sugar and the poached fish, stirring gently so as to break into large pieces. Remove fish and puree from pan and reserve.

Soak the noodles until soft ~ about 4 minutes in hot water, or slightly longer for thicker varieties. Drain. Meanwhile, add any remaining oil to pan and heat over medium high flame. Briefly fry the chickpea flour, chili and pepper, then increase to high and add the noodles and cook for 3 minutes, stirring all the time. Add the reserved poached fish ingredients, and stir through.

Sprinkle the fried salted fish atop, and garnish with freshly chopped coriander/ cilantro. Serves 4-6

How to Crisp-fry Noodles

Crunchy chow mein-style noodles are available pre-packaged, but you can also make them yourself. Not all noodles are suitable for frying, however. Do not fry dry *mein* wheat noodles without first parboiling and drying, although this process can be difficult, time consuming and prone to spoilage during the drying phase. Better yet, fry thin fresh Asian wheat noodles or even easier, pre-cooked Hokkien noodles. Gently pry apart without adding oil, then deep fry.

RICE STICKS, RICE VERMICELLI
& BEAN THREAD/GLASS NOODLES
All can be fried direct from the packet.

FRESH NOODLES
Fry directly from packet in hot oil ~
about 350°F/180°C in a wok or deep fryer.

DRIED EGG NOODLES
Parboil noodles in a large pot of boiling water for a minute, or until just soft; drain. Separate the noodles by spreading them out onto a lightly oiled baking sheet and dry well. Heat oil to 350°F/180°C and deep fry small amounts at a time, until golden brown ~ about 1-2 minutes. Use chopsticks or tongs to turn periodically.

Noodle Salads

nan gyi a-thoke

Combining noodles and fresh salad ingredients creates a delicious combination of crunchy textures, suiting hot climes. Street-side stands abound, with miscellaneous mounds of diverse rice and wheat noodles (page 202) varying in thickness and color, blended by the vendor to taste. Sometimes they are mixed with a hot meat sauce, other times simply a vinegar dressing, usually thickened with ground peanuts or roasted chickpea/besan flour. If the flavor doesn't equate to what you nostalgically remember, it's probably the lack of MSG, which locals use copiously. Alternatively, add a couple teaspoons of vegetable- or chicken powder, bearing in mind that these tend to be quite salty.

Always have Salty Pickle (page 283) prepared for quick assembly, plus a condiment of chopped fresh coriander/cilantro sprigs with minced garlic and salt. Barely moisten with oil or water.

Monti Salad

monti a-thoke

This Mandalay specialty can be made variously with wheat- or egg noodles or thick rice stick noodles. This recipe is a meatless version, although Fish Cakes (page 64) and cooked shredded chicken suit.

7 oz (200 g) packet dry rice sticks or thin wheat noodles

1/3 cup (25 g) crisp fried onion/shallot (page 41 or store bought)

1/4 cup (20 g) crisp fried garlic (page 41 or store bought)

1/4 cup (60 ml) Seasoned Oil (page 42)

1/2 teaspoon (2 ml) salt

1/4 teaspoon (1 ml) turmeric powder

1 tablespoon (15 ml) chickpea flour (besan/gram) roasted

1 tablespoon (15 ml) freshly squeezed lime or lemon juice

1 tablespoon (15 ml) fish sauce

2-3 teaspoon (10-15 ml) chili flakes in oil (Chili Fry, page 292)

3 leaves Chinese (Napa) cabbage, thinly sliced

1 cup (75 g) bean sprouts

6 green onions (scallions/ spring onions) coarsely chopped

1/2 bunch (50 g) fresh coriander (cilantro) coarsely chopped

Lime or lemon wedges, to garnish

Boil the noodles as per recipe directions: rice sticks for 4 minutes; wheat noodles slightly longer; Hokkien noodles need 1 minute in boiling water.

Drain and assemble noodles in a salad bowl; toss with crisp fried onions/ shallots and garlic, plus Seasoned Oil, salt and turmeric. Stir in chickpea flour, and lime or lemon juice and fish sauce. Add chili to taste. Toss with the cabbage, bean spouts, and green onions. Top with fresh coriander/cilantro sprigs and garnish with additional lime or lemon wedges, plus extra fried chilies and adjust seasoning with table dipping sauce (page 287). Serves 4-6

VARIATION: RAKHINE MONTI
The far western state of Rakhine is lauded for crisp salad freshness. Decrease oil by half. Omit the chickpea flour, add strips of seeded long green fresh chili and 1 tablespoon (15 ml) tamarind puree instead of lime or lemon juice.

Mandalay Festival Noodles
myee-shae

These up-country noodles are typical festival fare, sold at stands around the showground. Vary the specific sprouts according to market availability, although the combination of crisp bean sprouts and tender onion shoots makes a terrific flavor combination. Salted soy beans (paste or sauce) and fermented tofu are available in Chinese Asian markets, often in bottles. Both are very pungent and briny. Chinese pickled mustard (actually a cabbage) often comes in plastic tetra packs, but sometimes direct from vats. Or better yet, prepare Salty Pickle (page 283) and use in place of the pickled mustard here.

1 lb (500 g) skinless and boneless chicken breast

About 1-2 cups (250-500 ml) stock or water, boiling

Vegetable oil, for frying

1/4 cup (30 g) sticky (glutinous) rice flour

1/2 cup (65 g) plain rice flour

1/2 lb (250 g) pork loin, sliced into thin strips

2 tablespoon (30 ml) white vinegar

2 garlic cloves, minced

1/2 inch (1.2 cm) knob fresh ginger, grated

1 tablespoon (15 ml) chili flakes in oil (Chili Fry, page 292)

1 tablespoon (15 ml) fermented tofu (optional)

1 tablespoon (15 ml) dark soy sauce

1 tablespoon (15 ml) salted soy beans

7 oz (200 g) packet rice sticks

2 tablespoons (30 ml) chickpea flour (besan/ gram) roasted

1-2 teaspoons (5-10 ml) Asian chili powder or hot paprika

1/2 cup (85 g) coarsely chopped pickled mustard leaves or Salty Pickle (pages 283, 365)

1 carrot, peeled and shredded

1/2 bunch (50 g) fresh coriander (cilantro) sprigs

1 cup (75 g) bean sprouts
½ punnet onion spouts
1-2 teaspoons (5-10 ml)
   freshly ground pepper

1-2 teaspoons (5-10 ml) salt,
   to taste
lime wedges, to garnish

Put the chicken breast in a small saucepan and pour boiling stock or water atop. Over medium low heat, simmer the chicken till just done ~ 5-7 minutes. Remove from water and shred the meat; reserve both the meat and broth separately. (Alternatively, use left-over cooked chicken such as a supermarket roast, skin removed.)

Meanwhile, heat oil for shallow pan frying or deep frying, ensuring that the oil comes no more than one-third up the side of the pan, lest it overflow. Combine the two rice flours, and dredge the pork slices. Fry a few pieces at a time until crispy ~ 2-3 minutes. Drain on absorbent paper and set aside.

For the dressing, whisk together the vinegar, garlic, ginger and 1 tablespoon/ 15 ml of the chili oil and flakes. Add the preserved tofu if using, pressing to mash it into the dressing, followed by soy sauce and salted soybeans. (If the beans are whole instead of a paste, mash as well.) Mix well.

Plunge noodles into a large pot of boiling water and cook for about 4 minutes or as per packet. Drain and toss the chickpea flour plus chili powder with the cooked noodles, followed by pickled mustard, carrots and dressing. Cut the fresh coriander/cilantro into 2 inch/5 cm sprigs; add. At the last minute, toss in cooked meats and sprouts with additional fried chili flakes on the side. Taste for seasoning and garnish with lime wedges. Serve at room temperature in summer, or in colder climes serve in individual bowls ladled with a little hot stock to moisten. Serves 6

from *Peeps at Many Lands* (1909)

Scott's Market

Named originally after James George Scott, the British civil servant who introduced soccer to Myanmar, this city center market is a must-see tourist attraction of somewhat indifferent rambling colonial architecture and lean-tos.

Inaugurated in 1926, with later add-ons over the years, including a relatively new annex across the street (largely selling medical equipment), there's nearly some 1,700 shops crammed in a partial city block. Here's the city's best collection of antiques, handicrafts, clothes, jade jewelry, paintings, lacquer ware, wood carvings, tapestries, silverware, brassware and silk and cotton fabrics. All are juxtaposed against cobblestone laneways of yesteryear, and a humble outdoor food court in the market center, offering tea and local snacks served from low-slung plastic tables and chairs.

Locals will tell you that prices are higher here due to its foreign tourists, but you are just as likely to spot natives shopping for prescription spectacles, music and videos, sandals and textiles, plus, for investment, gems and gold. Upstairs is a veritable rabbit warren of haberdashery, and nary a tourist to be seen.

Post independence, Scott's Market was renamed Bogyoke Aung San in honor of martyred national hero General Aung San (father of Aung San Suu Kyi). It's just a short walking distance from the Sule Pagoda and Traders Hotel, plus the city's largest Indian market Kone Sae Tan, where one succumbs to the aromas of spice, in the heart of the city's commercial Indian quarter. On the street side, one is regaled by samosas, dosas and Disney-like exquisitely colored desserts. Inside, it's an oven of aromas, well worth the sweat.

Aung San Bogyoke is closed on Mondays and public holidays, and during the April "New Year" Thingyan water festival this is the first place to start throwing pitchers of water over unsuspecting shoppers ~ usually a day earlier than the rest of the city. So beware!

"The bazars are a great attraction, and provide the people with their main centres of gossip."

~ Sir A. C. Lothian, *A Handbook to India, Pakistan, Burma and Ceylon* (1955)

SALAD DAYS
Vegetables & Salads

အသုပ်နှင့်ဟင်းသီးဟင်းရွက်များ

"*Besides being made into salads, vegetables are "fried." This is not fat frying. Only the seasoning, consisting of a small quantity of chopped pork or shrimps, crushed garlic and ngapi, is fried in the merest fraction of sesamum oil, then the bean sprouts, cabbage or what not, chopped small, are spread over it.*"

   -- Mi Mi Khaing, *Burmese Family* (1946)

Vegetables & Salads

Lethoke is Burmese for "mixed by hand," and countless colonial recipes listed titles such as *Tomato Lethoke, Cucumber Lethoke,* and the like. Such dishes are typically bound with roasted chickpea flour or peanut meal and flavored oil, fish sauce, powdered dried shrimp, lime or tamarind, fresh green chilies or dried red chili powder, shrimp paste, and crispy fried shallots and garlic, or sometimes simply well sauteed onion. Wow!

As they say in local parlance locals like their salads *chin-chin, ngan-ngan* and *sut-sut* ~ sour, salty and hot. Furthermore, *lethoke* are not restricted to just vegetable salads, known as *lethoke soan:* there's also meat, rice, and noodle versions, as well. The reason for using one's hands is to ensure very thorough mixing, versus light tossing, and slight bruising is not discouraged. You can see this done daily at roadside stalls with vendors crouched on a low stool in front of their portable stand. As eating with hands is traditional in the country, locals have no qualms watching vendors use their fingers. Alternatively, don plastic gloves, as salad utensils may provide too light a touch.

Seasoned oil typically flavors Burmese vegetables, with fried onion and garlic showered as a final garnish. Vegetables and salads are frequently lightly bound or sprinkled with crushed dried peanuts and/or toasted sesame or roasted chickpea flour. Basically, it comes down to the regional agriculture: for example eastern Shan state prefers ground peanuts, western Rakhine chickpea flour.

Asian greengrocery is full is misnomers, mis-translation and misuse, yet these plants are at the pacesetting edge of cookery today. In the West, there are so many arbitrary decisions as to whether the plant is called by its Chinese, Vietnamese, Thai or even Latin name, that it can render recipes almost unintelligible. Consequently, Anglicization is used here wherever practicable. But don't let pedants distract you from buying, trying and experimenting.

BLANCHING VEGETABLES

Blanching means to briefly immerse in boiling water. Here, vegetables are plunged into a rapidly boiling pot, and removed immediately once the water just begins to boil again. Blanching rids vegetables of raw taste, improves texture and color, and is necessary prior to freezing vegetables to stop continued aging.

1 Cut vegetables into the desired size. Plunge prepared vegetables into a large pot of rapidly boiling water set over a high heat. Blanch for 30-60 seconds, or until the water again boils rapidly.

2 Drain and immediately plunge into a bowl of iced water to stop cooking. This also sets the color.

Some cooks prefer to add salt or sodium bicarbonate to the cooking water, both to improve flavor, and to enhance the color. This is optional, and in the latter case, harms nutrition.

La Phet
Fermented Tea Leaves

The Burmese contend that theirs is the only Asian country that both drinks tea as a beverage and eats the leaves as a dish. While this is debatable (with esoteric recipes occurring across the continent), it's safe to say that Myanmar is unique in its daily, indeed ubiquitous, consumption of tea leaves.

Made by fermenting steamed, hand-twisted and pressed tea in the ground for a year, the leaves take on a slightly sour and brackish flavor with a dark moist texture. But it's only afterwards that the real work begins. Specialist tea distributors transform the mulch with natural formulations, highlighting its essential bittersweet, sweet, sour and hot-sour essences. At home, it's up to the cook to toss the salad with myriad ingredients from fried pulses and seeds, crisp onion and garlic, seasoned oil and, for an even lighter touch, shredded cabbage and tomato. Well prepared, it is neither hot nor biting and balances the pungent tastes of the fermented leaves with a mild touch of acidity.

In local lore, fermented tea as a salad "vegetable" is king, while mango reigns over fruits. Like the French reliance on cheese, *la phet* fermented tea leaf in Myanmar occupies an essential, de rigueur place at the table. Not just to Burmese, but seemingly to all the country's ethnicities. As the aphorism goes: "to offer betel, tobacco and *la phet* means hospitality and welcome," whether as an accompaniment to tea for visiting folk or at the end of a meal. And no party, feast, festival or wedding is complete without its proffer.

SUBSTITUTIONS Overseas, *la phet* is sold pre-packaged in specialist Burmese stores, usually with all the ingredients separately packaged for easy last-minute assembly. If you can't obtain *la phet:*

⊝ Swap pickled ginger for tea leaf. *Gyin thou* is made using fresh young ginger or pickled ginger, well drained and shredded. (Japanese pickled ginger comes in both yellow and dyed red, and is suitable here although it's slightly sweeter.) Proceed with the same side ingredients.

Ⓙ Unfortunately, substituting reconstituted dried green tea leaves does not work

"This condiment is as regular a crown to a Burmese dinner as cheese is to an English one, and with the same idea, possibly erroneous in both cases, that it promotes digestion. It is almost exclusively produced in Taungbaing, in the Shan country, by a hill tribe called Rumai, better known by the Burmese name of Palaungs. The Burmese mix with it salt, garlic and assafoetida, douse it in oil and add a few grains of millet seed. The leaves forming the basis are the leaves of an actual tree as distinguished from the bushes of China.

~ Shway Yoe (Sir James George Scott)
The Burman, His Life and Notions (1882)

Tea Leaf Salad
la phet a-thoke

There's essentially two ways to eat *la phet*. Commonly, a circular sectioned lacquer-ware tray is offered with fermented tea leaf in the center surrounded by various condiments. The first diner spoons a small portion of tea to his or her mouth, followed by various accompaniments of choice. The tray is then passed around, to share, including the spoon.

A variant tea leaf salad, increasingly popular today, is pre-mixed, by tossing the leaves with the same ingredients. This is done at the last minute to ensure crispness and freshness. It also allows the optional addition of fresh ingredients like sliced tomato, shredded cabbage and paper-thin slivers of lemon or lime (peel and flesh).

Don't feel you need to add all the ingredients below; decide on market availability. And vary quantities to taste. Crispy fried onion and garlic are easily found in Asian groceries, or make your own. Apart from oil or Seasoned Oil (page 42), no actual dressing is required for tea leaf salad. Add fish sauce or lemon juice only when including fresh ingredients. A relatively small portion of fermented tea easily serves 4-6 persons when garnished with the following:

DRY INGREDIENTS

Crisp fried onion or shallots (page 41 or store bought)

Crisp fried garlic

Crisp fried baby fava/ broadbeans

Crisp fried chickpeas

Fried peanuts, crushed or chopped

Roasted sesame seeds

Dried shrimp or floss

FRESH INGREDIENTS

Garlic, thinly sliced

Ginger, peeled and thinly sliced (preferably young ginger)

Lemon or lime, cut into small thin pieces

Fresh green or red small chilies, cut into thin rings

Tomato, coarsely diced

White cabbage, shredded (ensure it is very fresh)

DRESSING INGREDIENTS

Seasoned Oil (page 42) or cold-pressed peanut oil or untoasted sesame oil

Salt

Freshly squeezed lemon juice

Fish sauce

Potato & Mint Salad

ar luu nae puccy nan thoke

Potatoes appear to have been introduced to colonial Burma in the 1880s, as there are no prior market references to the crop. But how fortunate that was! Arguably the country's potato crop are today Asia's tastiest ~ from standard French Fry chips to curry and mash. We encountered this delicious salad in the Shan hills of Kalaw, where it was served refreshingly cold straight from the refrigerator. It immediately struck us as a contemporary adaptation, well worth repeating.

4 potatoes in jacket (about 1 1/2 lb/750 g)

1-2 teaspoons (5-10 ml) salt, to taste

1 teaspoon (5 ml) finely ground white pepper

1/4 cup (60 ml) Seasoned Oil (page 42)

1/2 bunch (50 g) fresh mint, leaves finely sliced/ chiffonade (pages 262, 358)

Boil potatoes in skin, until tender ~ about 20 minutes. Drain, cool slightly, then peel and discard skin. Cut potatoes into large cubes and while still warm season with salt and pepper and add oil. Cool to room temperature, then gently stir in mint. Serve at room temperature, or refrigerate until ready. Serves 4-6

Pickled Asparagus Salad

ka nyut thoke

Local asparagus grows as long as 2 feet/60 cm and tends to be quite woody. Peel stems if tough. You can use pickled spears in this "Nouvelle Shan" recipe, but rinse or soak briefly so that they are only mildly sour. White cloud mushrooms and/or brown tree ear fungus are added more for texture than flavor, creating a beautiful presentation. Although not his recipe per se, we credit this combination to Swiss chef Boris Granges, a long-time resident of the country.

2 oz (60 g) fresh cloud or tree ear mushrooms/fungus

7 oz (200 g) asparagus spears

1/2 cup (125 ml) rice- or white vinegar

1 teaspoon (5 ml) salt

Pinch Asian chili powder or hot paprika

2 carrots, peeled

3 tablespoons (45 ml) Seasoned Oil (page 42)

1 teaspoon (5 ml) sesame seed, toasted, black or white or a combination

Tomato, for garnish (optional)

Trim mushrooms, removing core, and rinse. If using dried mushrooms, soak in hot water for 15 minutes and drain.

Cut asparagus into 2 inch/5 cm lengths and plunge into boiling water. Bring once again to the boil, then drain in a colander; do not refresh. Put asparagus into a bowl and toss with vinegar, salt and chili powder while it is cooling.

Cut carrots into sticks similar in size to the asparagus and plunge into a pot of boiling water; cook for 3 minutes, drain and mix with the asparagus.

To serve, arrange carrots and asparagus on a plate, top with mushroom and drizzle with Seasoned Oil. Sprinkle with sesame. If desired, garnish with sliced tomato. Serves 6

Long Bean Salad

pae tount shae thoke

Long beans, also known as snake- or yard-long beans, grow about 1 foot/ 30 cm in length. Fresh beans spring when held horizontally in a bunch, and black tips do not indicate age. They are eaten raw or quickly blanched. If substituting standard string beans or runner beans, slice lengthwise as well as crosswise.

1/4 cup (30 g) dried shrimp
1 lb (500 g) long beans, cut into 2 in (5 cm) pieces
1-2 lemons or limes, freshly squeezed
1 tablespoon (15 ml) fish sauce
1/4 teaspoon (1 ml) turmeric powder

2 tablespoons Seasoned Oil (page 42) or vegetable oil
Salt, to taste
1/3 cup (25 g) crisp fried onion/shallot (page 41 or store bought)
3 tablespoons (45 ml) sesame seeds, toasted

Rinse shrimp briefly with boiling water, drain and pat dry. If large, pound or chop; small shrimp can be added as is. Bring a large pot of salted water to the boil and blanch the beans for 3 minutes. Drain, refresh under cold water and squeeze dry with your hands; they should be slightly bruised.

Blend the lemon juice and fish sauce with the turmeric and combine with oil. Toss the green beans to coat, and taste for salt. Immediately before serving, top with crispy onion, sesame seeds, and shrimp.
Serves 4-6

Wing Bean Salad

pae zaung war thee thoke

Wing beans are four-sided, with frilly edges. They can be eaten both raw and cooked. If unavailable, substitute standard green beans or long beans.

500 g (1 lb) wing beans, cut in half crosswise

3 tablespoons (45 ml) Seasoned Oil (page 42) or vegetable oil

3 tablespoons (45 ml) sesame seeds, toasted

1/4 cup (30 g) finely chopped peanuts, toasted

1 tablespoon (15 ml) fish sauce

1 teaspoon (5 ml) salt

Bring a large pot of salted water to the boil and blanch the beans for 3 minutes. Drain, refresh under cold water and squeeze dry with your hands; they should be slightly bruised.

Blend the oil, sesame, peanuts and fish sauce. Just before serving, toss through the beans. Serves 4-6

VARIATION Substitute asparagus spears cut in equal lengths. Boil for just 1 minute, then spread out to cool; do not refresh in cold water, nor squeeze to bruise.

HINT An attractive way to serve a selection of Burmese salads is to line them in small piles or mounds on a long fish platter, each garnished with its own topping. As Burmese salads typically have scant liquid dressing to sop into each other, this works a treat.

Lemon Salad & Citron Salad
shaut thee thoke

Myanmar lemons and larger citrons are slightly less sour than varieties sold overseas. If your local citrus is especially tart, adjust seasoning with an additional pinch or more of sugar. Alternatively, substitute grapefruit and pomelo. Although not authentic, replace shelled cooked prawns for the dried shrimp called for here, using as much as 2 lb/1 kg.

1/2 cup (60 g) thinly sliced pink or golden shallots

1/4 cup (30 g) dried shrimp (optional)

4 large lemons or citrons

4 leaves white cabbage, shredded

1/2 teaspoon (2 ml) shrimp paste

1 teaspoon (5 ml) chickpea flour (besan/gram) roasted

1 teaspoon-1 tablespoon (5-15 ml) white sugar, to taste

3 fresh green long finger chilies, or 1-2 tablespoons (15-30 ml) chili flakes in oil (Chili Fry, page 292)

1-2 tablespoons (15-30 ml) Seasoned Oil (page 42) or Chili Oil (page 292)

1/4 bunch (25 g) fresh coriander (cilantro) sprigs, coarsely chopped

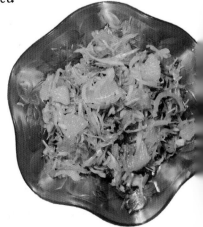

Peel and thinly slice shallots; soak in iced water for a few minutes then pat dry.

If using, soak the shrimp in water for about 15 minutes; drain and pat dry.

Peel away all membrane and skin from lemons or citrons, and break into small segments. Use a knife to cut the flesh between the membrane segments. (See also Technique, page 367) Just before serving, combine with all the ingredients and garnish with fresh sprigs of coriander/cilantro. Serves 6

VARIATION: WITH CRISP FRIED ONION
Omit the fresh onion or shallot. Quickly fry thinly sliced onion and garlic (page 41) until golden and crisp, or use store bought. Drain, and garnish at last minute atop the lemon salad. Drizzle with seasoned oil for additional flavor.

Tomato Mixed Salad

kha yan chin thee thoke

Here tomatoes complement cabbage and sweet salad onions, garnished with crisp-fried garlic and imbued oil. Myanmar onions are pink-blushed, but red onions are used here for added sweetness. They are typically soaked in iced water prior to consumption. If available, use white "salad onions" (page 367). If deleting the dried shrimp, increase fish sauce. As a variation, substitute roasted chickpea flour (besan/gram) for the peanuts.

1/2 cup (60 g) thinly sliced pink or golden shallots or salad onions

1 lime, freshly squeezed or 2 tablespoons (30 ml) white vinegar

1 teaspoon (5 ml) salt

4 small tomatoes, cored and thinly sliced (8 oz/250 g)

4 leaves white cabbage or Napa/Chinese cabbage, shredded

1 tablespoon (15 ml) fish sauce

1 fresh green long finger chili, seeded and sliced

1/2 bunch (50 g) fresh coriander (cilantro) coarsely chopped

1 tablespoon (15 ml) chopped peanuts

1 heaping tablespoon (20 ml) dried shrimp, crushed (optional)

2 tablespoons (30 ml) Seasoned Oil (page 42) or vegetable oil

1/4 cup (20 g) crisp fried shallot/onion (page 41 or store bought)

Soak shallots in half the lime juice and salt and prepare the vegetables. Assemble the tomato, cabbage and soaked onion in a serving bowl or plate. Drizzle with fish sauce and remaining lime, then mix with chili, fresh coriander/cilantro, peanuts and, if using, dried shrimp. At the last minute, toss in oil and crispy fried shallots. Serves 6

Bamboo Shoot Salad

hmyit thoke

Bamboo shoots are universally loved across East Asia, but not so favored by Western palates. Part of the problem is the strong smell, which is remedied by boiling prior to use. You rarely find fresh bamboo shoots overseas, so use canned, or even better, those which are vacuum-sealed in plastic bags, or straight from the brining crock. Bamboo shoots come whole or pre-sliced.

7 oz (200 g) can bamboo shoots, drained

4 fresh green or red long finger chilies, or 1 bell pepper (capsicum)

1/2 cup (60 g) thinly sliced pink or golden shallots, or salad onion

1 lime, freshly squeezed (2 tablespoons/30 ml)

1 tablespoon (15 ml) fish sauce

1 teaspoon (5 ml) salt

Pinch sugar

5 oz (150 g) shelled cooked prawns/shrimp, de-veined (about 12 medium-sized)

1/2 cup (125 ml) coconut milk

1/2 bunch (50 g) fresh coriander (cilantro) sprigs, coarsely chopped

Bring the bamboo shoots to a boil in a large saucepan of water; drain and begin again with fresh cold water. Bring to the boil, lower heat slightly, and cook for 20-30 minutes; drain and rinse. If whole, cut the shoots into thin strips.

Prepare the chilies by cutting in half lengthwise and discarding seeds; slice into long, thin strips. Briefly marinate chilies and shallots or onion in lime juice, fish sauce, salt and sugar. Coarsely chop the shellfish. When ready to serve, toss all ingredients together. Serves 6

HINT If using frozen shrimp, thaw with the cooling bamboo shoots. It's quicker.

Cauliflower & Asparagus Salad

pan gyaw be nint ka nyut thoke

This showcases the myriad flavors of Burmese salads ~ infinitely versatile, substituting (or combining) variously cucumber, cabbage, long- or green beans, daikon radish, even bean sprouts. (Blanching times will vary, and tender vegetables such as sprouts or leafy cabbage require immediate refreshing in chilled- or ice water.)

1/2 cup (125 ml) white vinegar

1/2 head cauliflower, broken into florets

2 carrots. peeled and cut into 2 inch (5 cm) long sticks

8 oz (250 g) asparagus, trimmed and cut into 2 inch (5 cm) lengths

1 teaspoon (5 ml) salt

1/4 cup (60 ml) Seasoned Oil (page 42) or vegetable oil

1/2 teaspoon (2 ml) turmeric powder

1 teaspoon (5 ml) sugar

2 tablespoons (30 ml) black and/or white sesame seeds

1/2 cup (35 g) crisp fried onion/shallot (page 41 or store bought)

1/4 cup (20 g) crisp fried garlic (page 41 or store bought)

Prepare the vegetables: Bring a large pot of water to the boil with half the vinegar. Plunge the cauliflower and carrot into the pot and cook for 2 minutes. Remove with a slotted spoon, then add asparagus to the same water; cook for just 1 minute. Drain but do not refresh; spread to cool and sprinkle with salt, plus remaining vinegar. Just before serving, toss with remaining ingredients, adding crisp fried onion and garlic last. Serves 4-6

VARIATION Blanch vegetables as above, then stir fry the vegetables with seasonings, and serve hot. Garnish with crisp fried shallots and garlic.

Burmese Mixed Vegetables
thee sone gyaw

Asimple, refreshing dish of greens, bamboo, okra and beans. Eat as a cold salad, or serve as a warm vegetable side dish variation below.

About 3 oz (75 g) baby
  spinach leaves, mizuna or
  watercress
4 oz (120 g) can sliced
  bamboo shoots, drained
8 long beans or 5 oz (150 g)
  green beans, cut into 1 inch
  (5 cm) pieces
8 okra
2 tablespoons (30 ml)
  Seasoned Oil (page 42)
  or vegetable oil

1 tablespoon (15 ml) fish
  sauce
1 teaspoon (5 ml) salt, or to
  taste
2 tablespoons (30ml) sesame
  seeds, toasted
1/4 cup (30 g) finely chopped
  peanuts, toasted
1/3 cup crisp fried onion/
  shallot (page 41 or store
  bought)

Stem, then rinse the leafy greens well under several changes of water, especially spinach as it notoriously retains grit. Reserve for final assembly.

Drain the bamboo shoots, rinse well, then boil in a large saucepan of water for 20-30 minutes to remove the sharp taste and smell. Drain and soak in cold water until ready to assemble. Begin anew with fresh water and plunge the beans into boiling water for about 3 minutes; remove with a slotted spoon, drain and refresh under cold water to stop further cooking and to retain color. Boil the okra for 3 minutes in the same water; drain, rinse and cut in half.

When cool, toss vegetables with the oil and fish sauce, plus salt to taste. Toss again with the toasted sesame seeds, peanuts and crisp fried onions. Arrange a bed of salad greens, top with vegetables. Serves 6

VARIATION: BLANCHED GREENS
Instead of fresh salad greens, substitute hearty leafy green vegetables such as bok choy, gai lan/flowering Chinese broccoli, or mature spinach leaves, separating leaf from stem, as stalks take slightly longer to cook. Cut into serving-size pieces, blanch in a pot of boiling water for 1-2 minutes, drain and refresh; pat dry. Then proceed as above.

Stuffed Eggplant & Aubergine
kahyan thee hnut

This recipe comes from Myanmar's far west Rakhine State. Palm-sized eggplants/aubergine (also known as *brinjal*), usually white and green speckled, are the norm there. If using smaller, long thin purple or gray-green varieties, double the quantity, but merely slice in half lengthwise instead of quartering. Rakhine chilies, unlike varieties popular elsewhere in Myanmar, are small and lantern-shaped, equivalent to fiery habañero or Scotch bonnet.

8 smallish eggplants/ aubergine (5 oz/150 g each)

1 tablespoon (15 ml) Asian chili powder or hot paprika

2 medium onions, finely chopped (1 1/3 cups/175 g)

5 large garlic cloves, minced

1 teaspoon (5 ml) freshly grated ginger

1 teaspoon (5 ml) turmeric powder

1 tablespoon (15 ml) salt

1 tablespoon (15 ml) shrimp paste

1/2 cup (125 ml) vegetable oil

1 3/4 cups (400 ml) stock or water

1/2 cup (25 g) dried shrimp or pork, powdered or floss (optional)

Soften the eggplants by gently whacking them on all sides with a wooden spoon; do not crack the skin. Depending on their size, halve or quarter them lengthwise, leaving stalk end uncut so that the two halves remain attached. Gently scoop out the fleshy center, but retain the pulp next to the skin intact for structural support; chop to a pulp.

Combine the pulp with ground chili, onion, garlic, ginger, turmeric, salt and shrimp paste (not floss); blend well. Spoon this mixture into the skin shells. Reform to recreate the whole eggplant and tie with twine to retain shape.

Heat the oil over medium heat in a Dutch oven or wide-bottomed frypan. Fry the eggplants in a couple of batches; turn to cook lightly on all sides, about 3 minutes. Place all back into the pan, add stock or water and partially cover; simmer over moderate heat turning once. Cook until most of the liquid is absorbed and only oil remains ~ about 20 minutes, or longer for larger eggplants. Remove lid during final 5 minutes cooking to allow sauce to thicken slightly.

Unbind the eggplant parcels, and arrange on a serving platter. If using, top with dried shrimp or pork floss. Serve warm or at room temperature. Serves 8

Potato Curry (in Three Ways)

ar luu hin

In this master recipe, parboil potatoes to hasten cooking. For longer stewing, begin with raw potatoes. And for a slightly crisp variation, fry potatoes beforehand. For best flavor, source alleppey turmeric, not Madras.

$1/2$ cup (125 ml) oil

2 small onions, thinly sliced ($2/3$ cup/120 g)

6 medium potatoes ($1^1/2$ lb/750 g) peeled

$1/2$ teaspoon (2 ml) turmeric powder

1 teaspoon (5 ml) mustard seeds, toasted

8 curry leaves

About 2 teaspoons (10 ml) salt

Heat oil in a large saucepan over medium-low flame and cook the onions slowly until very golden ~ about 20 minutes. Lower flame, lest they burn.

Meanwhile, slice the potatoes lengthwise into quarters, and parboil them in a pot of salted water ~ about 5 minutes. Drain, but retain some of the cooking water for the stew.

In a medium saucepan over moderate flame, add turmeric and potatoes to the cooked onion and water to just cover. Add mustard seed and curry leaves, if using. Add reserved cooking liquid just to cover, and simmer uncovered until tender and thick ~ about 20 minutes. Adjust seasoning. Serves 4-6

RAW POTATOES
Proceed as above, adding more water or stock as needed while cooking potatoes until soft ~ as long as 1 hour, depending on the variety. (This especially suits European waxy varieties like Kipfler.)

FRIED POTATOES
Dust quartered potatoes with plain rice flour. Heat oil and fry until lightly golden on all sides ~ about 5 minutes. Remove and set aside. Add more oil, fry onions as above, then add fried potatoes and water to cover, plus seasonings. Bring to the boil, lower heat, and simmer without lid until gravy thickens and potatoes are tender ~ about 30 minutes.

Savory Mash

ar luu chay hnut

A colonial-era classic from chef Albert Bernard at the Candacraig Hotel in former Maymyo. Mint, tomato and onion make it a deliciously different side dish to roast beef or even fried chicken. Boiling potatoes in their skins gives better flavor, but to save time, peel and add the skins to the boiling water.

1¼ lb (625 g) potatoes
½ bunch (50 g) mint,
　leaves only, finely sliced/
　chiffonade (page 262)
1-2 tablespoons (15-30 ml)
　tomato puree, or 1 small
　tomato, freshly chopped

1 small onion, finely diced
　(⅓ cup/45 g)
4 oz (½ cup/125 g) butter
1 teaspoon (5 ml) salt
1 teaspoon (5 ml) freshly
　ground white pepper
Pinch freshly grated nutmeg

Boil potatoes in their jackets. When tender ~ about 20 minutes ~ drain and cool slightly. When not too hot to handle, hold in a tea towel and rub the skin off; alternatively, use a paring knife to pull away the parchment-like skin.

While the potatoes are cooking, prepare the mint, tomato and onion; set aside for quick assembly later.

Mash the potatoes and while still hot, stir in the butter, mint, tomato and onion. Add salt and pepper to taste. (It's essential to combine all ingredients while hot, allowing flavors to meld.) Sprinkle with nutmeg, and keep warm until ready to serve. Serves 4-6

HINT Do not puree potatoes in a blender, lest they turn gluey. Use a specialty masher, or simply press through a potato ricer. Although our grandmothers prided themselves for their smooth and creamy mash, modern cooks espouse lumpy smashed potatoes. In fact, it's even easier!

Hill Station Mushrooms

taung paw mho hin

Before the days of air conditioning, hill stations were high altitude retreats for colonials escaping the searing heat of summer. In such climes, wild mushrooms grow best. If available, use meaty wild varieties, such as pine and cultivated king oyster. Large field or Portobello mushrooms also suit, as do standard button champignons.

2 medium onions (8 oz/250 g)
2 garlic cloves, chopped
$^{1}/_{2}$ inch (1.2 cm) knob fresh ginger, grated
$^{1}/_{3}$ cup (90 ml) vegetable oil
1 teaspoon (5 ml) Asian chili powder or hot paprika
$^{1}/_{2}$ teaspoon (2 ml) turmeric powder

$^{1}/_{2}$ teaspoon (2 ml) salt
1 lb (500 g) mushrooms, halved or quartered
$^{1}/_{4}$ cup (60 ml) water
1 tablespoon (15 ml) fish sauce
1 small bunch watercress
Lemon or lime

Pound or finely chop the onion, garlic and ginger together until pureed; alternatively use a blender, adding some of the oil to help it mix well. Add chili powder, turmeric and salt. Heat oil in a large saucepan on medium heat, and cook the puree for several minutes, stirring regularly lest it stick. Increase heat to high, add mushrooms, stirring to coat well, then add water and fish sauce; boil uncovered until the liquid is absorbed ~ about 30 seconds at most.

Arrange the watercress on a small platter, and spoon the warm mushrooms directly atop. Squeeze with fresh lemon or lime. Serves 4-6

Gourd Fritters

bu thee gyaw

This dish, along with Chickpea Fritters (page 193), are arguably the two most popular crisps in the country. These are best deep fried in a wok, where the oil can pool deeply to ensure uniform coating and crispness. Here winter melon or edible gourd is called for, but vary according to market availability (see also *Gourd*, page 363). Serve as a snack with dipping sauce (page 287) or to garnish myriad dishes, such as Mohinga stew (page 206).

1 lb (500 g) peeled and prepared gourd/winter melon, or summer squash
1 cup (150 g) plain rice flour
1/2 cup (75 g) sticky (glutinous) rice flour
1 tablespoon (15 ml) baking powder

1 teaspoon (5 ml) salt
1/2 teaspoon (2 ml) turmeric powder
1 cup (90 ml) water
Oil, for deep frying

Use young gourd or winter melon, as they are more tender. Pare away the skin and slice into ⅓ inch/1 cm fingers or sticks.

Sift together the dry ingredients, then stir in water; blend well. Heat oil in a wok over medium high heat. It should be about 4 inches/10 cm deep. Use fingers or chopsticks to coat one piece at a time in the batter and carefully drop individually into the hot oil; do not overcrowd. Turn over mid way through cooking. When golden ~ about 4 minutes ~ remove with a slotted spoon and drain; repeat with remaining. Serves 6

What! beer manufactured in Rangoon? Yes: and very
good beer too, in so far as colour, flavour, and creaming
qualities are concerned. The ingredients employed in
the manufacture of the beverage are brought together
from various sources: sugar from Penang -- for malt
does not seem to be deemed necessary; hops from
England, -- it may be from some of those rich and
beautiful fields along which the railway runs, in
the vicinity of Canterbury and of Maidstone. Yeast once
"started," propagates itself rapidly on the spot; and isinglass
where with to clarify the "brew," is manufactured from some
kinds of fish, captured in the adjoining rivers and their estuary."

-- Charles Alexander Gordon, *Our Trip to Burmah, With Notes on
that Country* (1875)

Barbecue Favorites

Char-grilled foods are popular accompaniments at Myanmar beer "stations." Typically unrefrigerated cabinets line the footpath outside a shop, and imbibers pick and choose among the selection, such as whole fish, sausages or dried meats. But it's the simplicity of vegetables that excel.

GRILLED LADY'S FINGERS (OKRA) / YONE PA TAE THEE A-KIN
Soak wooden skewers in water to prevent charring. Skewer 4 or 5 okra crosswise on a stick; repeat with a parallel skewer. Brush lightly with fish sauce and oil and grill on the barbecue or under an oven broiler about 8 inches/20 cm from the heat. Turn occasionally, until just softened ~ about 5 minutes. Sprinkle with salt and freshly ground pepper.

CHARRED CORN WITH LEMON
PYAUNG PHOO IN NINT THAN PAE YO THEE
A typical beer snack, and perfect for the barbecue. Shuck fresh ears of corn. Brush lightly with oil and grill over coals or under an oven broiler about 8 inches/20 cm from the heat. Turn occasionally, until lightly golden on all sides. Use a knife to cut the corn from the cob, sprinkle with salt and a pinch of Asian chili powder. Squeeze with fresh lemon or lime and serve.

SKEWERED MUSHROOMS / MHO KIN
Clean button mushrooms (page 365) and skewer them on sticks; brush lightly with oil. Grill about 8 inches/20 cm from heat turning often ~ 3-4 minutes total. Sprinkle with salt and pepper and serve with chili sauce.

GRILLED QUAIL EGG / NGONE AU KIN
Fresh quail eggs in the shell, as well as cooked and shelled in a can, are available at Asian markets. If fresh, merely boil for about 3 minutes in gently simmering water, cool and peel. Canned eggs are drained and gently rinsed. Skewer 3 or 4 eggs per stick, brush with seasoned oil and merely re-heat. Sprinkle with Asian chili powder and salt.

GRILLED BEAN CURD / PAE PYAR KIN
Use hard bean curd, cut into 1 inch/2.5 cm pieces, and thread onto skewers. Brush lightly with oil and sprinkle with Asian chili powder and freshly ground pepper. Cook for a minute or so on each side, until hot throughout. Sprinkle lightly with salt.

Three or four curries are presented to the guest, with fried
fish and meat, and sometimes cakes made of rice-flour and
jagra, a species of sugar made from the palm.

~ Father Vincenzo Sangermano, *The Burmese Empire A
Hundred Years Ago* (1893)

Myanmar Assar-Asa

There are several sorts of generic *sar thauk shaing* Burmese eateries, from humble hawker stalls to tea shops, local food shops and more upmarket restaurants catering both to locals and foreigners alike. But a favorite remains the basic Myanmar rice and curry restaurant, *hta min shaing*. These restaurants typically offer a cafeteria-style range, with a plethora of dishes cooked and set behind a glass partition. (In the hygienic West, health authorities would designate it a "sneeze guard.") Just pick and point to your favorites, and the establishment will round out the offerings, ensuring that you get "a balanced meal" as mothers are wont to say.

Myanmar Assar-asa is the term for such a Burmese spread, and it's a veritable feast. As a non-Burmese speaking tourist, one can sit down to receive a truly extravagant *hta min hin* or *hta min nae hin* set menu without even ordering! Or go just outside the kitchen where the selection rests, and point. Rice reigns as king, and half a dozen or so side dishes crown its glory. A standard menu includes pulses, such as butter- or soy beans cooked with turmeric, or a lentil dal: clear broth gourd soup or sour tamarind soup; light and mildly spicy *a-thoke* salad of raw fruits or vegetables, or mildly tart salads from pennywort, to citron, to crisp-fried chicken skin; one or two curries, variously of fish, chicken, prawns, or "mutton" (actually goat); and concurrently a relish or sambal eaten with raw vegetables. Finally, there's salty Bate Chin sauce (page 287) used to season like salt and pepper

Cooks prepare the sumptuous spread in the early morning, and serve throughout the day. Consequently, late morning and lunch is the best time to head to a local roadside eatery for Myanmar *assar-asa* at its freshest. Better yet, dishes are replenished for free. As such a meal mostly attracts locals and not "wealthy" foreigners, its cost is typically just a few dollars.

Throughout the meal, a weak Chinese-style green tea, *la pey yay chan*, is offered for free, and at the end hard lumps of jaggery palm sugar taken. Otherwise, sweets are typically served at a tea house, but not at the end of this meal. Surprisingly, savory *la phet*, or fermented tea leaf salad, is eaten in place of dessert. Here, green tea leaves are steamed and buried to mature for six months, then washed and pounded with garlic, and tossed variously with sesame seeds, nuts, fried beans or peas, dried fish and fried garlic and ginger. An unusual, yet delicious, finish to a meal, and fittingly, more like a digestive.

SOUP KITCHEN
Broths & Soups

ဟင်းခါးနှင့်အရည်သောက်ဟင်း

"*Every housewife should examine the contents of the stockpot every day, and every evening the contents should be poured into a clean bowl and set in a cool larder til next morning. This for up-country places. In the Delta it is hardly safe or desirable to keep any bones, etc., from one day to the next. You can make your soup fresh every day, but you ought to watch it.*"

-- M. Fraser, *The Burma Guides Cookery Book* (1932)

Broths & Soups

In the olden days, lack of refrigeration made stock bones potentially hazardous. But the pungency of locally-traded spices helped cloak any untoward aromas. Likewise, colonials avoided cream, milk, bread and flour in any dish destined as leftovers, as these tend to sour quickly in the humid tropics. By contrast, sago or tapioca proved a popular ~ and less risky ~ thickening agent. Hence the almost ubiquitous presence of a sago container accompanying canister sets of flour, sugar, salt and tea found today in Australasian antique stores.

Burmese soups, *hin ga*, in contrast to Eurasian recipes, are typically clear broth based, and accompany a meal to moisten and cleanse the palate and are not served as a separate course. They are often sour, to cut the unctuousness of oily dishes. Such soups are considered indispensable to an authentic repast ~ especially as little or no water, wine or drink of any kind accompanies a traditional Burmese meal. Conversely *hin cho* is closer to a "stew." Heartier thickened soups and stews generally fall under the *hin* or "curry" category, more of a main than an accompaniment.

You are likely to see stock favored especially in hotels and select restaurants. Most home and street cooks use plain water. This has as much to do with refrigeration and habit, as actual taste preference. That being said, all these recipes are enhanced by using stock instead of water. Conversely, locals are likely to add powdered chicken cube or a large spoonful of MSG. In any case, Burmese stocks are generally thin in flavor and definitely don't dominate a dish with the rich aroma of, say, the proverbial Jewish chicken soup. These stocks are meant to be light and clean, with minimal flavor, and more like flavored water than as a stand-alone soup. Indeed, you can easily use a diluted chicken or fish stock without detriment in most dishes. In fact, Eurasian stocks are richer, and may overpower the delicate nuances of Burmese soups, stews and curries.

A good rule is to dilute commercial stocks by 50 per cent ~ in other words, 1 part stock per 1 part water. Chicken broth is the most versatile, although a light fish stock works surprisingly well in all dishes. Hearty beef stock should only be used in beef dishes. Simmering ~ where the water literally quivers just below boiling point ~ produces a clearer brew; rapid boiling results in cloudy stock. A general rule is to bring liquid to the boil then reduce heat to low or medium low and continue simmering.

Basic Broth from Myanmar
hin cho

1 Boil 1 small peeled onion and 3 slivered garlic cloves in 4 cups (1 liter) lightly salted water; reduce heat and simmer covered until tender ~ about 20 minutes.

2 Add ¼ cup (30 g) pounded dried shrimp, or 8 whole shrimp shells and heads; simmer with a pinch of turmeric ~ about 15 minutes ~ then strain. Or use unsalted dried fish. (In some inland regions, meat stocks prevail instead of shrimp or dried fish. In this case, add lemongrass, fresh coriander/cilantro roots or stems, and a few slices of ginger for more fragrance, and a couple of spoonsful of soy sauce. Such meat stocks require longer slow stewing.)

3 Add herbs and vegetables of choice. Season with fish sauce and pepper. Optionally, thicken with a little chickpea flour (besan/gram), or soy bean flour, or roasted rice flour. Strain when ready to use.

HINT Turmeric invariably is added to seafood to counter any fishy smells. Don gloves and rub onto the fish prior to use. Turmeric may also be rubbed onto chicken pieces as a marinade prior to use.

VARIATIONS

 BEEF & CHICKEN Add Chinese celery to stock

PORK Add Chinese 5-spice

FISH Add sawtooth coriander (eryngo leaf/long coriander)

Eurasian Stock

hin yay

Asian stocks are weaker than Western counterparts and taste watery on their own. But they complement within a dish, without overriding other flavors. An old boiling hen makes the richest stock, but carcass bones work equally well. Add pork rib bones for added taste. For a gelatinous texture, include a pig's trotter and chicken feet. Begin with cold water, not hot, to extract more essence from the meat. Soy sauce is commonly added with pork to improve aroma.

2 lb (1 kg) boiling hen or chicken bones

1 lb (500 g) pork ribs

8 cups (2 liters) cold water

1 inch (2.5 cm) knob fresh ginger, thinly sliced

3 green onions (scallions/ spring onions) lightly bruised

1 tablespoon (15 ml) soy sauce

Place the bones and meat in a stockpot and cover with cold water. Place over high heat and bring to the boil; skim the impurities and foam which will come to the top. Drain and rinse, then cover again with cold water. Add ginger, green onions and soy. Bring to the boil, then lower heat and simmer for 2-3 hours, partially covered. Strain and refrigerate.

Spoon away the fat which congeals on the surface. Alternatively, float a paper towel atop the hot stock, then discard as the fat is absorbed into the paper; repeat. Store stock frozen for months in small sealed containers or refrigerated for several days, until ready to use. Makes about 8 cups/2 liters

Colonial Stock
hin ga

Unlike native stocks and broths, this incredibly rich concoction is a flavorsome meal in itself. Generally, the meat and vegetables are so overcooked that they are strained and relegated to animal feed. But oh, what a stock! For this recipe, invest in an excessively large pot, or use a canning vessel. It's well worth making a great quantity, then freezing portions in small plastic containers for later use in sauces, stocks and soups. Have your butcher saw beef bones into large but manageable pieces, about 2 inch/5 cm thick marrow bones are best. Char bones under the grill before adding to stock for enhanced flavor. Do the same with halved onions, grilling the cut side until blackened. Calf's foot or pig's trotters add a more gelatinous texture.

10 lb (4.5 kg) beef bones

5 lb (2.5 kg) boneless beef knuckle or shin, diced

1 calf's foot or 2 pig trotters, parboiled

1 lb (500 g) chicken giblets: hearts and gizzards, no liver

1 lb (500 g) whole piece prosciutto or Westphalian-style ham

3 large onions, peeled

6 cloves

4 carrots, whole

1 large turnip (1 lb/500 g) peeled and halved

2 parsnips (7 oz/200 g) peeled and left whole

4 celery ribs, especially leaves

4 inch (10 cm) piece of mace (optional)

2 bay laurel leaves

1 small bunch (25 g) fresh thyme

1 small bunch (25 g) fresh marjoram

1 bunch (100 g) fresh curly- or flat-leaf parsley

2 tablespoons (30 ml) peppercorns

Grill the bones under a broiler; alternatively bake in a hot 400°F/200°C oven for about 1 hour, turning mid way. In a huge stockpot, combine all meats and bones, and cool water to cover. Bring to the boil over high heat, then immediately lower to simmer for 6 hours, uncovered. Stock should not boil rapidly, lest it clouds. Add herbs and vegetables ~ studding each onion with 2 cloves ~ and simmer another 2 hours, then strain. Use as a stock or soup base, or boil with fine sago pearls for a thickened soup.

TECHNIQUE: BLANCHING OR PARBOILING MEATS

This is done to remove strong flavors and aromas by skimming off floating impurities. Meat is placed in cold or room-temperature water then quickly brought to the boil, until scum rises; use a slotted spoon or wire mesh to remove. By contrast, when parboiling vegetables, water is brought to a rapid boil first, before plunging in the vegetables; drain and refresh.

Pink Lentil Soup

pae ni lay hin cho

Pink lentils suit this simple soup, as they literally disintegrate into a light puree, here lightly redolent of cumin. Standard gray lentils take longer to cook and the resulting soup will be darker and heavier. Do not substitute slow-cooking brown or Puy lentils here.

³/4 cup (135 g) pink lentils
2 tablespoons (30 ml) oil
1 medium onion, thinly sliced
  (²/3 cup/90 g)
2 garlic cloves, minced
2 teaspoons (10 ml) ground
  cumin
1 bay laurel leaf
6 cups (1.5 liter) stock

1 carrot, diced
1 tablespoon (15 ml) fish
  sauce

To GARNISH

Sprigs fresh coriander
  (cilantro) coarsely chopped
Crisp fried onion/shallot
  (page 41 or store
  bought)

Rinse the lentils, taking care to remove any grit or stones. Place in a medium saucepan and cover with water. Bring to the boil over high heat, reduce to medium and simmer covered for 20 minutes, or until barely tender. Be careful, as the lentils are prone to froth and boil over; drain.

Heat the oil in a medium saucepan over moderate flame and fry the onions and garlic until barely tender and wilted ~ about 3 minutes. Add cumin and bay in the final minute, then stock, carrot and cooked lentils. Bring just to the boil, lower the heat and simmer for 20 minutes, until the lentils begin to fall apart and the soup slightly thickens. Add fish sauce just before serving and garnish. Serves 6

Roselle Soup

chin poung ywet

No Burmese cookbook is complete without a recipe for roselle soup, although its chief ingredient is difficult to procure overseas. Hibiscus leaves can be found in Fijian or Pacific island markets, as well as at select Indian grocers. If unavailable, try souring with fresh sorrel or strained tamarind puree to taste, and substituting chayote/choko or pumpkin leaves for texture.

2 tablespoons (30 ml) vegetable oil

1 small onion, finely sliced (⅓ cup/45 g)

3 garlic cloves, minced

Pinch turmeric powder

Pinch Asian chili powder or hot paprika

4 cups (1 liter) stock or store bought fish stock or fumet

4 oz (125 g) fresh roselle/ hibiscus leaves

1 tablespoon (15 ml) fish sauce

Heat the oil in a large saucepan over medium low heat and gently fry the onion and garlic with turmeric and chili powder until transparent ~ about 3-5 minutes. It should not brown.

Add stock, bring to the boil, then toss in fresh leaves and cook for just a few minutes. Turn off the heat and allow to cool slightly; add fish sauce. Serves 4-6

from The Silken East (1904)

Chicken & Kaffir Lime Broth

kyet thar chin sat hin cho

Shan and T'ai influenced, this rich chicken broth is redolent of citronella from its fresh kaffir lime julienne. Best to use tender young leaves here, but with tough big leaves, merely crumble them into the soup, do not cut into fine shreds; then eat around it, or remove before serving.

5 cups (1.2 ml) rich chicken broth

1 tablespoon (15 ml) fish sauce

Salt and white pepper, to taste

4 kaffir lime leaves, shredded into paper-thin julienne

About 3 tablespoons crisp fried onion/shallot (page 41 or store bought)

1-2 fresh green or red small chilies, seeded and finely chopped (optional)

Lime wedges

Bring the stock to a boil, and season with fish sauce, salt and pepper. Add kaffir lime leaves and remove from the heat. Ladle the hot soup into bowls and garnish with crispy fried onion and fresh chilies. Accompany with lime segments, squeezing into individual bowls to taste. Serves 4-6

TECHNIQUE: CHIFFONADE

Kaffir lime leaves have a tough rib vein running down the back. Hold the leaf in one hand, folding the leaf inward, lengthwise in half. With the other hand, gently pull the stem upward and along the rib vein to remove and discard. Cut into a fine julienne or chiffonade by stacking several leaves atop one another, and tightly roll into a cigar shape. Hold firmly, while slicing circular end crosswise into fine shreds.

Fish & Vermicelli Soup

kyar zam hingha

A last minute sprinkle of pepper makes this soup truly fiery.

3 tablespoons (45 ml) vegetable oil

2 small onions, finely sliced (²/₃ cup/90 g)

4 garlic cloves, minced

Pinch turmeric powder

¼ teaspoon (1 ml) Asian chili powder or hot paprika

1 lb (500 g) fish fillet, smoked or fresh, such as catfish/basa

4 cups (1 liter) stock or water

1 cup (100 g) finely shredded white cabbage

4 oz (125 g) cellophane- or glass noodles (bean thread vermicelli)

1 tablespoon (15 ml) fish sauce

2 teaspoons (10 ml) freshly ground pepper

Heat oil in a saucepan over moderate flame. Fry onions and garlic for a few minutes until soft, then add turmeric and chili, fish, stock and cabbage; lower heat and simmer partially covered for 15 minutes. The fish should break up, not stay in big pieces.

Meanwhile, soak vermicelli in cold water to soften. At the last minute, drain and add to the hot soup and cook for just a minute or two. Season with fish sauce and sprinkle liberally with pepper. Serves 4-6

from Peeps at Many Lands (1909)

Pickled Mustard Soup

kyet thar nint mone hnyin chin hin cho

This recipe takes its cue from both Shan and Bamar influences, but its origin is Chinese. Pickled mustard greens are made from *swatow* cabbage, cured in a simple sugar, salt and vinegar brine to retain a unique crunchiness with a sharp mustardy flavor. Available in Asian supermarkets, variously in large crocks, air-tight plastic bags, and canned. Extra rich stock makes this a double winner!

1 cup (200 g) coarsely chopped pickled mustard greens

5 cups (1.2 l) rich chicken stock

2 garlic cloves, thinly sliced

2 thin slices fresh ginger, minced

1/4 cup (60 g) tomato puree

Salt and white pepper, to taste

To GARNISH

Sprigs fresh coriander (cilantro) coarsely chopped

Crisp fried onion/shallot and/or crisp fried garlic (page 41 or store bought)

Drain the pickled mustard, then rinse very well. Squeeze firmly with your palm to extract moisture, then rinse and squeeze again; coarsely chop.

Bring chicken stock to a boil with garlic and ginger, and add pickled mustard, and tomato puree; adjust seasoning. Simmer partially covered for 1 hour and garnish with fresh coriander/cilantro and fried onion. Serves 4

VARIATION Pork belly with rind, and "soft bone" pork cartilage ribs, make delicious additions. Cut belly into lardons (thick slivers), or cut rack into individual ribs. Gently boil for about 1½ hours in total, adding more stock or water as needed.

Bamboo Shoot Soup
myit chin hin cho

The initial smell of bamboo shoot is likely to put you off, at least the first time. Yet this remains a local favorite, especially when made with fermented bamboo, a delicacy rarely served to tourists. Up-market eateries are wont to embellish this dish with rare ~ and endangered ~ shark fin.

8 oz (250 g) packet or can
  bamboo shoots (about
  1½ cups/375 ml) sliced

2 tablespoons (30 ml)
  vegetable oil

1 teaspoon (5 ml) shrimp
  paste

Pinch turmeric powder

½ cup (50 g) dried shrimp,
  pounded, or floss

4 cups (1 liter) stock

1 tablespoon (15 ml) fish
  sauce

Salt and pepper, to taste

To GARNISH
Lemon basil leaves
Lime wedges

Drain the bamboo and rinse well. Parboil or blanch three separate times in changes of water to remove smell ~ about 30 minutes total. Drain and rinse a final time and cut into thin strips if they are not already; squeeze.

Heat the oil in a large saucepan over medium-low heat and gently fry shrimp paste and turmeric for a minute. Add shrimp floss and prepared bamboo slices, cover with stock and bring to a gentle boil; cook a further 5 minutes and at last minute adjust seasoning with fish sauce, salt and pepper. Garnish with basil and lime. Serves 4-6

VARIATION: WITH PORK
Add thin slices of pork fillet, briefly marinated in fish sauce. Boil in the stock until done ~ just a couple minutes. For longer cooking meat, such as pork neck, dice and cover briefly with boiling water direct from the kettle. This helps remove any excess fat. Drain and add meat to stock; gently simmer for 1 hour or longer, until tender. Add cooked meat at the same time as bamboo and stock.

Gourd Soup

bhthee hingha

Use an edible gourd such as calabash, or winter melon (page 363, and variation opposite). Dried pork floss is available at East Asian groceries. Although optional, it adds a delicious element to this soup's presentation. For a very special flourish, add a pinch of pricey saffron.

8 oz (500 g) gourd or winter melon

5 cups (1.2 liter) stock

$^1\!/_2$ cup (60 g) dried shrimp, pounded (optional)

1 teaspoon (5 ml) freshly grated ginger

1 garlic clove, minced

1 tablespoon (15 ml) fish sauce

1 teaspoon (5 ml) salt

$^1\!/_2$ teaspoon (2 ml) freshly ground pepper

To GARNISH

About $^1\!/_4$ cup (20 g) crisp fried onion/shallot (page 41 or store bought)

About $^1\!/_3$ cup (15 g) pork floss (optional)

Fresh coriander (cilantro) sprigs very coarsely chopped

Peel and cut the gourd or melon into thin chunks, or grate.

In a large saucepan over medium flame, combine stock, optional dried shrimp, ginger and garlic. Bring to a boil and simmer for 5 minutes. Add the gourd and cook for 5-10 minutes more, or until tender. Season with fish sauce plus salt and pepper to taste. Garnish as desired. Serves 4

VARIATION: WITH PRAWNS AND GREEN TOMATO
Add shelled cooked (not dried) prawns at the end. They merely need reheating through, plus a few green tomato slices or 2 tablespoons/30 ml tomato puree.

Variation: Winter melon tureen

This is a classic Chinese presentation, long popular at high-end restaurants in Yangon and Mandalay. It requires a whole winter melon, clean-skinned and unscarred. Scrub skin with brush, and slice off cap top. The melon may be carved or chiseled for aesthetic presentation, but not too deeply. Scoop out seeds and pulp, but not flesh. Prepare soup as described previously, and place in melon to about three-quarters full; replace cap. Set melon in a form-fitting bowl and put this on a trivet rack in a very large and deep pot; steam for about 3-4 hours for a 5 lb/2.2 kg melon, or up to 6 hours for larger. Water should cover the bowl almost all the way up its side; add more water as necessary. During the final half hour replenish stock within the melon. Alternatively, steam the melon without the soup, and after cooking, pour prepared soup inside and serve. Use a sharp spoon to scoop slices of the melon flesh when serving, and add to soup.

HINT Create a hammock-like sling of string around the bowl before placing it into the pot. This allows for easy retrieval later.

Pepper Water
(The Original Mulligatawny)
rassam

The origin of the word Mulligatawny is a corruption of two South Indian words, *milaku* (pepper) and *tannir* (water). This vigorous version is a palate cleanser, best served after an Indian-style curry, rather than as a starter. We first tasted it in the former colonial hill station Maymyo ~ now Pwin Oo Lyin ~ where Dennis & Dolly Bernard of Aung Padamyar cook family dishes dating from a century ago. We've been returning to their restaurant every trip since! For a richer flavor with slightly subdued sour taste, substitute Eurasian or Colonial stock (pages 257, 258) for the water.

1/2 cup (80 g) dried lentils or peas

1/4 cup (60 ml) oil, preferably peanut- or un-toasted sesame oil

1 teaspoon (5 ml) brown mustard seed, toasted

1/2 teaspoon (2 ml) fenugreek seed

4 dried red small chilies, seeded

6 curry leaves, fresh or dried

1/2 cup (60 g) finely sliced pink or golden shallot

1 teaspoon (5 ml) cumin seed, toasted

6 garlic cloves, crushed but unpeeled

1 teaspoon (5 ml) black pepper, freshly ground

3 cups (750 ml) thin tamarind puree

2 teaspoons (10 ml) salt

1/4 teaspoon (1 ml) turmeric powder

1 medium tomato, coarsely chopped, or 1/3 cup (90 ml) tomato puree

1-2 tablespoons (15-30 ml) grated palm sugar, or brown sugar

4 sprigs fresh coriander (cilantro) coarsely chopped

Boil the lentils or peas in water to cover, until very tender and mushy ~ about 30 minutes. Drain, then press gently to extract excess water; reserve lentils. (Mild tasting pink lentils and field or pigeon peas all suit, but not strong flavored "blue boiler" peas or garden green peas.)

Heat the oil in a large saucepan over a medium-high flame. All at once, add the mustard, fenugreek, chili and curry leaves, immediately followed by shallots. Lower heat slightly, and stir until lightly browned ~ about 3 minutes. Remove with a slotted spoon and reserve. Add cumin, garlic and pepper, cooking for a further 2 minutes. Add tamarind, followed by 3 cups/750 ml water. Bring to a boil, adding salt, turmeric and tomato, followed by cooked lentils or peas and reserved fried spices. Simmer for about 20 minutes. Shortly before serving, taste and add just enough sugar to balance the sour taste; gently boil for a few more minutes, and stir in fresh coriander/cilantro. Soup should be thin and acidic; if too thick, add more water. Serves 6-8

"Mulligatawny soup is sacred to the Sabbath, and to the Sabbath breakfast in particular. No one would dream of having it at any other time; in fact, to do so would disintegrate the calendar, and whenever you enter the breakfastroom of a European house in Burma, and the fragrant odour of mulligatawny assails your nostrils, you can be quite sure, whether the church bells are ringing or not, that it is Sunday."

~Paul Edmonds, *Peacocks and Pagodas* (1925)

Anglo Mulligatawny

ma note thar nee

A classic Anglo-Indian soup that crossed the empire, to become a favorite among generations the world over. It bares scant resemblance to its predecessor, Pepper Water (see previous recipe). Some versions add pink lentils, but this recipe is thickened with chickpea flour alone.

$1/2$ cup (125 ml) oil

2 teaspoons (10 ml) cumin seed, toasted

1 teaspoon (5 ml) mustard seed, yellow or black, toasted

2 teaspoons (10 ml) coriander seed, toasted

1 tablespoon (15 ml) freshly grated ginger

6 garlic cloves, minced

2 tablespoons (30 ml) chickpea flour (besan/gram) raw

4 cups (1 liter) rich chicken stock

1 lb (500 g) boneless chicken thigh meat, sliced

2 small onions, diced ($2/3$ cup/90 g)

2 cups (500 ml) coconut milk

1 cup (250 ml) coconut cream

Pinch saffron threads

1 teaspoon (5 ml) Asian chili powder or hot paprika

2 teaspoons (10 ml) salt

To GARNISH

Crisp fried onion/shallot (page 41 or store bought)

Fresh coriander (cilantro)

Lime wedges

Heat oil in a pot over medium heat. Fry the cumin, mustard and coriander seeds for 30 seconds, until fragrant; remove with a slotted spoon and reserve.

Fry the onion, ginger and garlic in the same oil ~ 3-5 minutes. Add the chickpea flour and continue cooking for a couple minutes. Stir in chicken stock, and when just boiling add the chicken. Lower heat and simmer for about 5 minutes. At that point, add coconut milk and cream, and simmer, uncovered, for another 2 minutes. Add toasted spices plus saffron, chili powder, salt and garnish. Serves 6-8

Myitkyina Barley Soup

myit kyina hin cho

Myitkyina is a town in Myanmar's northwest Kachin state, and this soup was colonial formal fare. But unlike earthy Mulligatawny, this dish fell into relative obscurity over the decades. The soup is creamy white ~ hence the use of white barley, clear stock and white pepper ~ beautifully juxtaposing the contrasting colors of carrot and parsley. At banquets, carrots were cut into exquisitely miniature balls, but a fine dice is simpler. White pearl barley is paler than standard pearl barley and in Asia, commonly added to desserts; use here, if available.

½ cup (90 g) white~ or pearl barley
1 tablespoon (15 ml) butter
Pinch salt
6 cups (1.5 liter) chicken or veal stock
⅓ cup (40 g) diced carrot

1 egg yolk
½ cup (125 ml) cream
1 teaspoon (5 ml) salt
½ teaspoon (2 ml) finely ground white pepper
Pinch nutmeg
2 teaspoons (10 ml) freshly chopped parsley

Wash barley, put in pot with cold water and boil for 5 minutes. Strain and cover with 5 cups/1.2 liters fresh water. Add butter and a pinch of salt, and bring to the boil over medium heat; simmer partially covered for about 90 minutes, until very soft; add more water from kettle as it boils dry. Strain, discarding the cooking liquid, and rub barley through a sieve, or easier, puree in a blender. If using a blender, you may need to add some of the stock to puree sufficiently. Whisk the puree with the stock and re-heat over low flame.

In a separate pot, cook the carrots in boiling water until just tender ~ about 3 minutes. Strain and refresh; reserve.

In a mixing bowl, blend the yolk with cream, and gradually whisk in a ladleful or two of the hot stock. Ensure the remaining stock is barely simmering, then whisk the yolk and cream mixture back into the hot liquid all at once. Stir until the soup thickens slightly, but do not boil lest it curdle. (Preparation in a bain marie or double boiler over simmering water is a safer option.) Adjust seasoning and at last minute, add the carrots and garnish with parsley. Accompany with toast fingers. Serves 4~6

PANTRY PRESERVES
Chutneys, Condiments & Sauces

ကြာရှည်ခံစားစရာများ

"*Several of the recipes give ingredients which come from tins; these may be useful in jungle life.*"

-- M. Fraser, *The Burma Guides Cookery Book* (1932)

Chutneys, Condiments & Sauces

A well-stocked larder is the key to contented cooking, as nothing is more frustrating than having to dash off to the grocery for a missing ingredient or two. Spare a thought, then, for remote colonials whose shopping expeditions were rare by necessity. With no refrigeration nor freezing, their larders and pantries needed careful stocking, and seasonal produce was preserved and bottled to last throughout the year.

Traditional Burmese *htamine chin,* dried spice "sprinkles", are the perfect camp food, as they require no refrigeration and remained fresh over many weeks, in spite of such common ingredients as shrimp or fish. Most are combined with chili flakes, so be sure to source a relatively mild chili here, as Myanmar spice is closest to a combination of hot and mild paprika. Thai chili flakes may prove too hot, Latin American ones even hotter. Chinese flakes, especially from Yunnan suit perfectly. Chili powders can be hotter than flakes if they are ground with seeds, which is the hottest portion of the chili. Powders and pastes made with seeded dried chilies are best of all.

Burmese "quick fresh" condiments and chutneys are some of the world's best, but to be consumed on the day. They are less seen today, due to the country's changing demographics; but they suit a spicy curry from the Subcontinent as well as a barbecued meat in an overseas suburban backyard. By contrast, thin table dipping sauces like Bate Chin flavor foods at the table as readily as salt and pepper, or as easily as squirting soy sauce in China, fish sauce in Vietnam and Thailand, and thicker ketchup in America and Britain.

Colonials invariably remarked negatively about fish sauce, and all its derivatives. Made from the extract of salted putrefied fish, then brewed over several months to several years, it is wildly popular, indeed, ubiquitous across Southeast Asia. The brined sauce extract, as well as its solid fermented fish bits, are used. Similar brews have a long pedigree, tracing back to *garum* and *liquamen* of ancient Greece, Rome and Byzantium. And its closest Western equivalent today? Anchovy paste.

"There are few articles of food which meet with more energetic denunciation than the favourite Burman condiment, ngapi, which means literally pressed fish. . . The smell of ngapi is certainly not charming to an uneducated nose."

~ Shway Yoe (Sir James George Scott), *The Burman, His Life and Notions* (1882)

Fresh Coconut Chutney

ohn thee chin

½ fresh coconut, grated

1 small onion, finely sliced, or about ⅓ cup (45 g) finely sliced pink or golden shallots

1 teaspoon (5 ml) Asian chili powder or hot paprika

⅓ cup (20 g) coarsely chopped fresh coriander stems and roots

2 tablespoons (30 ml) white vinegar

½ teaspoon (2 ml) sugar

Pinch salt

2 tablespoons (30 ml) plain yogurt (optional)

Crack open the coconut and grate the flesh inside (page 306). You should have about 4 cups/400 g loosely packed. Squeeze in your fist to extract the first pressing of coconut cream; reserve for another use.

Combine the coconut with remaining ingredients and optional yogurt if using. Serve as a condiment. Makes about ½ cup/125 ml

Green Mango Condiment

tha yet chin

1 green/unripe mango (about 8 oz/250 g)

⅓ cup (45 g) finely sliced pink or golden shallots

1 teaspoon (5 ml) Asian chili powder or hot paprika

1 teaspoon (5 ml) white sugar

½ teaspoon (2 ml) salt

1-2 fresh small chilies, seeded and finely chopped

1 teaspoon (5 ml) freshly grated ginger

1 teaspoon (5 ml) white- or grated palm sugar

½ teaspoon (2 ml) salt

1 tablespoon (15 ml) freshly squeezed lime juice or white vinegar

1 tablespoon (15 ml) cream or yogurt

Peel and coarsely grate the mango. Combine with all the ingredients, and serve. Makes about 1½ cups/375 ml

Fresh Tomato Chutney
kha yan chin thee chin

This works with both green and ripe tomatoes ~ adjust sugar accordingly, but do not peel and seed green tomatoes.

4 medium tomatoes (1 lb/ 500 g) peeled, seeded and coarsely chopped

1 small onion, finely diced or about 1/3 cup (45 g) finely sliced pink or golden shallots

1 teaspoon (5 ml) Asian chili powder or hot paprika

2 teaspoons (10 ml) white sugar, or more to taste

1 tablespoon (15 ml) white vinegar

1/2 teaspoon (2 ml) salt

Prepare tomatoes (page 371). Combine all ingredients in a mixing bowl and stir lightly. Refrigerate until ready to serve. Makes about 2 cups/500 ml

Quick Pear & Coconut Chutney
pan the chin

Myanmar markets abound with luscious apples and nashi pear, mostly from neighboring Yunnan, China, although domestic production is growing. While nashi is rather innocuous, also try this recipe with tart Granny Smith (increase the sugar) or mildly sweet Pink Lady apples. The secret is juicy crispness, so "floury" fruit are not suitable.

1/3 cup (30 g) freshly grated coconut

2 nashi or apples (1 lb/ 500 g)

1 lime, freshly squeezed, about 2 tablespoons (30ml)

1/2 teaspoon (2 ml) salt

1 tablespoon (15 ml) finely sliced pink or golden shallots

2-4 fresh green small chilies, seeded and thinly sliced

Prepare fresh coconut (page 306). Peel, core and grate the nashi or apples, immediately tossing in lime juice and salt to prevent discoloration. Use your hands to gently squeeze and bruise together all remaining ingredients and serve as a condiment. Makes about 1 cup/500 ml

Mint Relish

pusinan chin

Round-edged peppermint tastes better than pointy spearmint. The latter tends to taste too herbaceous when ground.

1 bunch (100 g) fresh mint,
  leaves only
1 garlic clove, minced
2-4 fresh green small chilies,
  seeded and diced
$^1/_2$ teaspoon (2 ml) salt

1 lime, freshly squeezed
1-2 tablespoons (15-30 ml) oil
$^1/_3$ cup (90 ml) yogurt
  (optional)
Pinch white sugar (optional)

For coarse texture, do not use blender: Cut leaves in a chiffonade (page 262) and stir in garlic, chili, salt, lime and moisten with oil. Allow flavors to meld at least 30 minutes. Alternatively, combine the ingredients in a blender and process. Drizzle in oil as needed to help blend, and add sugar if too tart. This is delicious with grilled meats. Add yogurt if accompanying rice.
Makes about $^1/_2$ cup/125 ml

Cucumber & Yogurt Raita
the khwar thee chin

Reminiscent of an Indian *raita*, treat as an accompanying condiment ⁓ as much a salad as a cooling foil to rich dishes.

1 lb (500 g) cucumber
2 teaspoons (10 ml) salt
2 tablespoons (30 ml) freshly chopped mint
1 tablespoon (15 ml) freshly chopped lemon basil (optional)

1 tablespoon (15 ml) freshly squeezed lemon or lime, or white vinegar
1 cup (250 ml) plain yogurt
1/4 teaspoon (1 ml) white sugar

Peel the cucumber, then use a spoon to scoop out seeds and discard them. For a decorative appearance, score with a fork along all sides, then thinly slice about 1/8 inch/3 mm thick. Toss with half the salt and leave to drain in a colander for a few minutes; pat dry.

Gently stir together the cucumbers with all remaining ingredients. You can prepare this several hours in advance. Makes about 2 cups/500 ml

Salty Pickle
sar yay sein chin

This is a popular table sauce accompaniment to Shan Noodles (page 210), but it is an equally delicious garnish to most soups and stews. Although this condiment easily keeps for a week or longer in the refrigerator, it is always safest to briefly blanch or even microwave raw garlic intended for long storage, as it is prone to botulism.

$1/2$ cup (85 g) finely chopped Chinese pickled mustard (page 365)

2 oz (60 g) cloud- or tree ear mushroom/fungus

1 carrot, peeled and shredded, or finely diced

2 garlic cloves, minced

2 teaspoon (10 ml) salt, preferably non-iodized

$1/4$ cup (60 g) store bought chili paste (sambal olek)

Rinse the mustard greens well, then dice. Rinse the mushroom/fungus, trim and remove core. If using dried mushrooms, soak in hot water for 15 minutes and drain. Briefly blanch the carrots, and drain. Combine all ingredients, spoon into a sterilized jar and store until ready to use, as it improves with age. Makes about 1 cup/250 ml

Fresh Prawn & Tomato Balachaung

pazun thoke ngapi gyaw

Classic balachaung consists simply of dried shrimp and chili flakes. This recipe uses fresh prawns instead, resulting in a richer, earthier, condiment. Sprinkle on rice, eating in small portions.

1/3 cup (90 ml) vegetable oil

1 cup (125 g) finely sliced pink or golden shallots

1 bulb (70 g) garlic, cloves finely sliced

2 teaspoons (10 ml) chili flakes

1/2 teaspoon (2 ml) turmeric powder

1 teaspoon (5 ml) shrimp paste

3 tablespoons (45 ml) white vinegar

1/2 lb (250 g) cooked prawns or shrimp meat, finely chopped

1/2 teaspoon (2 ml) salt

1 tablespoon (15 ml) tamarind puree

1 medium tomato, peeled, seeded and chopped

In a wok or frypan, heat oil over medium heat. Add the shallots, stir periodically and fry until slightly crisp. Remove with slotted spoon, drain and reserve. Repeat with garlic slices.

Fry chilies and turmeric momentarily in the same oil. Take care that the oil is not too hot, lest it burn the chilies; they brown very quickly. Strain through a sieve, reserving oil as Seasoned Oil in other recipes. (Any residual oil in the pan from frying chilies will suffice here, so do not wipe clean with paper towel.) Dry fry the shrimp paste in same pan then add vinegar. Add prawns and salt, toss for 1 minute over medium-high heat, add tamarind and tomatoes and fry until excess liquid cooks away ~ 3-5 minutes; stir constantly. Remove from heat and stir in reserved fried chili flakes, onion and garlic. Makes about 2 cups/500ml

Whitebait Sambal

nga chouk htaung gyaw

Use tiny dried *ikan bilis* fish for this recipe, available un-refrigerated in Asian supermarkets. Do not used tinned anchovy, nor frozen whitebait. Prepare at the last minute to ensure crisp flavor. This is an ideal accompaniment to Coconut Rice (page 156).

1/4 cup (20 g) dried anchovy/whitebait (ikan bilis) page 356

1/3 cup (45 g) finely sliced pink or golden shallots

1/2 teaspoon (2 ml) shrimp paste

2 teaspoons (10 ml) tamarind puree

1/4 teaspoon (1 ml) sugar

Pinch salt

1/2 lemongrass, white part only, finely chopped

2 tablespoons (30 ml) vegetable oil

1 tablespoon (15 ml) water

1 green onion (scallion/ spring onion), thinly sliced

Pour boiling water over the dried fish to clean, then drain immediately. Spread out to pat dry.

Combine shallots, shrimp paste, tamarind, sugar, salt and blend into a rough paste with crushed lemongrass; add oil and water to moisten and bind. To finish, stir in dried fish and green onion. Makes about 1/3 cup/90 ml

Sauces

a-chin-yei

Ubiquitous as salt and pepper at the table, sauces and dips are ideal accompaniments for barbecued meats, grilled vegetables, and fritter snacks. Ever versatile, many can be used as a salad dressing on raw leafy lettuce or blanched vegetables. In neighboring countries, from Thailand to Vietnam, similar condiment sauces are watered down and sweetened with sugar, but not commonly so in Myanmar.

Bate Chin

table sauce

This is the simplest and most common table sauce, made variously with fish sauce, soy sauce, lemon- or lime juice (bottled or fresh) or vinegar. It goes with practically everything, but especially with shrimp crackers, tempura, fish and curries. Sometimes a little water is added to dilute, other times a pinch of sugar and a squeeze of fresh lime. Local males contend that Bate Chin arouses the passions and increases stamina, jokingly dubbing it *thote bodei*.

1/3 cup (90 ml) fish sauce or
soy sauce

6 fresh green or red small
chilies, thinly sliced

5 small garlic cloves, thinly
sliced

Combine all ingredients together, allowing flavors to meld. This is made fresh daily, as colors and textures deteriorate when left longer. Makes about ½ cup (125 ml)

BATE CHIN SHALAKA
Substitute rice- palm- or coconut vinegar, or bottled lime juice, for the fish- or soy sauce.

Tamarind Sauce

ma gyi chin yay

6 fresh coriander (cilantro)
roots or stems

1/3 cup (90 ml) thin tamarind
puree

1-2 fresh green small chilies,
seeded and finely chopped
or pounded

1 small garlic clove, minced

1/4 teaspoon (1 ml) grated
palm sugar or white sugar

1/4 teaspoon (1 ml) salt

Pinch ground coriander seed,
toasted

If fresh coriander/cilantro roots are unavailable, use stems. If you have a stone mortar and pestle pound until blended; if not, combine everything into a blender and puree. If too thick, add up to ¼ cup/60 ml or more water; allow flavors to meld. Makes about ½ cup/125 ml

Cooked Tomato Sauce

kha yam chin thee hnit

We came across this delicious sauce years ago at Mar Lar Thein Gi restaurant in Bagan, where vivacious Daw Yin Yin Htay and husband U Paw Lar cook up that town's best tucker. Well worth a detour, as Michelin would state.

1/4 cup (60 ml) vegetable oil

2 teaspoons (10 ml) shrimp paste

8 medium tomatoes, coarsely chopped (about 3 lbs/ 1.3 kg)

2 small onions, finely sliced (2/3 cup/90 g)

1 teaspoon (5 ml) Asian chili powder or hot paprika

1/2 teaspoon (2 ml) salt

1/2 teaspoon (2 ml) turmeric powder

1/4 cup (25 g) dried shrimp, pounded (optional)

About 1/2-1 cup (125-250 ml) water, as needed

1-2 teaspoons (5-10 ml) white sugar (optional)

Heat oil in a large saucepan over moderate flame. Add the shrimp paste, tomatoes, and onion in that order, and stir for a few minutes. Add remaining ingredients, using only half the water and no sugar yet. Bring to a rapid boil, lower heat, cover and stew for about 30 minutes. Stir occasionally to prevent scorching and add additional water as needed. Oil should start to pool at the top, when done. After about 30 minutes, taste and add sugar if too tart. (Off-season tomatoes will require this; fully ripe summer tomatoes probably will not.) Serve as a side dish. It's particularly good with grilled meats and boiled pulses and Scotch Eggs. Makes about 1¹/₂ cups/375 ml

Mounted Butter

Made like classic mayonnaise, this yesteryear recipe is delicious with Maynmar's bounty of char grilled seafood. Clarified butter is separated oil from the whitish milk solids (page 357). Cool to room temperature, but do not chill as it easily solidifies.

2 egg yolks
1 tablespoon (15 ml) freshly
squeezed lime or lemon
juice
1 teaspoon (5 ml) dry
mustard powder

1 teaspoon (5 ml) salt
Pinch Asian chili powder or
hot paprika
3/4 cup (200g) clarified
butter, melted but not hot

Ensure your bowl and all ingredients are at warm room temperature, not cold. Whisk the yolks until quite frothy ~ about 2 minutes. Whisk in the lemon or vinegar and all the seasoning, then very slowly drizzle in the clarified butter drop by drop while beating briskly. It should become emulsified and thick. Makes 1 cup/250 ml

Sweet Mayonnaise

Sweetened condensed milk is a mainstay across Southeast Asia, not only in the region's ubiquitously milky-sweet teas, but here as a thickening base for mayonnaise. The recipe caught early European settlers' fancy with similar recipes still prepared as far afield as New Zealand.

2 eggs
1 3/4 cups (450 ml) sweetened
condensed milk
4 oz (1/2 cup/125 g) butter,
softened

1 tablespoon (15 ml) dry
mustard powder
1 teaspoon (5 ml) salt
3/4 cup (175 ml) white
vinegar

Beat whole eggs till frothy. Combine all ingredients together in a medium bowl and beat with a mixer for a few minutes till mayonnaise consistency. If needed, add a spoonful cold water to thin. Makes 1 1/2 cups/375 ml

Buttermilk Mayonnaise

Buttermilk gives this mayo a special tang, and was especially prized by European settlers, as it was not as perishable as fresh milk, and lasted longer in the days of ice boxes. Although slightly cumbersome, this recipe guarantees mayonnaise-like emulsification. But don't cook the egg yolk over direct heat, as it is likely to curdle. Scalding means to heat just below the boil. It is reputed to add flavor to milk, but its original justification was to pasteurize raw milk.

2 tablespoons (30 ml) corn starch (cornflour)
2/3 cup (175 ml) buttermilk
1 cup (250 ml) vegetable oil
1 tablespoon (15 ml) white vinegar

1 teaspoon (5 ml) salt
1 egg yolk
1/2 teaspoon (2 ml) dry mustard powder
1/2 teaspoon (2 ml) finely ground white pepper

Dissolve corn starch with a spoonful of the cold milk; set aside. Scald the remaining buttermilk, but do not let it boil. Immediately remove from heat and stir in 2 tablespoon/30 ml of the oil plus, corn starch, vinegar and salt. Return to medium low flame, and whisk constantly until thickened ~ about 3 minutes; remove from heat.

Lightly beat the egg yolk in a small bowl, then slowly drizzle some of the hot sauce into the yolk, always whisking. Then reverse, by whisking the blended yolk back into the sauce. Set the saucepan in a larger bowl of ice water and continue whisking for a few minutes, until just tepid but not cold. Remove from water bath and slowly drizzle in remaining oil, whisking constantly until thick and emulsified. (Do this initially drop by drop, lest it curdle.) Finally whisk in mustard and pepper.
Makes 1 1/2 cups/400 ml

Chili Fry

nga youk thi gyaw

Fried chili flakes are a traditional table accompaniment, just as Westerners have pepper. Save the resulting chili-infused oil for later use ~ traditionally the oil is used as a base for curry, and it's particularly tasty with stir-fried vegetables. For best results, begin with un-toasted sesame oil, or peanut oil.

2 cups (500 ml) vegetable oil   1/2 (2 ml) teaspoon salt
1 cup (100 g) chili flakes

Have a strainer with heat-proof bowl standing near your stove, ready to strain (and cool) the ingredients as they cook instantly. Heat oil in a wok over medium-high heat to almost smoking. Add chili flakes to the hot oil, then immediately remove from heat and strain; reserve chilies; add salt. You can serve fried flakes dry, or return to oil once it cools; both are traditional practice. Chili Fry keeps for a couple weeks at room temperature or until oil turns rancid. Serve as a relish or table seasoning. Makes about 1¼ cups/300 g

Balachaung
dried shrimp & chili fry

This is a classic Burmese accompaniment, sprinkled on rice or eaten alongside fresh crudités such as lettuce, raw eggplant, cucumber, sprouts and crisp broccoli florets. Use the smallest dried shrimp for this recipe, almost krill sized. For a colonial-era canape, press Balachaung onto cold buttered toast or bread fingers.

1 cup (125 g) dried shrimp

2 cups (500 ml) vegetable oil

2 tablespoons (30 ml) chili flakes

1/3 cup (45 g) finely sliced pink or golden shallots

5 small garlic cloves, thinly sliced

1 teaspoon (5 ml) freshly grated ginger

1/4 teaspoon (1 ml) turmeric powder

1 tablespoon (15 ml) shrimp paste

If you have a heavy mortar and pestle, pound the shrimp until coarse mealy texture. You can also do this in a blender.

Have a strainer with heat-proof bowl standing near your stove, ready to strain (and cool) the ingredients, as they cook instantly. Heat oil in a wok over medium-high heat to almost smoking. Add chili flakes to the hot oil, then immediately remove from heat and strain; reserve chilies. Return oil to heat and quickly fry shallots until crisply golden, stirring constantly to achieve uniform color ~ about 2-3 minutes. Strain again, then repeat, frying garlic and ginger in the same oil, and strain once they turn golden. Reserve 1/4 cup/60 ml of the oil for the next step, save the rest as Seasoned Oil for use in other recipes.

Do not wipe your wok. Add reserved cooked oil, re-heat, and fry the turmeric and shrimp paste followed by the dried shrimp. Fry, stirring furiously for about 2 minutes. Strain and combine with previous fried ingredients. If properly cooked dry, this should easily keep for weeks at room temperature, covered.

"I am not aware that any Englishman has been equally enthusiastic with regard to balachong, but there is no doubt that ngapi seinsa. . . is identical with this much used substitute for anchovy sauce, and is often brought direct from the Burman bazaar by Madrasi butlers, who declare it has come all the way from Penang, and charge correspondingly."

~ Shway Yoe (Sir James George Scott) *The Burman, His Life and Notions* (1882)

PROOF of the PUDDING
Sweetmeats & Desserts

အချိုပွဲနှင့်သစ်သီးခြောက်

"I made cakes with exceeding great vigour and confidence during almost the whole of my stay, but nobody ate them save myself from bravado, the dogs from greed, and unsuspecting strangers from innocence."

-- Beth Ellis, *An English Girl's First Impression of Burmah* (1899)

PUDDING: To North Americans the word connotes a custard-like confection. In Britain and the Commonwealth, pudding has a broader meaning, signifying dessert. As in "What's for pud?"

Sweetmeats & Desserts

IT'S not just after meal times that one can indulge in these favorite sweets. Indeed, as in most of Asia, the concept of meal-end "pudding" is alien. Instead, a digestive-like fermented tea leaf is more appropriate.

Consider these tasty delicacies equally for mid-morning or afternoon tea, as well as dessert. Or indulgently as a bedtime snack. After all, that's what prestige hotels offer at turn-down service. (And frustratingly, usually spotted after brushing one's teeth at night.)

Myanmar dishes are sweetened variously with palm sugar or jaggery (of varying age and color), white cane sugar, and caramelized cane sugar. Market stalls abound with a plethora of sugar varieties, and counters are piled high with candied fruits and crystallized vegetables like pumpkin and gourd. Local cake and candy shops do a brisk trade, both from bees flying in for an easy nectar fix, but especially with local Myanmar clientele. Many dishes are made with agar agar, a natural gelatin-like firming agent made from seaweed. While it is considered a vegetarian gelatin substitute, it does not have the same spring; indeed agar has a stiff over-set consistency. Conveniently, it sets without refrigeration.

Myanmar sweet cakes and puddings are more likely steamed as baked. Most steamed cakes are cooked without a cover, but to the overseas palate, the end result is better when encased with plastic cling wrap or parchment paper.

The region's plethora of tropical fruit means rich pickings: jams suitable for breakfast, plus condiments for a typical Burman repast at any time of day. Equally, we're tempted by nostalgia in the afternoons, when historic hotels serve a very English menu of tea sandwiches and cakes with jam. Sitting amongst the tiered trays on the table, one feels transported back to the Golden Age of Travel.

Jams and jellies should be cooked until they reach about $8°F/5°C$ above water boiling point. Although $212°F/100°C$ is the world standard for boiling, this differs considerably, depending on altitude. An easier gauge is to cook until the desired thickness -- that is, a perfect spreading consistency. For preserves, wide mouth saucepans work best, as they allow quicker evaporation, leading to brighter color and fresher flavor.

Rich Semolina Cake

shwe kyi sa-nwin ma kin

One of the country's most famous desserts, this moist cake is sometimes cooked without eggs, becoming more like an Indian *kasari* pudding; but we've always found such variations disappointing. Other versions use oil instead of butter, and it is especially good made with cold-pressed nut oils, particularly macadamia oil. Semolina cake is traditionally sprinkled with white poppy seeds ~ indeed, some recipes call for quantities in the batter itself, giving a delicious crunch, but alas, these are not commonly available overseas; black poppy seeds are hardly used in Myanmar cooking. Both fine- and coarse semolina can be used here, and toasting semolina prior to cooking greatly improves flavor.

2 cups (350 g) semolina
1 1/2 cups (400ml) coconut milk
4 oz (125 g) butter or 1/2 cup (125 ml) oil
2 cups (460 g) white sugar
1/2 cup (75 g) golden raisins or sultanas

3/4 cup (90 g) finely chopped cashews, toasted
1/4 teaspoon (1 ml) salt
3 eggs, well beaten
1 tablespoon (15 ml) poppy seed, preferably white

Toast the semolina on a baking tray in a high oven for about 10 minutes. Stir or shake occasionally so it browns evenly.

In a large saucepan over medium heat, combine coconut milk, butter or oil and sugar, until dissolved. Slowly add the semolina, stirring constantly so that lumps do not form ~ about 5 minutes. Keep stirring until the mixture just begins to bubble; add fruit, nuts and salt. Lower heat slightly and keep stirring for another 10 minutes. This mixture gets very stiff, but not unmanageably so; the batter will come away from the pan sides. Remove from heat, quickly beat in eggs mixing well, and transfer mixture to a deep, buttered oven-proof dish, about 8 x 8 x 2 1/2 inch deep (20 x 20 x 6 cm). Sprinkle with poppy seeds and bake in a preheated 325°F/160°C oven for 25 minutes, or until set. Insert a knife or toothpick in the center to test if it is done; it should emerge clean.

Cool in pan for several hours or overnight and serve at room temperature. Cut with a sharp knife into small squares, diamonds or wedges. If desired, top with coconut flakes or raisins soaked in sugar syrup. Serves 8-12

Coconut Semolina Pudding

sa-nwin ma kin

Bake this a day ahead, as it improves in flavor. This dish is much more pudding like, and less cakey, than Semolina Cake.

1¹/₃ cups (175 g) semolina

4 cups (1 liter) coconut milk or cream

²/₃ cup (150 g) white sugar

1 teaspoon (5 ml) salt

¹/₃ cup (35 g) golden raisins or sultanas

¹/₄ cup (60 g) butter or ghee

2 egg whites, stiffly beaten

¹/₃ cup (60 g) whole or halved blanched almonds

2 teaspoons (10 ml) sesame seeds

2 teaspoons (10 ml) white poppy seed (optional)

Toast the semolina on a baking tray in a high oven for about 10 minutes. Stir occasionally so it browns evenly.

Heat coconut milk in a large saucepan over medium flame. When it is just boiling, lower heat and stir in the semolina, sugar and salt, continuing to stir constantly for about 10 minutes. When ready, the mixture will start to pull away from the sides of the pan. Remove from heat and stir in raisins, then gradually fold in butter and beaten egg whites. Return pan to heat and cook over moderate flame, stirring in one direction only. Again, the mixture should pull away from the sides of the pan ~ about 3 minutes. Pour into a buttered 8 x 8 x 2 ¹/₂ inch (20 x 20 x 6 cm) deep oven dish and bake and sprinkle with almonds, sesame- and poppy seeds. Bake in a preheated 325°F/160°C oven for about 25 minutes, or until fully set. Cut into small squares. Serves 8-12

Coconut Blancmange

ohn yo

Blancmange was a mainstay of colonial desserts and remains timelessly popular today. Unlike set custard, it is made without egg and therefore can be cooked directly atop flame without risk of curdling, but be careful lest it scorch. Using palm sugar slightly discolors the namesake white or "blanc," but adds better flavor. This recipe benefits from the addition of an optional teaspoon of pandan extract/essence.

1/4 cup (30 g) corn starch (cornflour)

2 1/2 cups (625 ml) coconut milk

1/4 cup (55 g) grated palm sugar or white sugar

Pinch salt

1 teaspoon (5ml) pandan extract/essence (optional)

About 1/4 cup (30 g) Sweet Grated Coconut (page 322 or store bought) or freshly grated coconut

Fresh berries, to garnish (optional)

Stir the corn starch with 1/2 cup/125 ml of the coconut milk to make a paste. Heat remaining coconut milk, sugar and salt in saucepan and bring to a boil. (If using palm sugar, boil to dissolve sugar, then strain mixture to remove any grit. Return to pan.) Whisk in the corn starch paste, stirring constantly; lower heat and gently boil for a few minutes, until thickened. This allows the raw flavors of the starch to cook out. Add pandan flavor now, if using. Pour into a slightly wet 3 cup/750 ml pudding mold or 6 individual molds; refrigerate until set ~ at least 5 hours. Do not cover for the first hour to allow quick cooling, but later wrap with plastic to prevent drying out.

To serve, unmold the blancmange and top with coconut, and if desired, fresh berries. Serves 6

Add a couple of drops red or green food coloring while cooking: split portion in half, dying one or both. Allow bottom half to barely set first in refrigerator ~ about 1 hour. Meanwhile keep second portion warm, atop a double boiler to prevent setting. (Do not continue cooking, merely keep warm.) Then top bottom portion with second color and set fully. Un-mold and serve.

Coconut

Fresh coconuts are full of water, feel heavy and will slosh loudly when shaken. A slight sloshing sound indicates an old coconut, so avoid.

Coconut cream is the first pressing from freshly grated coconut. Subsequent thick and thin coconut milk is made by adding water ~ either hot or room temperature ~ then squeezing to extract the resultant liquid. Coconut milk is sometimes made from dried coconut, but is less satisfactory. Generally speaking, the less watery liquid in the can, the richer the coconut cream or milk. Shake in the store to discern the difference, but do not shake cans at home before using. Rather, stand and let the thick milk rise to the top before opening and spooning off. Make sure not to confuse sweetened coconut milk, which is sometimes labeled "cream of coconut."

Coconut water is the viscous liquid inside fresh coconut and should never be confused with coconut milk and cream. Coconut water is now fashionable as a health drink.

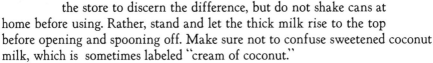

TECHNIQUE: GRATING FRESH COCONUT

Traditional coconut graters were typically sculptured wood in the shape of an animal, with a large protruding spike or grater at its snout. Cooks would crouch atop, while scraping a half shell. More contemporary versions are merely made of wrought iron.

Hand-held models work in the same manner. Firmly hold one half shell in cupped hand, while grating the coconut flesh away. There are two grater shapes: one slightly resembles a citrus zester, creating strips instead of crush. It is identifiable by its round or circular blades. The second is an actual grater, producing fleshy pulp. The former is best for garnish strips, the latter for extracting coconut cream.

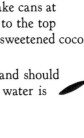

Small hand appliances also work, and resemble miniature versions of commercial machines. One model attaches to the counter, when the coconut half is held against the concave blades, while moving the handle with the other hand to create a whirling blade.

1 Pierce the eyes of the coconut with a nail; drain the interior water.

2 Traditionally, villagers crack a coconut's hard shell by holding in one hand, while scoring with a machete or heavy knife along the circumference., using quick sharp blows. As this is dangerous for a beginner, it is best to crack with a hammer, drop onto concrete until it splits, or use a hack saw. Ideally, you should end up with two complete halves. Grate as described above.

TECHNIQUE: COCONUT CREAM & MILK

1 Take freshly grated coconut and squeeze firmly with your hand. Alternatively, press it though a China cap or Chinois with a wooden pestle. This is the richest pressing, known as cream, and works best with mushy, finely grated coconut, but not coarser coconut shred. Easier still, puree shredded coconut in a food processor or blender, then press or squeeze.

2 Pour about 2 cups/500 ml boiling water to cover the squeezed flesh and stir till cool. Strain and firmly squeeze to extract coconut milk. Do not blend the two pressings. One coconut should extract 4 cups/1 liter liquid.

The remaining coconut pulp is generally discarded, but can be sugared and dried in the sun or in a very low oven, until fully desiccated. (See Sweet Grated Coconut page 322) As most of the rich fat has been extracted, it will not be as full-flavored.

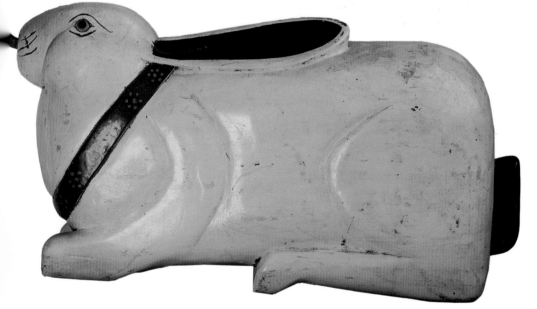

Tapioca Pudding
tharku

This classic dessert has no flavor from the actual tapioca, merely texture. Pre-soaking small tapioca allows for faster cooking time and uniform texture.

1 cup (190 g) small pearl
  tapioca (sago) well rinsed
  or soaked
1 cup (220 g) grated palm
  sugar or brown sugar,
  firmly packed

Pinch salt
1/4 cup (60 ml) coconut
  cream
Freshly grated coconut,
  or desiccated coconut, to
  garnish

Bring 6 cups/1.5 liter or more of water to a boil in a large saucepan set over a high flame. When boiling, gradually pour in the tapioca, stirring occasionally to prevent sticking to pan bottom. Small pearls take about 30 minutes to cook, both floating when done, and turning from white to totally translucent; drain. (Instant tapioca mixes will cook quicker.) Add more boiling water from kettle if it boils dry.

Meanwhile, dissolve palm sugar in 2/3 cup/175 ml water in a saucepan over medium-high heat. Once it boils and all sugar has dissolved, remove from heat to cool. Add salt and cooked tapioca, allowing flavors to meld for at least 30 minutes, or longer.

If refrigerated, the tapioca will set, so it is best served at room temperature. Spoon into bowls and top each with a couple of spoonsful of coconut cream and a light sprinkle of grated coconut. Serves 4-6

VARIATION: PANDAN FLAVORED

Scrunch a fresh pandan leaf to extract essence, and add to coconut cream plus an additional 2 tablespoons (30 g) sugar. Heat in a saucepan over low heat till sugar dissolves, then cool. Blend this into the finished tapioca dish. Small bottles of pandan extract/essence are available at select Asian markets, usually next to food coloring and vanilla; if substituting for fresh leaf, add just a few drops.

Everywhere along the roads these night bazars are common. Generally a couple of women smoking sit beside them, as represented -- their stock-in-trade a tray of miscellaneous sweetmeats. Often there are long lines of these bazaars in the streets.

-- Charles Alexander Gordon, *Our Trip to Burmah, With Notes on that Country* (1875)

Creamy Coconut Fudge

ohn malain

The Burmese title signifies rich coconut cream that has floated to the top. A specialty of Mandalay sweet merchants lining Zeygio Market, this delicious fudge is sinfully addictive. Agar agar is a seaweed based "gelatin," essential here to set the fudge.

1¹/2 cups (400 g) sweetened
  condensed milk
¹/2 cup (50 g) desiccated
  coconut
¹/2 cup (125 ml) coconut
  cream

¹/3 cup (75 g) grated palm
  sugar
1 tablespoon (15 ml) agar
  agar powder

In a medium saucepan, heat together the condensed milk, coconut and coconut cream over moderate flame.

Separately, in a small saucepan melt the palm sugar with 1 tablespoon (15 ml) water; stir in agar powder to dissolve and immediately add to the coconut mixture. Lower flame to medium-low and continue stirring for 5 minutes. This can scorch easily, so be vigilant. An indication of when ready is the mixture starting to pull away from the sides of the pan when stirred. The longer you can cook without scorching, the richer the final result. Pour into an oiled or parchment paper-lined 8 x 12 inch (20 x 30 cm) dish. Press gently and allow to cool and set, then cut into small squares. Makes about 50

HINT If using agar agar sticks instead of powder, soften in water, squeeze, then stir into the hot dessert to melt, as if using softened gelatin sheets.

Tamarind Granita & Sorbet

man gyi thee yay kel chit

Slightly bracing, this palate cleanser works both between courses as well as at the end. Granita is coarse, crystallized ice, made by simply semi-freezing fruit liquid and puree on a shallow tray, scraping periodically during setting. Using an ice-cream machine for sorbet creates a smoother texture. For best flavor, use syrup from candied ginger, either commercial or page 321.

¹/₂ cup (100 g) tamarind pulp
1 cup (250 ml) sugar syrup (page 349)

Pinch salt
¹/₂ egg white (optional)

Soak the tamarind pulp in 1 cup/250 ml tepid or boiling water, until the pulp is soft and loosens from the pods. (Older tamarind pulp, if very hard, requires hotter water.) Strain the pulp from the pods and add sugar syrup and salt. Pour onto a non-reactive (non-aluminum) flat baking tray and place in freezer until nearly set. Scrape periodically to create a sludge, preventing it from freezing solid. (Using a stainless steel egg slice works particularly well for scraping.) For sorbet, use an ice-cream freezer, adding optional egg white; process until frozen. Makes about 2 cups/500 ml

VARIATION: LONGAN SORBET
Select Chinese groceries sell dried longan pulp, which is mildly sweet and vaguely similar to litchi/lychee and rambutan. Soak 3 oz/100 g longan pulp in 1¹/₂ cups/375 ml hot water till soft, then puree in a blender with a pinch of salt and 1 tablespoon/15 ml lemon juice. Add ¹/₃ cup/90ml sugar syrup (plain, or from making candied ginger and pomelo, or pineapple jam). Transfer to an ice-cream machine, add ¹/₂ egg white and process till frozen. Makes about 4 cups/1 liter

"When we were constipated, my mother gave us a sherbet of tamarind, sweetened with jaggery -- the cooked sugar juices of the palmyra palm -- both of which are purging."

-- Mi Mi Khaing, *Burmese Family* (1946)

Fried Bananas

nget pyaw gyaw

Cooked banana recipes work best with small sugar- or ladyfinger bananas, as they stay firmer during cooking. When using longer Cavendish bananas, halve the length and be extra careful when turning in the oil, lest they break. For a variation, instead of sprinkling fried bananas with sugar, top with the coconut milk sauce from the next recipe ~ or use both.

6 sugar/ladyfinger bananas or 3 standard-sized bananas, un-peeled	1/2 cup (125 ml) ghee, or vegetable oil
About 3 tablespoons (45 ml) sticky rice flour (optional)	1 tablespoon (15 ml) white sugar, or more to taste
	2 tablespoons (30 ml) sesame seeds, toasted

Peel bananas and if using long standard-sized bananas, halve crosswise. Prick the flesh lightly. For a slightly crisper crust, lightly dust the bananas with sticky rice flour.

Heat ghee in a fry pan over medium-high flame and gently lower the bananas into the oil. Decrease heat to medium and cook for about 3 minutes on first side and 2 minutes turned over. Drain on absorbent paper and sprinkle with sugar and sesame. Serves 6

VARIATION: BANANA FRITTERS
Prick banana as above, then lightly dust with corn starch/cornflour or tapioca flour, then dip in Tempura Batter (page 191). Fry in a great quantity of oil, until golden; drain on a rack and sprinkle with white sugar. Optionally, add 2 tablespoons/30 ml sesame seeds to the batter.

Steamed Banana with Coconut Milk

nget pyaw baung

This is a deliciously simple finale to a meal. The recipe works best when bananas are slightly under-ripe, otherwise they are prone to mush.

3 standard-sized bananas or 6 sugar/ladyfinger bananas, un-peeled

1½ cups (400 ml) coconut milk

⅓ cup (75 g) grated palm- or white sugar

½ teaspoon (2 ml) salt

A few drops pandan extract/essence (optional) or 1 pandan leaf, scrunched

TO GARNISH

Freshly grated coconut

White poppy- or sesame seeds, toasted

Prick banana skin with a thin needle all over to avoid any possible popping or minor explosions during cooking. (Don't be alarmed: Baked potatoes in their jackets have similar problems.) Cook bananas in a covered steamer over rapidly boiling water until the skin begins to break, about 3 minutes. Or, cook bananas in a pot of boiling water for about 2 minutes. Remove bananas from heat, cool immediately under cold water, then peel. Cut large bananas in half crosswise. Small bananas can be left whole or sliced lengthwise. Handle carefully, as they are now delicate.

Meanwhile, combine coconut milk, sugar, salt and optional pandan in a saucepan over medium flame; stir to dissolve. Reduce heat and simmer gently for about 3 minutes. Remove from heat and serve either hot or room temperature, pouring over cooked bananas at table. Garnish with grated coconut, or sprinkle with toasted poppy- or sesame seeds. Serves 4-6

VARIATION: PUMPKIN & TARO
Pare, cut into large chunks and steam until just tender. Add to sweetened coconut milk, and proceed as above.

Almond Cookies
yang-yen bang

This cookie has long been popular in Yangon's Chinatown, and is now even more so in Mandalay. Traditionally they are made with lard, which creates a uniquely tender flakiness.

2¹/2 cups (300 g) all-purpose (plain) flour, sifted

1 teaspoon (5 ml) baking powder

³/4 cup (175 g) white sugar

¹/4 teaspoon (1 ml) salt

7 oz (200 g) lard, softened

1 egg

2 tablespoons (30 ml) water

1 teaspoon (5 ml) almond extract/essence

TO FINISH

¹/3 cup (40 g) whole blanched almonds

1 egg yolk beaten with 1 tablespoon (15 ml) water

Measure sifted flour, then sift again with the baking powder; whisk in sugar and salt.

Use an electric beater on slow to mix lard and egg until light; add water and almond extract. Gradually beat in the flour until the mixture draws away from the sides of the bowl. Finally, knead with your hands until firm and dense ~ about 1 minute. Cut the dough ball into 3 portions and lay on a lightly floured surface. Use your palms to roll into 1 inch/2.5 cm thick cylinders; wrap with plastic film and chill for 1 hour.

Cut the cylinders into 1 inch/2.5 cm pieces and press in your palm to flatten to ¹/4 inch (6 mm). Arrange about 1 inch/2.5 cm apart on a parchment-lined baking sheet. Press 1 almond flat onto each cookie. Brush with egg glaze and bake in a preheated 350°F/175°C oven until golden ~ about 15 minutes. Makes about 25 cookies

HINT Lightly brush baking paper with butter to give cookies a buttery aroma.

Coconut Macaroons
ohn thee besakit

Across Southeast Asia, canned sweetened condensed milk is a mainstay. Historically, sweetened milk preceded evaporated milk, with sugar not only inhibiting bacterial growth, but also producing natural thickening properties. While some 60% of water is removed in both evaporated and condensed milk, the latter can be made even thicker by further cooking, creating what the Spanish call *dulce de leche* ~ or candy of milk. Using freshly grated coconut in this recipe makes all the difference. But as quantities vary when grating a coconut, if required, adjust final quantity by adding desiccated coconut.

1 coconut, freshly grated
(about 4 cups/400 g)
1¹/₃ cups (350 ml) sweetened
condensed milk

Pinch salt
¹/₂ teaspoon (2 ml) vanilla
extract (essence)

Crack coconut in half, drain liquid (reserve for another purpose), then grate the meat (page 306). You should have 4 cups/400 g. Squeeze to extract any milk, then partially dry the grated coconut slightly in the hot sun for about 30 minutes, or rub with a tea towel to extract any excess moisture. (Coarse grated coconut does not allow good milk extraction here, while finely grated will. Conversely, coarse grated meat produces a chewier macaroon.)

Place milk in the top of a double boiler. Add salt, cover tightly and cook for 1¹/₂ hours over hot water ~ until thickened and golden in color. Do not open lid while cooking, but do replenish with water below as necessary. Cool milk slightly, then stir in vanilla and coconut.

Drop a teaspoonful on a parchment- or baking paper-lined baking sheet 1 inch/2.5 cm apart. Bake in a preheated moderate oven at 350°F/175°C for 10-12 minutes, or until very lightly golden. Cool slightly on the baking sheet before removing, as they are very fragile. Store in an air-tight container. Makes about 20

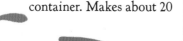

Sesame Cookies

hnan pyit

These cookies are surprisingly popular in Bagan. First popularized by one of the local lacquerware shops, which gave free samples to customers, they were copied by other shops and finally restaurants. Yangon bakeries have since taken notice. For best flavor, lightly toast the sesame first, as short cookie baking times do not allow for sufficient browning of the seeds. Also try the thin lacy roof tile variation.

3 oz (¹/₃ cup/100 g) butter
1 cup (230 g) white sugar
1 egg
Pinch salt
1¹/₂ cups (180 g) all-purpose/ plain flour

¹/₂ teaspoon (2 ml) vanilla extract (essence)
1 cup (125 g) sesame seed, lightly roasted

Use an electric beater to cream the butter and sugar until light and mounted. Beat in the egg and salt, then hand stir the flour, vanilla and three-quarters of the sesame seeds.

Cut the dough ball in half and chill for 30 minutes. Lay dough on a lightly floured surface and use your palms to roll each into 1 inch/2.5 cm thick cylinders. Cut into ³/₄ inch/2 cm pieces, and roll these into the remaining ¹/₄ cup (30 g) sesame seeds.

Line a baking sheet with parchment- or baking paper and arrange the cookie dough, allowing space in between. Each cookie should be slightly smaller than a walnut. Bake in a preheated 350°F/175°C oven for about 12-15 minutes or until the cookies are hard and lightly browned. Do not overcook, lest the sesame burn. Makes about 50

VARIATION: FLORENTINES & TUILES

Crisp, thin lacy cookies are made by decreasing flour to $^1/_2$ cup/75 g. Stir all the sesame into the batter; do not reserve any for later coating. As these will triple in size, drop by the teaspoonsful far apart on the baking sheet. Bake for 7-10 minutes, or until thin and lightly browned. Remove from oven and leave on sheet for a few minutes to slightly harden, then use a spatula to remove and cool on a rack. Optionally, lightly coat the bottom of the cookies with melted chocolate.

For curved "roof tile" *tuiles* do not cool in pan; rather, remove immediately with spatula and cool on a rolling pin to form a curve. For best presentation, do not turn them over.

Pineapple & Coconut Jam

nar nat ohn thee yo

This is a favorite candy sold at Mandalay's Zeygio Market, where sweetmeat vendors line the alley, each selling similar treats, but each with its own loyal clientele. This jam is traditionally served thick, more like a candy, and it is best to weigh the prepared pineapple and sugar, as they should be the same quantity by scales not volume. To use, put a couple spoonsful in a mug of boiling water to make a warming tea. Likewise, it is excellent on porridge oatmeal as well as crumpets, pikelets and pancakes, or as a spread on toast.

1 fresh pineapple (about 4¹/₂ lb/2 kg) peeled, cored and chopped

About 3-4 cups (690-920 g) white sugar

4 cloves

1 cinnamon quill (about 2 inch/5 cm long)

Pinch salt

1 cup (65 g) desiccated coconut

1 tablespoon (15 ml) white poppyseeds, ground (optional)

Prepare the pineapple: you should have about 6 cups/900 g. Measure equal quantities by weight of pineapple and sugar, and put into a wide saucepan over medium heat; add cloves, cinnamon and salt. Boil gently for about 45 minutes, stirring occasionally. Add coconut and optional poppyseed, then remove from heat. Pour through a coarse mesh, and save the excess syrup for another use; do not drain it completely, rather leave the pineapple slightly moist. Allow the pineapple jam to cool and turn sticky, then wrap in plastic until ready to serve. Makes about 3 cups/750 ml

VARIATION: PINEAPPLE & ALMOND JAM
Substitute an equal quantity coarsely ground blanched almonds for coconut and poppyseed, and proceed as above.

CAUTION Although traditionally used for cooking preserves, unlined copper pots must be thoroughly cleansed prior to use to remove metallic toxins. Scour with acidic vinegar (or lemon) and coarse salt until brightly colored; rinse well, then use immediately.

Candied Pomelo Peel

than payo thee say pyae

Peel does not mean solely the pared thin outer skin or zest; here it also includes the inner white pith. This recipe is perfect for both voluptuously thick-skinned pomelo, as well as lemons, limes, grapefruit, oranges with thick rind and pith. HINT chop candied rind and serve as a breakfast alternative to marmalade.

1 lb (500 g) citrus rind
  including pith
1/2 teaspoon (2 ml) salt
About 2 cups (460 g) white
  sugar

Powdered sugar (icing/
  confectioner's sugar)
  (optional)

Make certain there is no fruit flesh on the skins. Remove peel as described in Technique (page 367) and cut into wide strips and blanch in a large pot of boiling water with salt ~ about 3 minutes for thinner peel, 5 minutes for thicker. (A big pot is important, as you want excess water to dilute bitterness in the peel.) Drain, spread the peel on a rack and leave in the sun for several hours. (Alternatively place in a very low 100°F/50°C convection oven for 1 hour.) Place peels in a metal bowl ~ but not plastic as it may melt, nor glass as it can crack.

Prepare a heavy syrup from the white sugar and 2 cups/500 ml water: In a medium saucepan over high heat, stir the sugar until dissolved, then bring to the boil. Stop stirring once it boils and rinse the pan sides occasionally with a brush dipped into cold water to prevent crystallization. Boil for 15 minutes or until at the soft ball stage, then immediately pour over the peel. (Do not let the syrup cool or set before, as it will harden.) Leave for several days, but occasionally turn the pieces for uniform coverage.

Alternatively, boil thick skins directly in the syrup, although this results in a stronger tasting, slightly bitter candied rind. (Some palates prefer the bite!) After blanching and drying rinds, put into saucepan with the syrup and cook for 15 minutes. The result will not be as thick as a soft ball, but similar to the syrup when candying ginger.

After soaking for several days, use a slotted spoon to lift out the peel. Place on drying trays ~ a rack with a parchment paper-lined tray below is ideal. It will be sticky. Dust with powdered sugar. This will keep for months in the refrigerator, or canned in sterilized jars.

Candied Ginger in Syrup

gin say pyae

In former days, Moulmein was famed for producing the nation's finest and largest ginger, but no longer in present-day Mawlamyine. Use seasonal fresh young ginger here, recognizable by its pale parchment-like skin. (Best months are mid-summer to autumn.) Mature ginger, which is available year round, has a darker shinier skin and requires peeling. Whatever sort, ensure it is fresh, not wrinkled. Try this variously sliced into boiling water to make a tea, atop ice-cream or as a snack. Although simple to prepare, you will need to begin several days in advance.

1 lb (500 g) fresh ginger,
preferably young
3 cups (700 g) white sugar

Prick the ginger stems with a needle all over, and soak overnight in cold water; drain and cover with fresh water until ready. (Repeat over several days.)

Put the ginger in a large saucepan and cover with fresh water. Bring to the boil, drain and blanch again using fresh water.

Make a thin syrup with 2 cups/460 g of the sugar and 4 cups/1 liter water. Stir the sugar till dissolved then bring to the boil and remove from heat. (Do not stir after it boils, lest the sugar crystallize.) Cool, add ginger, and soak overnight.

Remove the ginger from syrup and reserve; bring the syrup to the boil once again. Remove from heat and, when cool, add the reserved ginger; soak for 24 hours.

Remove the ginger again, and set aside. Add another 1 cup/250 g sugar plus 2 cups/500 ml water to the syrup, and bring to boil. Add ginger to the syrup and bring to the boil once again. Reduce heat to low and barely simmer, uncovered, for 3 hours or until very thick and the ginger is well glazed. Pour into sterilized bottles and seal. This will keep several months in the refrigerator.

VARIATION: CRYSTALLIZED GINGER
Remove ginger pieces from syrup and slice lengthwise into thin strips. Place pieces on a rack in the sun to dry until slightly tacky. Sprinkle with crystallized white sugar, dry again, then lightly dust with powdered/confectioners' sugar before serving.

Sweet Grated Coconut

ohn yo

This recipe is so easy to prepare. It keeps well refrigerated, and is the perfect topping to sweets, garnished candies and as a snack. It's an ideal accompaniment with afternoon tea. And once you've mastered cracking and grating a fresh coconut, you will never go back to packaged sweetened coconut!

1 ripe coconut, grated   *³/₄ cup (175 g) white sugar*

Crack open the coconut and grate the flesh inside. You should have about 4 cups/400 g (page 306).

Loosely crumble the coconut mass into the top of a double boiler and add sugar, mixing lightly. Over medium heat, bring the water below to a boil, then cover and cook the coconut for 1 hour. Add more boiling water as necessary, but do not open the lid so as to preserve the heat within. Remove from the heat and spread out on a parchment paper-lined tray to cool, then leave for several hours in the sun to dry fully. Makes about 5 cups/1.2 liter, loosely packed.

VARIATION Add a few drops pandan extract/essence or 1 crumbled fresh pandan leaf and cook as above. Alternatively, store the candied coconut in a tightly sealed container with a scrunched pandan leaf.

* QUICK SWEET COCONUT Toss freshly grated coconut with white sugar and knead well ⁓ until sugar crystals dissolve. It is ready to serve immediately.

Locally, sweetened coconut is delicious mixed with tender young pounded sticky rice, especially as a breakfast cereal laced with coconut milk. The rice grains are first steamed and dried, then pounded. Such pounded rice is available across the region ⁓ from Vietnam where it is sold green hued, to Cambodia where its known as *om bok*. (Seasonally available in Asia only, not overseas.)

Jaggery & Puffed Rice

pouk pouk sote

Puffed rice is obtained from popping rice still in its chaff. It typically begins with stirring in a large, handleless bell-mouthed wok, or *moe byae dae*. Sand and oil are heated to create an even higher temperature, then the rice is added. Unlike popcorn, the kernels do not pop like projectiles, merely puff. The rice is then sieved ~ first to remove the sand and secondly to remove the chaff. Puffed rice is found in health food stores or use crumbled puffed rice crackers for a close equivalent. Breakfast cereals can also substitute, although they are much crispier.

2 cups (440g) grated palm
   sugar or firmly packed
   brown sugar
1/4 teaspoon (1ml) salt

1/4 cup (60 ml) water
3 cups (60 g) puffed rice

Combine sugar, salt and water in a small saucepan and over high heat stir until dissolved; stop stirring once it boils. Brush sides of pan with wet brush to prevent crystals forming. Boil for a few minutes until a treacle-like consistency. Watch carefully as palm sugar is prone to burn much quicker than cooked white sugar. Remove from flame, and immediately stir into the puffed rice. Working very quickly (it helps to have four hands now), stir to combine, then take two lightly oiled tablespoons to scoop clusters ~ about the size of a ping pong ball~ and drop onto parchment paper. Do this immediately, while the mixture is still warm, before it cools and hardens. Store in a tightly covered container where it will keep for a few days. Makes about 25

VARIATION: WITH PUFFED CORN
Substitute unseasoned popcorn. Preferably it should be air-popped, not in oil. Do not include any un-popped kernels. Alternatively, use crumbled corn puff crackers.

Halwa

Domestic Burmese tourists traveling via Pathein rarely return to Yangon empty handed. A delta capital, Pathein is in the middle of the country's richest rice region and boasts some 12 artisanal makers of Halwa, a sticky concoction of ground glutinous- and plain rice combined with coconut milk and the finest grades of sesame oil, peanut oil and ghee or butter. This region, once the world's largest producer of rice, highlights its most famous grain as a basic ingredient.

The original halwa (variously *halawa* or *halvah*) originated thousands of miles away, as a wheat- or semolina-based sweet, probably in Persia (now Iran). Early versions predominated with crushed sesame and nuts, but in neighboring countries it took on different guises: In India it's based on milky fudge-like *khoya*, and often includes vegetables such as carrot or zucchini/courgette; Syrian and Armenian halwa consists of semolina and milk plus almonds, walnuts or pine nuts and is sometimes marbled with chocolate. Rice-based Myanmar halwa might be the most unique version of all, with vast quantities of cold-pressed unctuousness.

The work is time consuming and laborious. For hours at a time, workers man oar-length shovels stirring cauldrons of boiling sugar syrup, continuously scrapping the bubbling mass in giant woks over roaring fires. In their scant free moments, they are stoking the fires with wood, and the result is a true sweat shop. Many work barefoot, occasionally stepping on sparking coals.

More oil and butter is progressively added whenever the mixture starts to stick, and the final product is a unctuous gluey mass pulled and cut into bite-size portions with scissors. And it's surprisingly perishable. Ghee, or clarified butter, renders the delicacy prone to rancidity. Refrigeration lengthens shelf life, but affects its consistency. Besides, in a land of few fridges and frequent power outages, that option is irrelevant. So eat within the week, which is usually not a problem.

*There is also a long-lasting dry version for sale to distant corners of the country. Here, the batter is cooked longer ~ for $2^1/_2$ hours ~ then baked slowly to dry for several more hours and finally cut into bits. It stores for a month.

QUAFFING
Libations, Brews & Beverages

ပျားရည်နှင့် ရမကာ

"The usual beverage of the Burmese is pure water. Formerly, indeed up to the commencement of the present Emperor's reign, they were allowed the use of wine, or rather to make themselves intoxicated; for it is considered no more sin in these countries to drink to the greatest excess than to take a single draught of wine."

‑Father Vincenzo Sangermano, *The Burmese Empire A Hundred Years Ago* (1893)

A Tea Primer
Black, Green & Semi-Fermented

Not all black teas are alike. Indeed Chinese, and Indian (English-style), black teas are polar opposites. Both black varieties allow for long transportation and storage without going stale. Green tea, by contrast, oxidizes quickly and should be used within six months of purchase. Indian black brews benefit from the addition of milk and sugar, but Chinese tea is drunk straight. Now here's where the confusing part really begins:

Britain introduced black tea drinking to Southeast Asia via their plantations in Ceylon and the Subcontinent. Before that, the only tea sipped in the region was Chinese, usually black, sometimes green, and occasionally *pu-erh*. And always straight. *(Pu-erh,* a fermented dark tea renowned for its decades' longevity, is the neat exception: in the Himalayas it is the foundation for the famed Butter Tea.) Today, Southeast Asian teas are ubiquitously drunk with copious amounts of sweetened condensed milk and usually additional sugar -- with sometimes powdered and canned evaporated milk as well. In Thailand and parts of nearby Yunnan, it brews to a brilliant orange hue. But in Myanmar the best is akin to Indian black style and it is sweetened, heavily. As for the straight brew, it's relegated to serving as a watery "chaser" gulped like water as a palate cleanser.

"A Proper Tea"

"**P**roper" is the expression used by the English to connote a loose-leaf tea brewed in the pot. And nothing can be deliciously further from generic tea bags, whether cheap paper 'flo-thru' designs or expensive fabric mesh. Tea bags use the cheapest grade "dust" or "finings," unlike the hand twisted whole leaves of epicurean lore.

1 Heat the pot. Chinese black and semi-fermented tea leaves are rinsed with boiling water prior to brewing; English black tea is not. Both reasons have little to do with hygiene and more to do with temperature. Black fermented teas require boiling temperature, or 212°F/100°C. A pre-heated pot decreases heat loss from the kettle, and likewise rinsed tea pre-heats both the pot and the leaves. Semi-fermented tea, such as oolong, is brewed around 200°F/90-95°C, but rinsed. Green tea is not rinsed, as it requires a much lower brewing temperature lest it turn bitter. As a general rule, the higher the grade the lower the heat, here typically brewed at 140-180°F/60-80°C.

2 Add a heaped teaspoon (hence the name) per cup, plus one for the pot. Add water and cover immediately and steep from 3-5 minutes. A tea cosy helps insulate the pot in a cold room, but should never be an excuse for allowing your tea to brew for too long.

3 Turn the pot in a circular motion three times to disperse the leaves, causing them to sink. ("Coffee floats, tea sinks," goes the adage.)

4 Pour, strained through a tea sieve, directly into cups. Add milk and sugar, to taste. That pretentious drivel about first pouring milk in the cup is an affectation, and creates a cold cup. It was Nancy Mitford who noted the class divide around tea drinking with her enduring concept of U and non U; stir more than twice and you are definitely the latter.

Milk Tea
la pey yay

Like Indian and Ceylon teas harvested for English consumption, Burmese *la pey yay* is brewed black tea, pure but not so simple. The best comes from the highlands of Shan state. It is finely ground, but not quite "dust," allowing for quick, strong brewing in a cloth sock. Afterwards, it's stirred with sweetened condensed milk. There are numerous variants, from very sweet to very milky and in between. (By contrast, in neighboring Thailand, milk tea boasts heaped teaspoons of instant milk plus evaporated milk, and even more sugar, plus the sweetened condensed milk.) Milk tea generally comes with *yay nway chan,* a free weak green or black tea chaser for free, similar to a glass of water.

Myanmar tea houses are like a trip back to Charles Dickens, with indentured-servitude boys attending the shop in quick step formation. (Just lately, girls seem to have broken that "glass ceiling.") Many faces are decoratively adorned with *thanaka,* the cooling yellow-white bark paste ubiquitously worn throughout the country. Outwardly, they seem happy and content at their school of life. But one should never tip them, as it implies hidden desire.

Especially popular early morning, but also at lunch and again late afternoon, tea houses are the place to come for quick snacks like Indian Poori (page 168) samosas and nan, fritters (page 189) and simple curry set dishes, or sweets like crème caramel and semolina cake (page 301). Less common at a tea house are one-dish meals like mohinga; such are more likely found at specialist, albeit humble, shop-front eateries.

Tea House Steeping

There's typically two ways to brew English-style black tea Burman fashion. The local ratio is as much as 1 heaping tablespoon per serving, although stronger grades may require just a heaped teaspoon per serve.

Add tea to cold water in a kettle and bring to the boil. Typically, the tea is placed in a cloth- or muslin "sock" with wire hoop serving as a giant tea bag, sitting atop the kettle. Once it boils, lower heat and simmer for 15 minutes. Remove tea or strain and serve with sweetened condensed milk.

Twice Brewed Tea

The term *nutphew* means "two times", and this commercial style is stronger and better, but rarely prepared at home, only at select top-notch tea shops. Because of its robust strength, milk is a must.

1   Place tea in its specialty "sock," then lower tea into boiling water in a kettle. Lower heat and simmer for 15 minutes. (If you do not have a similar sock, merely brew loose in the pot. Remove tea, or strain, and simmer the resulting brew a further 15 minutes.

2   Blend with both sweetened condensed milk and canned evaporated milk. Classically "pulled," meaning blending the tea by pouring from one cup to another at great height, results in a frothy top. Milk is first added to a cup and swirled to coat the bottom. Pour tea from the kettle into the cup -- from as high as a yard or meter away. (Caution: this is not for the untrained, as a missed shot results in scalding.) Pour from first cup into a serving cup of same size -- again at a distance, to create frothing

Myanmar Steeping at Home

At home, the standby brew is weak *yay nway chan*. It takes the place of water; indeed, it's safer for regular consumption than standard water, as it's boiled. Typically a mere teaspoon or two is scattered atop just boiled water in a large thermos canister, then left to steep all day to mask any tainted water flavors. Leaves will sink to the bottom. Such teas are usually cheap, even using the stems and smoked twigs from other plants. On one occasion, we purchased a bag at a roadside bus stop, to take overseas. But once brewed at home, friends remarked on its unmistakable fragrant aroma of hemp! Denatured, hopefully.

"It is in tea shops that people exchange news and, when it is not too dangerous an occupation, discuss politics. In fact there is an expression 'green tea circle' which implies an information discussion group."

~ Aung San Suu Kyi, Letters from Burma (1995)

Ordering in a Tea House

Please bring 1 cup of _____

    Tad quek _____ Yu pe ba   တစ်ခွက် ယူပေးပါ။

tea with milk

    La pey yay   လက်ဘက်ရည်။

standard milky tea

    La pey yay pon man   လက်ဘက်ရည်ပုံမှန်။

green tea (served like water, at no charge)

    Yay nway chan   ရေနွေးကြမ်း။

strong tea (less milky)

    La pey yay kya saik   လက်ဘက်ရည်ကျစိမ့်။

mildly sweet milky tea

    La pey yay cho bauk   လက်ဘက်ရည်ချိုပေါ့။

sweet milky tea

    La pey yay cho saik   လက်ဘက်ရည်ချိုစိမ့်။

very sweet milky tea

    La pey yay Kyauk Pa Daung   လက်ဘက်ရည်ကျောက်ပတောင်း။

Coffee
kawfee

Coffee came late to Myanmar, and instant granules still prevail. Local versions are made of finely ground coffee powder roasted with dark caramelized sugar. They are slightly bitter, but not as strong as European chicory roast.

Of particular note is a unique brew known as *Singapur*. It is coffee brewed with tea, not water, then sweetened with condensed milk.

Water Jugs
ye-o

In villages and cities alike, huge earthen jugs, or *ye-o*, shelter in small huts along roadsides. Typically, an enamelware plate or lacquered conical cap serves as lid, and a cup or two sits atop or nearby. As an act of merit, volunteers daily fetch the water from a local well, sometimes the tap, but it is never purified. Thus, although it is free to all passers-by, tourists should exercise extreme caution. The porous nature of these jugs creates a cooling seepage of liquid on its exterior. While the inside is rinsed and scoured regularly to prevent putrification, the exterior may turn mottled green with innocuous algae.

Some villages are particularly renowned for the quality of their vessels, many adorned with intricate geometric designs. Of special repute are wares from the clay of delta village Twante, due west of Yangon, and especially from up-country Bagan. Every four to six weeks a barge plies Yangon's pier offering a floating market of regional specialties from the north. Heavy pottery is off-loaded onto the dock near Botaung Paya, with other goods from *thanaka* bark to toys and local sweets sold on board.

As everyone has had a sip from the community water jug, a particularly witty slur is to brand promiscuous girls with the term *ye-o*.

Mango Lassi
thayet thee dain chin

Creamy yogurt makes the best drink, so eschew low-fat varieties and go for a full-cream pot-set brand. On the other hand, buttermilk (which is skimmed) makes a deliciously tangy alternative. Traditional lassi is served at room temperature, but is most quenching when all ingredients are cold.

2 mangos (about 1 lb/500 g) peeled and flesh mashed

¼ cup (60 g) white sugar

½ teaspoon (2 ml) vanilla extract (essence)

2 cups (500 ml) plain yogurt or buttermilk

Ice cubes (optional)

Place all ingredients together in a blender and puree. (Add ice cubes for a slurry.) Serve as is, or alternatively, over ice cubes.

VARIATION: WITH GREEN MANGO
Use unripe mangoes, for a more complex sweet-sour flavor dynamic, stewing first in sugar syrup (2 cups/500 ml water per 1 cup/230 g white sugar) for about 30 minutes. Initial cooking of mangoes creates a quality akin to pectin in a jam.

Pineapple Cooler

nar nat thee than pa yar yay

This is a perfect hot day's refresher. Best to make this with chilled ingredients, so that the ice cubes take longer to melt.

1¹/₂ cups (375 ml) pineapple juice or crushed pineapple

2 cups (500 ml) brewed tea, at room temperature or cold

¹/₄ cup (60 ml) freshly squeezed lime juice

Ice cubes

About 1-3 tablespoons (15-45 ml) Sugar Syrup (page 349) to taste

Fresh mint sprigs, to garnish

Combine pineapple, tea, lime and ice, either stirring together or blitzing in a blender to create a foamy texture. Sweeten to taste with sugar syrup and serve in glasses garnished with sprigs of fresh mint.

Tamarind Punch

ma gyi phaw yay

For fresher flavor, make this from packaged tamarind pulp instead of prepared store bought tamarind puree or tamarind water. Best of all, buy tamarind pods, shell yourself and use this pulp; both sweet and sour pod varieties work here, but adjust sugar accordingly. Salt is commonly added to fruit to pique its sour-sweet flavor.

1/2 cup (100 g) tamarind pulp
2 cups (500 ml) water
1/2 teaspoon (2 ml) salt
1 cup (250 ml) Sugar Syrup (page 349)

Ice cubes
About 2 cups (500 ml) soda water or sparkling mineral water
1 lime, cut in slices, to garnish

Soak the tamarind pulp in tepid water until the pulp is soft and loosens from the seeds. (Older tamarind pulp, if very hard, requires hot water.) Strain the pulp and add salt and sugar syrup.

Meanwhile, fill a large jug with ice and add the tamarind blend. Top with soda water, stir briefly, and serve in glasses packed with more ice and garnish with lime. Serves 4

"It is as well to take as little ice as possible.
It is usually full of microbes, the more venomous for their imprisonment. Drinks may be iced, but should have no ice in them. The digestion will also correspondingly benefit."

-- Sir J. G. Scott, *Burma A Handbook of Practical Information* (1921)

Lemon, Lime & Bitters

To this day in the Antipodes, this colonial-era "virgin" mocktail remains popular in pubs and bars. While it's believed the world's first commercially-marketed soft drink was flat and cloudy lemonade or squash, it wasn't until the late 18th century that carbonation came to the fore. "Impregnating water with fixed air" became all the rage, and a century later phosphates, or phosphoric acid, was added to lemon juice, creating fizzy lemonade. Confusingly, "lemonade" is the word used to describe carbonated clear lemon in Commonwealth countries, but "squash" ~ as in squeezed ~ means the cloudy refreshment. Conversely, in North American fresh lemonade invariably means squash, while trademarks like 7-Up and Sprite mean the gaseous clear soda pop variety.

Carbonated lemonade, such as Sprite or 7-Up

2-3 dashes Angostura bitters
Ice

Pour lemonade over ice to fill, and add bitters, allowing it's color to slowly float down the drink. Serves 1

"Do not drink lemon squashes, even when they are offered you by your dentist."

~Sir J. G. Scott, *Burma A Handbook of Practical Information* (1921)

Pegu Club

This was the house cocktail of colonial Rangoon's most prestigious club, oft labeled the real seat of Burmese colonial government due to its prestige membership. (It notoriously stuck to a no-Asians members policy well into the 20th century.) Built in 1871 predominantly of teak, it is one of the city's oldest colonial buildings left standing, and was long derelict. But perhaps it's the cocktail that proves the club's truly enduring legacy, making its name famous well beyond Asian borders. Not surprisingly, it was a mainstay at celebrated watering holes like Harry's New York Bar in Paris. As for the gin, it's more likely that Plymouth gin ~ high proofed and heavily imbued with botanicals ~ was originally used in the East, but London dry gin was later substituted to suit expatriate palates.

The oldest known existing Pegu Club recipe is from an edition of Harry McElhone's cocktail book of the Roaring '20s, consisting of 1 dash Angostura Bitters, 1 dash orange bitters, 1 teaspoon (5 ml) Rose's lime juice, and "$^1/_6$ Cointreau, $^2/_3$ gin." Other contemporary versions called for 2 oz gin, $^3/_4$ oz Curaçao and $^3/_4$ oz lime juice, plus both orange and Angostura bitters.

Debate continues about the correct sort of lime. As Britain's Navy was saved from scurvy by their daily ration of Rose's Lime Juice, this cordial became ubiquitous from the mid 19th century onward and presumably flavored the original cocktail. Modern versions use fresh lime, which skews the palate. So while it's not clear if fresh lime or lime cordial was used for this drink at its namesake club, it is apparent that sufficiently sweet liqueurs are essential. Even here, changing tastes and popularities of brands are taking a toll. While technically a triple sec, popular Cointreau is not sweet enough on its own in this mix, but inexpensive generic triple sec is sufficiently sugared. Likewise, once-fashionable white Curaçao (bitter orange citrus) requires the addition of sugar syrup, especially if using fresh citrus.

Rose's Lime Juice dates from 1867 when the British Merchant Shipping Act mandated daily lime rations for sailors to prevent scurvy. This led to the sailors' nickname "limeys". It was eventually introduced to American consumers near the turn of the last century. Ironically, lemons have more natural anti-scurvy qualities than limes.

1 oz = $^1/_2$ jigger
or about 20-25 ml

The Strand's Pegu Club

bago aeain

As re-adapted by Yangon's dowager hotel, for those seeking a trip down history's carriageway.

1 jigger (45 ml) gin
1/2 jigger (20 ml) triple sec
1/2 jigger (20 ml) fresh lime juice

1/4 jigger (10 ml) sweet red vermouth
Ice

Put all ingredients together in a cocktail shaker with ice and jiggle vigorously. Strain into a cocktail glass. Serves 1

"The Pegu Club seemed to be full of men on their way up or down, and the conversation was but an echo of the murmur of conquest far away to the north."

~ Rudyard Kipling, *From Sea to Sea* (1899)

Gin Pahit

Bitters are believed to improve appetite, hence its popularity in pre-dinner cocktails. Like the famed gin-and-tonic with its quinine warding off malaria, Angostura bitters was oft reputed (albeit falsely) to have similar medicinal properties owing to its alleged ingredient of cusparia or Angostura bark. In reality, there is no Angostura/cusparia in Angostura bitters; rather, it's named for the Venezuelan town of its origin. Long ago production relocated to Trinidad. Once popular, orange bitters is hardly available these day, but in days of yore was a common substitute for Angostura bitters.

Pahit is named after the Malay word for bitter, and it's debatable how much bitters was added to original mixes. These days a mere few squirts from the bottle into a jigger of gin should suffice, but in olden days it was reportedly 3 parts gin to 1 part bitters. That's probably incorrect, however, as The Strand's former sister hotel in Singapore, Raffles, serves it two parts London Dry gin and 3 dashes Angostura Bitters ~ and without ice. As their publicist explains: "Traditionally it is served without ice in a martini glass. However we have a few guests who have their preferences so we do also serve it in a rocks glass with two cubes of ice."

> *"an agreeable life, luncheon at this club or that, drives along trim, wide roads, bridge after dark at that club or this, gin pahits, a great many men in white drill or pongee silk, laughter, pleasant conversation; and then back through the night to dress for dinner. . ."*
>
> ~ W. Somerset Muagham, *The Gentleman in the Parlour* (1929)

Pink Gin

This is similar to Gin Pahit and often the same. Most important of all, is the swirl. The bitters goes in first ~ traditionally no more than 5 squirts, but less for today's palate. It's then swirled around the glass, and its excess discarded (similarly to throwing out vermouth in a very dry martini). Customarily served neat, but today's iced version is prosaically called Gin & Bitters.

Pimm's Rangoon

Pimm's Cup is an alcoholic spirit + fruit + herbal tonic. Originally concocted in Victorian times, it maintained its status until the mid 20th century. While the original *No. 1 Cup* ~ still the most popular ~ was gin based, other number variants used Scotch, brandy, rum, rye and vodka; most have been phased out, or are in limited production. The drink is now regaining favor, but few recall that its namesake cocktail was once *Pimm's Rangoon*. This nomenclature was probably an affectation of post-war America Trader Vic's, with nostalgic veterans longing for sensations of the Pacific and Asia. "The best years of our life," as they say.

1 jigger (45 ml) Pimm's
   No. 1 Cup
Ice
Ginger ale, to top

Lemon peel or zest
Twist of cucumber skin, or
   cucumber spear

Pour Pimm's in a highball glass over ice with ginger ale to top, and garnish.

VARIATION Substitute carbonated lemonade mixer for the ginger ale.

> 1 oz = 1/2 jigger
> or about 20-25 ml

Chili Sherry

This is more a cooking condiment than an actual drink, although a dash helps create a heavenly Bloody Mary. Formerly a culinary mainstay across British Asia and Africa, chilies are macerated in sherry ~ presumably to mask untoward flavors and smells of an opened bottle oxidizing in the tropical heat. The classic recipe uses sweet sherry, such as Bristol Cream, and just a few small dried chilis soaking in a bottle for at least a month, or much longer. Modern variants may call for some 20 or so fresh chilies in dry sherry. Typically, add a few teaspoons of the liquid during cooking to enhance stews, gravies and stir fries.

Rum Sour

rum nint than payo thee

At its simplest, this cocktail is a blend of rum, sugar and freshly squeezed lime. Other versions embellish with triple sec and bitters. A traditional sour glass looks a bit like a small, stemmed flute, widest at the top. While vaguely similar to a traditional champagne flute, it is smaller. Indeed, in most of Myanmar, this cocktail is still likely to be served in a shallow coupe, although there's now a trend to short tumblers, as pictured here.

While Mawlamyine was a distillery center for colonials as early as 1876, it was the re-birth of the Mandalay Rum factory up-country in the 1990s that reclaimed rum as Myanmar's national alcoholic drink ~ at least for the tourists. Otherwise, palm toddy spirit remains the country's most popular imbiber for the locals. Some commercial rum bottles boast 12 years provenance, but candidly, there's little flavor difference between these local distillates. There's also white rum but, while that clear variety blends especially well with tropical fruits and citrus, it remains little used.

2 jiggers (90 ml) rum
1 jigger (45 ml) freshly squeezed lime juice

1 tablespoon (15 ml) sugar syrup (page 349) or 1 teaspoon (5 ml) sugar
Ice

Combine all ingredients in a cocktail shaker with ice, shake vigorously, then pour into a glass. Serves 1

VARIATION Add 1 jigger triple sec or Cointreau plus 2 squirts Angostura bitters.

1 oz = 1/2 jigger
or about 20-25 ml

Sugar Syrup

tha kyar yi

Used to sweeten cocktails when sugar is unlikely to dissolve in a cold drink, this keeps well in the refrigerator for several weeks. Proportions may vary, depending on desired thickness. This version is relatively thin, to allow easy mixing. Store tightly covered. Palm and brown sugars can also substitute, but strain to remove any impurities. Alternatively, use the syrup from making candied pomelo and ginger (pages 320, 321).

1 cup (250 ml) white sugar
1 cup (250 ml) water

Combine sugar and water in a small saucepan over medium-high heat. Stir until the sugar dissolves, and the liquid is clear. Stop stirring and allow the syrup to come to boil. Brush the sides of the pan with cold water to prevent sugar crystals forming. Boil for 1 minute, then remove from heat and cool. (Do not stir while it boils, lest it crystalize.) Store refrigerated, tightly covered, in a jar. Makes about 1 cup/250 ml

'We must not be understood to speak of the juice of the grape, which does not grow in these parts, but of a liquor prepared from rice, or from the sugar of the palm, dissolved in water and distilled after a fermentation of two or three days."

~ Father Vincenzo Sangermano, *The Burmese Empire A Hundred Years Ago* (1893)

Wine & Myanmar Foods

Few subjects are as vexing in the East-meets-West culinary stakes as choosing wines to complement Asian flavors. The unctuous quality of Burmese dishes, plus chili and tart citrus, make any pairing doubly fraught. But perhaps most challenging of all is the concept of multiple courses taken simultaneously, as is the Burman fashion. In other words, finding a wine that suits all flavors, all dishes, all at the same time.

Break the rules! No wine really suits the richness of, say, Mohinga noodle soup at breakfast, or even coconut noodles or coconut rice. But you're unlikely to have to worry about this, unless you're indulging in an extravagant hotel early brunch. A local pork curry, especially with preserved mango, particularly suits a dry white or rosé; while an Indian-origin biriyani matches best with beer ~ and the colder the better. Generally speaking, near-frigid temperatures work best for both wine and beer, in hot climes. Or, as one might say in Australasian vernacular, add ice to your plonk and piss.

While Myanmar's still-fledgling local European-style wineries strengthen year upon year, its growers eschew a two-crop season, but likewise, endure the perennial threat of rot in a tropical environment. The region along Inle Lake, which has a temperate micro-climate and very cool evenings, is proving a bonanza. Some claim the *terroir* theory, saying it's best to drink local when visiting Myanmar as a tourist.

Most versatile are European grapes: from late harvest wines, whose sugars counter chili, to dry whites for aperitif, and big reds with meat dishes. But here ensure wines are well aged, or conversely, young, light and fruity. Sharp tannins work against most any Asian dish.

Instead consider Italian Primitivo and Amarone, Spanish Duero or even a South African Pinotage. Then there are French noble grapes. As an expat European restaurateur explained: "a wonderful Saint-Emillion or a Pauillac, I understand, is a bit out of place, but it brings lots of charm and magic."

A FEW HINTS FOR WINE PAIRING

e Consider red as more than an equal to white. In other words, don't fall for the fallacy that only fruit-driven whites suit Asian food. In truth, you're likely to spot more Asian diners quaffing red over their meal.

J Avoid tannin and wood. Eschew tannic reds, oaky chardonnays and young barrel-aged wines in general. (Well-aged wines are the exception.)

P Choose acidic wines. Acid softens the powerful flavor tastes of curry spice.

q Sweetness complements more local dishes than dryness.

Seek balance and harmony between the dishes and wine. It's the taste of a final recipe, not its main ingredient, that's primary when pairing recipes with alcohol. Foods with high protein traditionally call for red, but powerful and rich-flavored sauces suggest wine with a light body and sweeter taste. In other words, go back to the old adage: simple wine with complex food, simple food with complex wine.

Both white and red suit individual dishes, but residual sugar in white is a good foil to many Burmese recipes. (Whether you wish to drink cloyingly sweet Moselle or off-dry Gewürztraminer throughout an entire meal is another matter.) Slight sweetness is a nice balancing note to counter hot spices, and Riesling is oft recommended by the experts. Conversely, the austere rhubarb undertones and smell of *pipi de chat* in Sauvignon Blanc just don't suit. With a foot in each vat, rosé is regularly cited as the perfect plonk -- whether semi-sweet Anjou style, or drier Provence.

In regard to reds, the primary thing to avoid is strong tannin, which accentuates the burn from spices even more than high alcohol. Young gutsy Côtes du Rhône, or Shiraz, are poor examples. On the other hand, a well-aged Syrah proves absolutely ambrosial. Young, light fruity Grenache and Gamay (as in Beaujolais) are always safe bets, especially chilled.

Then there is the option of sparkling wines, from Champagne, Prosecco, Spumante, and the like. Old World European sommeliers concur that bubbles best suit Asian foods, yet drinking it throughout an entire meal is a minority palate. Opt for a demi-sec over brut, rosé even better. For lunch, one local confessed to favoring a light rosé or pink Champagne served in a large Burgundy glass with lots of ice cubes. "I may shock you, but this is very refreshing, and fancy!" And of course, its effervescence seems literally to lift the food -- and the mood.

LARDER
Provisions, Equipment
& Techniques

မီးဖိုဆောင်ရှိ စားစရာသို လှောင်ခန်း

"In Rangoon Bengalis are commonly employed to work in the kitchen because they are
more familiar with European tastes and habits, whereas with the Burmese one runs the
risk of being served one of the strong-smelling and not particularly appetizing sauces
of the country."

-- Adolf Bastian, *Reisen in Birma in den Jahren/A Journey in Burma 1861-1862* (1866)

ANCHOVY & WHITEBAIT, DRIED

Inaccurately and generically labeled anchovy for marketing convenience only, these matchstick sized, firm, desiccated fish are sold unrefrigerated, often under its Malaysian name *ikan bilis*. Fried or toasted as a snack, or tossed in salads, they are vaguely fishy yet mild in flavor, not salty. Western anchovies and whitebait are both much larger and not interchangeable, but Asian and New Zealand style whitebait are equivalent. Look for them on grocery shelves, not refrigerated. Some cooks prefer to quickly rinse (not soak), then dry fish in sun or oven, to ensure cleanliness.

ASIAN CHILI POWDER *see Chili*

BAMBOO SHOOT

Fresh bamboo shoots require timely preparation and are not used in this book. Canned or cryovac packaged shoots require thorough rinsing and long boiling to remove its briny flavor and strong aroma. Fermented/sour bamboo shoot is also popular in Myanmar, but not commonly available overseas; it is extremely pungent.

BANANA

While mango is arguably the queen of fruit, banana reigns as the most popular. Most prized locally is *Nantharbu*, slightly pot bellied with a pinkish-tinged old gold-colored skin, which could easily be mistaken for plantain. It is deliciously sweet, with an ambrosial creamy texture. Overseas, you are most likely to encounter long Cavendish; it's closest Burmese equivalent is *Pheegyan*. In overseas Caribbean, South American, African and Asian ethnic markets you are also likely to find small finger length varieties known variously as lady finger- or sugar bananas. They tend to be sweeter, but firmer for cooking. In Myanmar a popular small variety is *Sargalay*. Almost all of the banana plant is used, with the leaves for packing and steaming foods or as a plate in ethnic Indian restaurants; and the stalk an essential ingredient in Mohinga noodle soup.

TECHNIQUE

FOLDING BANANA LEAF PARCELS

Use a knife or scissors to cut fresh banana leaf into approximately 1 foot/30 cm pieces. Pass over a heat source to soften and lie flat with dull side facing you (bright green side to exterior). Put a portion of cooked rice at center and fold to overlap the two ends. Note: fold with the "ribs", not against them. Cup your hand under the open ends, one at a time. Bring up and inward, to fold over -- against the ribs. Secure with a toothpick.

BASIL

Small leaf lemon basil is the local choice, not standard sweet Thai basil, nor peppery holy basil. Save it for cucumber salad, and in seafood dishes, or as a ganja flavor substitute as in Bachelor Curry.

BAY LEAF

Burmese and Indian "bay leaf" has nothing to do with laurel. Although vaguely reminiscent in shape -- that is, long and pointed -- "Indian bay" comes from the cinnamon tree, and boasts a mild citrus-like flavor. It is an aromatic addition to rice and curry. European colonials used generic bay leaf in cooking; bay laurel is little used today in Myanmar. see also Cinnamon & Cassia

BEANS & PULSES

Cow peas, field beans, pigeon peas and butter beans, are all notoriously vague generic terms for popular dried beans used in Myanmar cooking. The local diet is rich in pulses, especially for savory dishes, but less so served sweetened -- as in countries further East. Most pulses and lentils are much smaller than Western counterparts: black beans and green mung beans/gram are about the size of a Puy lentil, while black-eyed peas only slightly larger. Dried beans, but not necessarily lentils, are best when soaked prior; they also require thorough boiling to remove toxins.

BEAN CURD *see Tofu*

BEAN SPROUTS
These deteriorate quickly, and taste strong with age, so buy fresh daily, and rinse well before using. Sprouts range from hair thin and delicate, to the more common thick mung bean sprout common in stir fries. When using the latter raw in a salad, quickly blanch in boiling water then soak in iced water till crisp. Purists remove both bean and hair like sprout. Some Myanmar curries are flavored with the pounded essence of sprouts.

BEANS, LONG
Also known as snake beans or yard-long beans, these have a mottled skin, and often have black tips. This does not indicate deterioration, and beans should be springy. Long beans are commonly bruised prior to eating raw, or briefly blanched. Substitute string- or green beans.

BREADCRUMBS
While a staple of colonial households, there is scant use of breadcrumbs in ethnic Bamar cooking today ~ unlike the Indo Chinese who readily adopted French bread into their cuisines. Substitute Japanese *panko* fresh and dried breadcrumbs. They are coarse and crustless, and absorb less oil during cooking, hence their lighter taste; they are available pre-packaged at most grocers.

FRESH BREADCRUMBS Use stale bread, as fresh is too soggy and tender. Best to use a French-style loaf, as it is dryer textured, or you can use white sliced. Remove crust, then warm bread in a low oven to slightly crisp. (You want it soft, not hard and crisp.) Use a serrated knife to cut into cubes. (Tearing may cause the bread to compress, so if using your hands be gentle.) A food processor is less successful than an electric blender, but do not overfill. Pulse in quick on off bursts until desired texture. Store tightly covered or in sealed plastic bags; crumbs freeze well.

DRIED CRUMBS are made using both the crust and meal of bread. Dry thoroughly in an oven, then grind. Food processors don't work as well here, best to use a meat grinder, blender, or crush with a rolling pin.

BUTTERED CRUMBS Heat clarified butter or a blend of oil and butter in a fry pan over medium high heat. When sizzling, add dried or soft crumbs and toss until golden ~ about 1-2 minutes. Remove with slotted spoon and drain on absorbent paper. They should be crumbly and not clumpy.

BUTTER & GHEE
Because of lack of refrigeration and short shelf life, fresh butter remains relatively rare. (Canned butter was and is available, exported especially from Australia or New Zealand.) During the colonial period, with its huge influx of Indians into Burma, ghee was common. This is less so today. Because of its low burning point, due to the presence of milk solids, butter is not a good frying agent ~ unless combined with vegetable oil. By contrast, clarified butter separates the whitish milk sediments from clear fat, allowing cooks to fry at higher temperatures. These same milk solids quickly render butter rancid, but clarified butter stores for weeks or longer, refrigerated in a glass jar with tightly fitting lid.

GHEE a form of clarified butter whose milk solids have cooked fully during prolonged heating, both to impart a distinct nutty flavor, and to make it less suseptible to rancidity. Most ghee is sold canned, without refrigeration. Like standard clarified butter, ghee can be used for frying without undue concern of burning. (This is not possible with pure butter.) Alternatively, substitute 3 parts vegetable oil and 1 part melted butter.

=== TECHNIQUE ===
CLARIFIED BUTTER

In a small saucepan, melt butter at low heat. Skim froth at top, then carefully pour the liquid golden oil from the pan, leaving behind sediment-like white milk solids.

CABBAGE
WHITE OR HEAD This is standard cabbage, dense with firm leaves. Although white

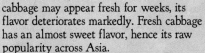

cabbage may appear fresh for weeks, its flavor deteriorates markedly. Fresh cabbage has an almost sweet flavor, hence its raw popularity across Asia.

CHINESE/NAPA (CABBAGE CELERY, WOMBOK) It is long and frilly, lighter in texture and taste than either white and Savoy varieties. Especially good in Burmese salads, prized for its fresh light texture.

CARDAMOM POD
There are three standard sorts: green, bleached white, and a bulbous lantern-like parchment-colored variety. The first two are of Indian origin, and popular in Myanmar. The third is restricted to Thai culinary use and Chinese apothecary. Many cooks contend that green pods are better than white, but market sales indicate otherwise. While the whole pod is ground, it is only the internal black seeds that lend flavor and aroma; the outside chaff is discarded after grinding.

CELERY, CHINESE OR ASIAN
Long spindly celery, used both raw and cooked. Confusingly, Asian celery varieties differ enormously in size, but not terribly in flavor or texture ~ in other words, such varieties are usually interchangeable. Vietnamese overseas grocers also sell a celery variety that resembles flat leaf parsley; it is often hydroponic. When unavailable, substitute flat leaf parsley, or standard celery leaves. Sometimes colloquially called "Chinese parsley" in Myanmar, it should not be confused with fresh coriander/cilantro, which also uses the term.

CHICKPEA Dried pulse, also known as Garbanzo beans, although such European sorts based on the Kabuli pea are much larger than local Desi (*chana dal*) variety. They are interchangeable, but cooking times may vary. Also available canned, which is pre-cooked.

CHICKPEA FLOUR (BESAN; GRAM POWDER; GARBANZO BEAN FLOUR) In Myanmar chickpea flour comes both raw and roasted. Raw is used when a dish is cooked further while roasted chickpea flour is added directly to salads, when no further cooking takes place. They are not interchangeable: raw flour gives a harsh taste to salads, while roasted flour turns slightly gelatinous when cooked.

=== TECHNIQUE ===
ROASTING CHICKPEA FLOUR & RICE FLOUR

Dry roast raw besan or gram flour in a non-oiled frypan or wok, stirring constantly over medium-high heat for a few minutes, or until a shade darker and slightly fragrant. Scrape from hot pan immediately, cool, and store in tightly sealed jar. Use similar procedure for rice flour.

CHICKEN SALT MSG is ubiquitous in East Asian cookery, and chicken salt is a flavored version. Equivalents are crumbled bouillon cubes, and trade names like Vegeta. There are some non-MSG flavor enhancer salts on the market, so it's worth seeking on supermarket labels. Alternatively, natural MSG is derived from seaweed.

CHIFFONADE A French term to describe fine shredding, especially of leafy greens and herbs. Stack several leaves atop one another, and tightly roll into a cigar shape. Hold firmly, while slicing circular end crosswise into fine shred.

CHILI Burmese food is not particularly fiery, although fried chilies flakes in oil are ubiquitously served at table to season dishes individually. As seeds are the hottest part of the chili, remove to decrease piquancy. Generally speaking, the smaller the chili the hotter; likewise, green is more fiery than red. When substituting dried chilies for fresh, pinch off stem, shake away seeds, then soak pods in warm water for 10-15 minutes, drain and proceed as directed. (Do not let your hands get in contact with the soaking water, as it may cause skin irritation.) The reason cooks prefer to use whole dried chilies vs chili powder is the seeds: ground powders include pod and seeds, while ground whole dried chilies have seeds discarded prior to grinding.

VARIETIES Although there are myriad chilies, both fresh and dried, three basic sizes dominate in the Burmese kitchen:
1. Finger-thick, long green and red chilies are the mildest, and most common.
2. Small lantern shaped chilies, resembling a cherry, are especially popular in the country's far west Rakhine state. Hottest of all, so use them sparingly.
3. Only slightly less piquant are medium chilies, about 1-1½ inches (2.5-4cm) length, similar to a serrano although the aforementioned are green, not red.

ASIAN CHILI POWDER As in neighboring Yunnan China, Burmese chili powder is made from long red chilies, which are less pungent than smaller varieties. Consequently, large measures are called for in these recipes, typically 1-2 teaspoons (5-10 ml), at which quantity cayenne red pepper or chili would destroy a recipe. To delineate this from cayenne, we use the term *Asian chili powder,* or *hot paprika.* Asian chili powder is far less piquant, nor is it equivalent to Mexican chili powder, which is a combination of herbs and spices. Hot paprika is vaguely equivalent, but because Hungarians have some eight grades, go for the dark red powder, not orange brown sorts like fiery *eros.* Generic *hot paprika* is generally available alongside *sweet paprika,* the latter which has little fire. A good ratio is 2 parts generic hot paprika to 1 part sweet paprika to equal Burmese chili powder. Do not use Spanish smoked paprika. Innocuous sweet paprika can be used as a color substitute to the safflower called for in these recipes.

CHILI FLAKES As above, but in coarser form. Used as a condiment when fried.

=== TECHNIQUE ===

CHILI OIL & ROASTED CHILI FLAKES

A standard condiment at the Burmese table. Select freshly milled chili flakes that are not too spicy. In a small saucepan heat 1 cup (250 ml) vegetable oil over moderate flame. Add equal quantity of chili, stirring constantly for 3-5 minutes, or until the chili turns dark but not burnt. Do not allow the oil to smoke, or it will taste acrid. Remove from heat and cool. Hint: for quick cooling -- especially important if you fear burning chilies -- pour through a strainer.
(see also Chili Fry, page 292)

CHILI PASTE, RED (SAMBAL OELEK) In its simplest form this is merely freshly ground chilies, perhaps with a bit of salt and vinegar, occasionally oil. Sometimes semi-fermented or semi-pickled, this sambal-like condiment is also used in cooking. It is made from milder red chilies instead of small hot varieties, and not as spicy as it looks. If unavailable, substitute Chinese fermented chili bean paste in cooked dishes.

CILANTRO *see Coriander, fresh*

CINNAMON & CASSIA Although slightly different, these two tree bark spices are often sold under the generic name *cinnamon,* which is more expensive and sold in smaller quills. Cheaper cassia bark is broader and coarser. Generally speaking cassia will have a more pronounced flavor and tends to work best in savory dishes; cinnamon delicately scents sweets, but this is not a hard and fast rule.

QUILLS These grow very long, and specialist spice merchants sell impressive quill bark of several feet/1 meter long. Average length used in these recipes is 2-3 inches/5-7.5 cm.

LEAVES Also known as Indian Bay leaves, these have a slightly citrus flavor. Although totally different in taste to bay laurel, the leaves come from related genus, and often listed as interchangeable.

CORIANDER, FRESH (CILANTRO, CHINESE PARSLEY) The leaf, stem and root of the coriander plant. Not to be confused with dry coriander seed. As a general rule, pound and cook with the roots; chop and add stems at last minute when frying and simmering; and save leaves for garnish. Slightly metallic in taste, its roots have both the best texture and arguably top flavor. (If your greengrocer cuts them off, which is especially common in North America, cause a ruckus!) Shan fresh coriander leaf is smaller than regular Burmese fresh coriander, but otherwise interchangeable. ERYNGO, SAWTOOTH CORIANDER, LONG CORIANDER Similar in taste to fresh coriander/cilantro, with long ridge-edged leaves. Especially used cooked in dishes, as its tough texture is resilient in broths. CORIANDER SEED Spice seed of the coriander plant; used especially in Indian and Chinese dishes, and as a popular spice rub on fowl. Local seeds, as in Thailand, tend to be smaller and browner than seeds sold overseas, but are interchangeable.

CURRY POWDER & MASALA

The two terms are interchangeable in Myanmar usage, and little used in ethnic Burmese dishes. Technically speaking curry powders are stronger and usually -- but not always -- need frying prior to use in a cooked dish. Fragrant masala spice is sprinkled at the end. The most common is garam masala. Refer to Curry Primer for suitable blends (pages 38-39). Whether a curry powder or a masala, dry spices benefit from roasting prior to cooking.

CHINESE 5-SPICE is locally called *pork masala*. A combination of star anise, fennel, cassia or cinnamon, cloves and variously brown cardamom, Sichuan pepper, black pepper, anise, nutmeg, ginger. It is used in Myanmar almost exclusively in pork dishes, and sprinkled atop Shan Noodles (page 210). Ethnic Chinese also rub it onto duck.

GARAM MASALA means "spice blend," although the term refers to a specific blend of fennel, cinnamon and caraway, plus pepper, cloves and green cardamom, with

Burmese versions adding cumin. Burmese Masala blends are interchangeable with curry powder, and used sparingly, except for Indian-origin recipes. (Indeed, Indian cooks would look askance at not personally blending their own spices.)

CURRY LEAF Fresh leaves and sprig of a specific tree, and not the same as curry powder. While not curry-flavored -- indeed, it tastes slightly of citrus -- it derives its name from being an ingredient in many curries. In Burmese ethnic cooking it is largely used with chicken, goat and beef, but surprisingly not fish, and is particularly common in Rakhine recipes.

DOUBLE BOILER (WATER BATH, BAIN MARIE) are all names for cooking over simmering water. This protects delicate ingredients that easily scorch or curdle when cooked over direct flame.

DUCK *see also pages 124-125* Unless well cooked till almost falling off the bone, duck meat tends to cook much tougher than chicken. Consequently, small chopped pieces are preferred in stews and curries. Otherwise, diners will find themselves fighting at the table with large carcass pieces. When roasting a whole duck, some varieties have scant breast meat, and are difficult to carve into beautiful slices. It may prove easier to joint a cooked roast with cooking shears or scissors.

TECHNIQUE
CARVING & DISJOINTING
A ROAST DUCK

With a large chef's knife and fork or tongs, cut the skin between the leg and breast, while pulling the leg out from the body to expose the joint. Cut forcefully through the leg joint. This will give you a leg+thigh "Maryland." Cut the knife forcefully at the joint attaching those two cuts. Repeat on other side. To cut the breast, score along the breast bone. Run the knife more deeply along the carcass bones, to remove entirely. (Some cooks prefer to remove the wish bone at end first, prior to

doing this.) At the wing, cut blade forcefully through the joint. Remove the breast and wing and slice breast, or serve whole.

DUTCH OVEN A covered casserole, or heavy cooking pot with tight fitting lid. Often set over fireplace or campfire coals for cooking, some models have legs, but those are not applicable here. Usually made of cast iron ‑ indeed, that is how the vessel derives its name, as the Dutch were first to produce a superior smooth forged metal which was exported to great acclaim. More common today are similar shaped pots of enameled cast iron.

DURIAN Tastes like heaven but smells like hell, goes the old adage about durian. This spiky fruit is pricey, and heavy. Not only that, it's precariously dangerous to harvest: typically, one man climbs to the high tree top with machete to pick the fruit, then throws it down to two workers holding a Hessian hammock to catch its fall.

EGGS Duck eggs are as popular as hen eggs, and preferred in baking cakes. Use them interchangeably, but note duck eggs larger size and adjust quantities accordingly.

=== **TECHNIQUE** ===
HARD BOILED EGGS
Throughout most of Southeast Asia, locals prefer a slightly runny interior yolk, with the exterior white fully firm. Cooking times will vary slightly due to egg size. Put room temperature eggs in a saucepan and cover with cold water; add a pinch of salt. Bring to the boil, reduce heat and simmer for about 5‑7 minutes, depending on egg size. Drain and refresh under cold water. For firm yolks, bring to the boil for 1 minute, cover and turn off heat immediately; sit in hot water for 12‑15 minutes, then drain and refresh under cold running water.

EGGPLANT (AUBERGINE, BRINJAL) Although long green eggplants are the

most common, you can substitute standard black varities, although the skin of the latter is especially tough in comparison. Green eggplants come up to 12 inches (30 cm) long and are commonly stir fried or stewed.

FISH SAUCE *see also Soy Sauce* The world's second most popular condiment is equally popular in Burmese cooking as soya or soy sauce. Made from the fermented extract of salted small fish or sprats, naturally‑brewed, acrid smelling fish sauce is a mainstay of Southeast Asian cooking, both for protein and salt in the diet. Myanmar fish sauce tends to be more robust than Thai and Southern or Central Vietnamese styles, although similar to strong Northern Vietnam fish sauce. Sometimes caramelized sugar is added, but otherwise labels should be specifically simple: just fish, salt, water and sugar. Eschew additional ingredients, and especially cheap chemical brews indicated by "hydrolyzed protein." Once opened, consume within 1 month, or refrigerate up to 6 months. After that, the flavor rapidly deteriorates.

USES Add to hot water as a consommé‑like tea; to soups and curries as a salt substitute while cooking; or as a table condiment, especially when diluted and combined variously with lemon, chilies and sugar to make the ubiquitous Bate Chin dipping sauce (page 287).

VARIETIES As in neighboring countries, there are several forms of progressively rotten or decayed fish used to flavor dishes. Standard fish sauce is comparatively innocuous, but not to the novice. You can also substitute shrimp paste to make dipping sauces, but literally rotten fish is authentic:

Fish sauce (standard salty) = *nganpya*
Fish sauce (without salt) = *nganpya‑ye*
Shrimp paste (fermented) = *pazun ngapi*
Fish paste (fermented) = *ngapi yay cho*

HINT a favorite table dipping sauce is made

of *ngapi yay cho*, with pounded garlic and chili. Substitute shrimp paste or even fish sauce.

FLOUR & STARCH *see also Chickpea Flour.*

Terminology between UK and US English differs markedly, leading to confusion. In North America, starchy powders that squeak when rubbed between fingers are considered "starch," while softer ground powders are called flour. European and Commonwealth usage, however, offers no such delineation, hence ground rice can be variously squeaky starch or soft flour.

WHEAT FLOUR a white flour, termed interchangeably as all-purpose or plain, depending on geography. Unlike wholemeal or whole-wheat flour, white flour has the germ and bran removed; while beige-white, further bleaching is common. Confusingly, Indian Atta flour (as used in Poori), is milled from the whole wheat grain, but it is extremely fine and slightly yellowish in appearance ~ and different to whole-wheat/wholemeal flours marketed overseas. The latter is rough with bran, and is not used in this book.

RICE FLOUR is made from either standard rice or sticky (glutinous) grain; the latter is a base for Asian cakes and dough. Rice starch is a slightly finer grade than commercial "ground rice." An even coarser grade of lightly toasted hand ground rice is also sold, sometimes parched prior to grinding.

GROUND WHOLE RICE is the sort blended in buttery shortbread, and not used here.

PLAIN RICE FLOUR gives a brittle crispness when dredged and fried, while sticky rice flour produces a slightly chewy crispness.

STICKY RICE FLOUR is especially used when making soft chewy dough, such as in Japanese mochi sweets. Both are relatively poor sauce thickeners; better are corn starch/cornflour, tapioca starch, and arrowroot. While these three are generally interchangeable, they do differ.

ARROWROOT thins once it boils, but creates a clear glaze, thus preferred in fruit desserts. It is commonly available as a powder, but lump arrowroot is available at Asian markets, and may require grinding in a mortar and pestle prior to use.

CORN STARCH/CORNFLOUR is blended in cold water prior to thickening a sauce; otherwise it lumps. Once boiled, it thickens.

TAPIOCA STARCH is more popular in Southeast Asia than corn starch and arrowroot. Use to thicken sauces, and also to bind pastes, as in fish cakes.

GARLIC

Bulbs of dried garlic ensure fresher flavor than pastes and dried flakes or powders. Both reddish-hued and white garlics are suitable, although the large elephant garlic is probably too mild. Conversely, cheap bleached Chinese garlic may render a raw condiment too pungent. When in doubt, source locally-grown and organic. Generally, the smaller the bulbs, the stronger the taste, which is why locals pay a premium for small cloves, despite the fuss in peeling. Standard garlic cloves used in this book are about the size of an almond. see also Crisp Frying Onion, page 41.

GHEE *see Butter*

GINGER

Beige to golden colored rhizome. Older ginger is more fibrous yet pungent. During summer, source a tender young ginger for garnishes, such as julienne strips. The latter is identifiable from its matt parchment like skin; older ginger is very glossy and golden yellow. Powdered or dry ginger is rarely used. As a rule, home cooks slice and fry; restaurants pound. Invest in a good ginger grater or Microplane for speed and ease. Although most flavor is retained in the parchment like skin, chefs often peel the rhizome before using; this is optional (and in the case of young ginger, not essential). If fresh ginger is unavailable, substitute 1/4 teaspoon (1 ml) ginger powder per 2 teaspoons (10 ml) grated ginger.

TECHNIQUE

CRISP FRYING GINGER
Differs slightly from onion and garlic. Cut into paper thin slices, then fry in oil over medium high heat until golden but not brown, turning regularly. Drain and cool, then chop finely. This also seasons the oil.

EXTRACTING JUICE
Finely grate, then press pulp through a fine sieve tea strainer. Commercial garlic and ginger extract or juice also suits.

GOURD, SQUASH & WINTER MELON

Edible wax gourd and winter melon are mainstays in Asian cooking, and available year-round in Chinese-Asian supermarkets. Also known as white gourd, winter melon grows round to oval, with a tough waxy white and green-mottled exterior. Not sweet, but delicious cooked, it's actually a summer vegetable. But this is not strictly a misnomer, as

it's hard skin -- akin to pumpkin -- allows cellaring long into winter. As it grows very large -- easily 10 lb/4.5 kg, it is often sold pre-sliced in segments. Always pare away the skin, unless using a whole melon as a tureen. Also use fuzzy melon, and long necked bottle gourd, although thinner skin means shorter storability. Calabash, a variety of "bottle gourd," is also dried for later use as a water receptacle. Fresh luffa, both smooth and angular-skinned, also suit. All require peeling and seeding, and can be used in curries and soups, but if too moist, they make poor fritters.

SUMMER SQUASH such as pattypan and zucchini/courgette are western substitutes, but generally taste stronger and slightly bitter compared to Asian counterparts. As summer squash are picked immature, their skin is tender and edible. Peeled chayote/choko can also substitute, although take care to wear gloves when processing.

GRAM *see Chickpea*

HONEY

As in most of Southeast Asia, honey is relegated to the medicine cabinet, or as a sweet on its own, but rarely used in cooking. A special treat is candied or calcified forest honey, gathered from abandoned hives, then eaten or sucked in chunks, or as medicine.

JAGGERY *see Sugar*

JICAMA/YAM BEAN

Also known as ice potato or Mexican yam, it is eaten both raw and cooked, adding little flavor, but lots of crunchiness. Typically it is soaked after preparation to remove excess starch, especially in a pickling brine. It is also sweetened in syrup and eaten as a candy.

JERKY

Dried and fried strips of goat, sold as pre-packaged snacks, but cheaper cow and buffalo are substitutes. (If truth be known, the latter are often dyed red to resemble goat meat, then palmed off as the more expensive.) The meat is cut into extremely thin narrow strips, then salted and dried in the sun. Strips are twined together then briefly deep fried. Small but wider flat strips are likewise twined, salted and dried, then fried with dried garlic slivers and chili pods. Even thicker dried meat is shredded and fried crisp with tomato sauce and served with rice.
SATE THAR CHOUT are round sticks.
SATE THAR PYAR GYAW are flat pieces which have been deep fried.

KAFFIR LIME, LEAF & FRUIT

Identifiable by its double helix leaf, fragrant kaffir lime leaves adds citrus flavor and aroma, not texture, and when eaten, should be sliced paper thin. Coarsely torn leaves are commonly added to soups, and pounded into curry pastes in eastern T'ai regions bordering Thailand. Sometimes available frozen, which is preferable to dried. Unlike standard lime, little if any juice squeezes from the fruit; rather, it is the pared peel that flavors. It is also used as a hair gloss.

LEMONGRASS These citronella-like stalks are a Southeast Asian mainstay. The bottom one-third white portion is of principal culinary worth, while its tough green stalks both color drinks and flavor tea. Use lemongrass stalks to to line the bottoms of cooking pots, preventing meat from scorching, while also imparting unique flavor to the cooking liquid. To store, stand upright in 1 inch (2.5 cm) water, or refrigerate in a plastic bag for up to 2 weeks. When very young, lemongrass is tender enough to eat finely sliced raw in a salad, while older stems are just used to flavor, not consume.

LENTILS, PINK & YELLOW These are variously whole, hulled and split. Pink and yellow lentils cook quickly, although yellow may require longer than pink. Their taste is very mild. Pink lentils in Myanmar are smaller and rounder.

MANGO RIPE Renowned as the queen of fruits mangoes vary in shape and weight from miniature to small "banana mango," to standard Kensington to giant prized Alphonso. These are extremely prone to bruising, and it is quipped that Asians devoted two millennia breeding out its fiber, while Florida growers took just a decade to breed it back in for better shipping. Ripe mango consumption is restricted to eating fresh, especially as a flavor in yogurt lassi (page 340), or cooked down to jam.
GREEN Unripe mango tree is used as both a souring ingredient and for crispness ~ often as a side dish condiment or salad. Or eaten as a snack with chili, sugar and salt. Sometimes interchangeable with green papaya, it is much firmer textured and more tart.

MASALA SPICE see Curry Powder

MUSHROOMS & FUNGI Myanmar is renowned for its myriad mushrooms, but fresh champignons can substitute in most recipes. Rinse fresh mushrooms quickly in several changes of water to remove grit. (Do not allow long contact with water.) Rinse and drain canned mushrooms before using, also reducing the quantity in the recipe by half. Dried mushrooms must be soaked in water to rehydrate, then rinsed thoroughly and drained.
SHIITAKE Also known as Chinese black mushrooms, these prized fungi have a meaty texture and are perfect for slow-cooked braises and soups. Colored dark gray to brown, they are available in varying grades from Oriental shops. Those with dark caps and deep, ivory-colored creases are particularly valued. When dried, the flavor is more pronounced than fresh, but faint compared to a European cep or boletus. Soak dried shiitake in hot to boiling water for about 20 minutes, and snip away the tough stems. Strain well, reserving soaking water to flavor stock
TREE EAR MUSHROOMS & CLOUD MUSHROOMS These gelatinous and tough fungi add special crunch, but little taste, to soups, salads and stir fries. Also known as black- and white fungus, wood ear, and jelly mushrooms. Soak dried fungus in warm water for 15 minutes or longer, then trim tough white core and stems before using. Merely trim and rinse fresh fungi. No discernible flavor, rather, they add texture and visual aesthetics.
OYSTER MUSHROOMS A good overseas substitute, thin and delicate, mild tasting.
STRAW MUSHROOMS Usually sold canned or dried, and occasionally fresh. Ideal for soups and curries or stews.

=== Technique ===
CLEANING MUSHROOMS
*Fungi harbor grit and require
thorough cleaning. Conversely, as
mushrooms are porous, they readily absorb
water, thus diluting their flavor when
soaked. Alternatively, brush mushrooms
with a soft bristle to remove grit.
This latter process prevents water
from diluting the exquisite
taste, and is especially appropriate
with fresh wild varieties.*

*1. Pare away the bottom of the
mushroom stems, as these are
either dried or dirty, or both.*

*2. Fill a large bowl or sink with cool
water. Plunge the mushrooms to rinse
vigorously, then immediately remove
to a colander and drain. Lift mushrooms
from water, as opposed
to merely draining, as sediment
falls to the bottom.*

*3. Place the mushrooms on a cloth or tea
towel and gently pat dry. Store at bottom
of refrigerator in paper or cloth bag,
but not plastic, lest they sweat.*

MINT By a wide margin, mint is the
most nutritional of any herb. Although its
taste is distinctly different, it can substitute
in most any Burmese dish where fresh
coriander/cilantro is specified, particularly
when used raw or uncooked. Choose
hearty round or blunt ended bright- or
light green peppermint, not darker fragile
spearmint. Lemon mint may also suit,
especially in seafood salads.

MUNG BEANS Dried mung beans,
or green- & golden gram, range from green
to yellow, and related black gram. Often
sprouted for additional nutrients. Whole
mung beans retain their color, while split
beans after hulling become uniformly beige
to yellow. They are sometimes confused
with yellow split peas (*channa dal*).
While all are mild in flavor and generally
interchangeable, cooking times vary.

**MUSTARD, PICKLED (SWATOW
CABBAGE)** Chinese in origin, this is cured
in a simple sugar, salt and vinegar brine
to retain a unique crunchiness with a
sharp mustardy flavor. Available in Asian
supermarkets in large crocks as well as in
air-tight plastic bags and canned. Rinse and
squeeze well before using.

**MUSTARD SEED, BROWN &
YELLOW** Indian origin, rarely used in
ethnic Burmese dishes, except pilaf.

MUTTON: GOAT This is a misnomer,
as in Myanmar usage it invariably
means goat, and with no reference to age.
Elsewhere, goat is available from Middle
Eastern butchers, or select European and
Asian butcheries. Female is milder in flavor
than male, but surprisingly, the goat taste is
much less pronounced than lamb. Substitute
yearling beef or lamb, although the latter is
practically unknown in Myanmar cuisine.

NON-REACTIVE POT OR BOWL
Certain metals react adversely with
acids like vinegar and citrus, leading
to discoloration and off-flavors. Avoid
aluminum, copper, and unlined cast iron
(such as woks and fry pans) when using
acidic ingredients. Stainless steel and
enamel-coated ware do not react. Likewise,
plastic bowls don't react to acids, but
they are not suitable for stiffly beaten egg
whites.

NUTS Whether as a beer station snack,
or ground atop salads, dried peanuts seem
ubiquitous in Myanmar, and when not the
regional local crop, chickpea flour/besan
substitutes.

PEANUTS Burmese peanuts are small,
closer in size to "Spanish peanuts." They
are prone to rancidity if not used shortly
after purchase. Peanuts come roasted, fried,
raw and dried. In almost all cases, peanuts
should be both shelled and hulled before
using. For salads, crushed dried peanuts are
preferred. Chinese dried peanuts are pre-
packaged and commonly exported (albeit,
usually in shell), so look in Asian groceries
if you cannot find in your supermarket.

=== Technique ===
TOASTING NUTS
*Nuts are best toasted in the oven,
as stove top roasting requires a vigilant
hand and is prone to burning.*

TOASTING *Spread evenly on a baking tray and bake in a preheated medium high oven for about 8-12 minutes, or until very lightly golden. (Times vary depending on size of the peanut.) Stir occasionally during toasting to ensure all sides brown evenly. Turn out of tray immediately, and cool.*

FRYING *Un-hulled peanuts -- that is, with the secondary papery skin not removed -- are typically fried. Heat oil in a wok over medium heat until almost smoking. Add nuts and fry, stirring regularly, for about 3 minutes. Remove immediately with a slotted spoon and drain. Pat with paper towels to remove all excess oil.*

OIL is a fixture in Burman cuisine, and most visitors find dishes swimming in it. Even neighboring ethnic groups, such as Rakhine, Mon and Shan, state that their own cooking is less oily than Burmese dishes. Consequently, ensure you are using a premium oil in these recipes, for both health and taste -- ideally unrefined, or cold pressed sold at health food stores. Also, Myanmar dishes are unctuous because the oil film protects food from spoiling in air, as there is little refrigeration. This is likely to change with the country's progressive advancement, yet it's another reason to ensure using a quality oil that does not solidify when cold. Recipes in this book may use less oil than is traditional, but without compromising their authenticity.

VEGETABLE- AND SALAD OIL are generic terms for any light-tasting oil, and specifically excludes strong-tasting oils such as olive, macadamia, walnut and hazelnut. ("Light" mild-tasting olive oil is an option, but it's not authentic to any East Asian cuisine.) Typical international oil varieties include blended vegetable, canola, peanut, safflower, sunflower, soybean, grape seed and rice bran oils. None should have a strong taste. (Caution: some Chinese peanut oils are toasted and overpowering.)

SESAME OIL (SESSAMUM, TEELSEED, GINGELLY, TIL) Along with peanut oil, one of the two preferred oils for Burmese cooking. Cold-pressed sesame oil from health food stores is best, and never substitute toasted Chinese-style sesame oil, which imparts a strong flavor and is likely to burn. On the other hand, sesame oil in select dishes is first toasted over the stove to enhance flavor. Because sesame oil foams during frying, cooks may add a spoonful of lemon juice to the cooking oil. Sesame oil is also prized for its medicinal benefits.

PEANUT OIL is the preferred oil of choice, along with sesame oil. For best results, use a cold-pressed or un-refined peanut oil from the health food store.

CANOLA OIL (RAPESEED) continues to gain a foothold, and cold-pressed canola from Yunnan is suprisingly good.

PALM OIL Increasingly popular as a cheap import, its use in Burman cuisine is detrimental to health, due to the local diet's high oil consumption. Ironically, colonial traders promoted a brand named Cocogem "as it preserves the richness of foods without imparting flavor of its own" -- in other words, innocuously bland, and the antithesis of fragrant cold-pressed oils preferred in Myanmar cooking.

OKRA (LADY'S FINGERS, BHINDI) Mucilaginous green pods, especially so when cut and stewed in a curry. More commonly grilled or barbecued as a beer snack.

ONION & SHALLOT While both are in the same Allium genus, onions and shallots differ, with shallots having more pronounced flavor. As smaller bulbs tend to have a stronger taste, Burmese generally eschew the large and jumbo bulbs preferred overseas. Local onions are generally pink blushed to yellow, never dark red and rarely white.

Generally speaking, use shallots raw in salads, but larger onions for cooking. Small to medium onions are preferred in curries and other cooked dishes. For crisp fried "onion," use pink or golden shallots only.

Myanmar recipes call for frying shallots and onion (plus garlic and ginger) at the beginning of cooking to flavor oil, then reserving them to add later to the finished dish.

GREEN ONIONS (SCALLIONS, SPRING ONIONS) Long fresh shoots of onion family. Milder than onions, a bulb may or may not form at its base, depending on variety. Technically, spring onions have a large bulb, while green onions do not, although the term is sometimes used interchangeably. Green onions may be regionally mis-labeled *shallot* which creates all sorts of confusion; but these are different and not interchangeable. Peel away wilted outer layers, trim off roots; otherwise, all of the plant is eaten. Add at last minute to cooked dishes, or as garnish.

SALAD ONION A fresh peeled large onion, regionally available in chilled supermarket produce stands. They tend to be milder than dried onions with papery skin, although sweet Walla Walla, Vidalia, Maui and Kununurra varieties all suit. Salad onions are not actually used in Myanmar recipes, but make good substitutes especially when used raw in salads, as they do not overpower.

HINT Soak onions in iced water, prior to adding raw to a salad. This improves crispness, as well as moderating strong flavor.

SHALLOT (ESCHALOT, FRENCH SHALLOT) Resembling clustered tiny onions, shallots come both brown or gold, and more commonly in Myanmar, pink to purple. As with garlic, larger bulbs taste milder than smaller cloves. Overseas, there is an elephantine variety, confusingly called "golden shallot," and while easier to peel, its flavor is much diminished.

WEIGHT Un-peeled small onions at store weigh about 2 oz/60 g each; 1 medium onion = 4 oz/120 g; 1 whole bulb pink or golden shallot = 2 oz/60 g.

TECHNIQUE

PEELING SMALL ONIONS & SHALLOTS

Use a paring knife to slice the top and tail of the bulb. Pour boiling water over the bulbs and allow to cool. Drain, and pinch the end of the bulb to extract the whole onion or shallot. Note: This method is not recommended when crisp frying onions and shallots, as it creates extra moisture.

PANDAN (pandanus, screwpine) Long green leaf popular throughout SE Asia, used especially to flavor desserts, but also in some savory dishes. Typically, It is scrunched and added to liquid dishes, or while boiling rice, and its extract/ essence used to flavor sweets. (If you see bright green cake at an Asian bakery, it is likely pandan flavor.) Store surplus fresh leaves in the freezer, or throw one into the back of your car window in the sun, as a natural air freshener. Technically, the word pandanus is restricted to thatched roofs and fencing.

PAPAYA, GREEN Unripe or green papaya (as well as mango) is grated and tossed into salads, and sometimes into stews or curries. On its own it tastes slightly astringent, but when blended with other ingredients, such as a fish sauce dressing, it becomes deliciously crunchy like tart apple. Do not substitute ripe nor semi ripe papaya. If unavailable, use green apple or nashi pear.

PONYEGYI Fermented soy bean powder; a staple in Burmese grocery stores. Typically, 1-2 tablespoons ground dried bean wafers are added to soups, noodles and curries, or as a condiment. Vaguely similar to miso.

POMELO *is drier in texture than grapefruit, and thus ideal for salads because it doesn't create running juices. It's also less bitter than grapefruit*

TECHNIQUE

SECTIONING GRAPEFRUIT & POMELO

1. Grapefruit is pared with a sharp knife to remove both peel and bitter pith. First slice off top and bottom of the fruit. Then pare away the sides of the grapefruit skin, barely cutting into the flesh. You will end up with a whole "naked" grapefruit. Insert your knife blade between the flesh of one section and its outer membrane, and gently cut to the "core" of the fruit. Repeat this process on its counter side to release the segment whole. Discard the membrane core or juice for other purposes.

2. Use a sharp paring knife to slice off top or cap of the pomelo -- about 1/2 inch (1.5 cm) into the skin, but not cutting into flesh. Cut vertical slices down the sides of the pomelo -- about four or five sections in all -- again, just cutting through the rind, but not into the flesh. Use fingers to pry away the thick skin. Then gently break the pomelo into sections, by plunging your finger into the dimpled core, then pulling out. Use a paring knife to help pull away any bitter pith.

RICE is the mainstay of Southeast Asian diets, and no meal is complete without its presence, either as rice noodles or steamed grain. Colonial Burma's delta region was prized as the rice basket of the British Empire, but today little is exported. As much of the colonial rice production was geared for overseas rice pudding consumption, the favored variety was round- or short grain rice. This is still prized, but its high price point means its use has greatly diminished, with medium grain the most popular today. Thai Jasmine and Chinese long grain rice are not popular. Unbroken grains fetch a premium, and rice from the previous harvest is especially favored, as new crop rice tends to cook soggy.

PLAIN RICE This is a catch-all term applied to standard white rice grains that are cooked similarly; in other words, short-, medium- and long grain. Jasmine is a variant strain of plain long grain rice.

MEDIUM GRAIN RICE Most commonly consumed today because it is considered lighter than long grain -- an especially important consideration when accompanying richly unctuous dishes.

STICKY RICE Slightly smaller in size, glutinous rice is chalky in appearance; it is soaked for hours prior to steaming over water. As its name implies, it clings solidly.

BLACK RICE Also a sticky variety, is generally relegated to dessert dishes. Soaking prior to use belies its color, as it's actually deep purple. Usually soaked then steamed, or sometimes boiled as a gruel-like pudding.

BROWN RICE is hulled or semi hulled. Cheaper than white rice, it is consumed particularly by the poor. Local lore claims it assists diabetics, which has become a major health concern of modern Myanmar.

RICE STARCH *see Flour & Starch*

SAGO *see Tapioca*

SHALLOT *see Onion*

SAFFRON & SAFFLOWER These are not interchangeable, although cheap safflower (bottom left) is sometimes sold as generic saffron. It is used as a natural coloring in stews and curries, but the richer red hue imparts no extra flavor. Alternatively, mild chili is ground with salt and sold in small packets labeled *yaung tin* for similar effect (left).

SAFFRON By contrast, true (and very expensive) saffron (bottom right) comes as strands or stamens, or as a powder. Its fragrance is overpowering, and only a little is used in cooking. For best results, dissolve in a spoonful of boiling water before adding to dishes. Some cooks also recommend grinding stamens prior to using, but this easily results in as much left behind in the mortar as in the dish. Because of its cost, little true saffron is used in ethnic Burmese cooking today, and rarely

in ethnic Indian cooking within Myanmar.

SCALLION *see Onion*

SOY SAUCE (SOYA SAUCE, SHOYU; PE NANPYA-YE) Imparts a salty, robust flavor to stir fries (especially those with a Chinese influence), stews and curries. It is also used in vegetarian dishes when fish sauce is inappropriate, such as in monasteries. When Burmese recipes call for generic soy sauce, use Chinese light style or *tamari;* otherwise dark-, and thick sweet are specified.
STYLES There are three basic soy sauces types: light, dark and sweet/thick. Standard Chinese soy sauce contains about 10% wheat, while Japanese shoyu has a much high ratio of wheat to soy bean -- nearly half. Traditional Japanese tamari contains under 10% wheat, but overseas brands now market wheat-free varieties. Confusion arises when Chinese and Japanese terminology conflict.
NATURALLY BREWED Most importantly, purchase only naturally-brewed brands; take special care by reading labels, as some brands promote blends of natural plus chemical brews. (By law, all Japanese shoyu is guaranteed naturally brewed.) Avoid any labels that list "hydrolized" as a component; moreover, soy sauce should contain few ingredients: water, soy, wheat, salt and sugar. All chemical additives and flavor enhancers are both unnecessary and undesirable. In countries where preservative sodium benzoate is banned, use within 1 month after opening, or refrigerate up to 6 months. After that, the flavor rapidly deteriorates.
LIGHT Japanese light- and Japanese dark shoyu are both similar in character to Chinese light soy. (Japanese dark is the ubiquitous Kikkoman sold overseas.) These styles are best at table when adding light saline flavor; but to be closest to Chinese/Burmese style, use tamari or Chinese light.
CHINESE DARK is preferred for cooking, when a more robust taste is desired, as in stir fry. Generic Japanese also substitutes.
THICK SWEET SOY SAUCE (KECAP MANIS) May or may not have soy as an ingredient, as it is basically cooking caramel. It is especially popular in slow braises and stews. Thick sweet brands vary from 0%

soy in Chinese "cooking caramel", to 2% in popular Indonesian brands, and some 20% soy in quality marques.

SPROUTS *see Bean Sprouts*

SHRIMP & PRAWNS Technically, shrimp are small prawns, and prawns large shrimp.
DRIED SHRIMP come in various sizes, from less than 1/4 inch (6 mm) to triple that size. Typically, large dried shrimp are sweeter, while small ones are saltier. They are sold unrefrigerated in Asian grocers. Soak for 15 minutes prior to using, but for best hygiene, rinse with boiling water, drain, then add to various dishes. Reconstituted dried shrimp should be refrigerated and used within a couple of days. If unavailable, omit entirely, or substitute chopped fresh shrimp. For shrimp floss and powder, do not soak; merely pound, or buy commercially. Less common are dried shrimp in the shell. Soak whole, retaining the shells for crunchy eating.

======= TECHNIQUE =======
DE-VEINING & BUTTERFLYING
1. *De-veining removes the gritty intestinal tract running along the back of fresh shrimp and prawns. This is done by pulling off the shell, then using a small paring knife to lightly score along its back, exposing the vein. Gently pull to remove.*
2. *Cutting shrimp deeply along its curled stomach, but not completely through, allows the meat to open up like a butterfly during cooking, hence its name. Butterflying works best with jumbo shrimp/ king prawns. For aesthetic reasons, do not remove the shrimp tail.*
==========================

SHRIMP PASTE (NGAPI) A pungent, darkly-colored, dense paste made from fermented prawn, and a valuable source of protein -- especially as it does not require refrigeration. Only a small amount is needed to flavor dishes, but ideally, dry-fry or bake in oven prior to use. When unavailable, delete or use anchovy paste

~ although the latter is very salty. It is also eaten as is, with fresh vegetables, or as a dipping sauce base.

=== TECHNIQUE ===
TOASTING SHRIMP PASTE

Toasting enhances the aroma, but it is an optional step for foreigners, who may prefer a subtler, less pronounced smell. Wrap a small amount of paste in a foil parcel and roast in a hot oven for about 10 minutes, or on the stove in a pan over medium high heat for 1 minute, stirring constantly. For large quantities, fry directly in an un-oiled non-stick skillet, turning vigorously as if making re-fried beans.

SESAME *see Oil*

SEMOLINA, COARSE & FINE
Derived from durum wheat, semolina's flavor improves with roasting, especially in cakes. Generally speaking, both coarse and fine varieties are used interchangeably in these recipes. Substitute cream of wheat porridge.

SPICES *see Curry Powder & Masala*

STOCK *see also pages 256-259*
Generic Burmese stock is weaker than Western counterparts. It is made variously with dried shrimp, chicken and/or pork, or just from vegetables. The safest bet is to use weak chicken stock throughout, or very watery fish stock/fumet, or water.

SUGAR & PALM SUGAR
The town of Kyaw Badaung near ancient Bagan is renowned for its sugar production, hence the term "kyaw badaung" style when requesting a very sweet tea. If palm sugar is unavailable, substitute an equivalent quantity of white sugar or firmly packed light-brown sugar.

PALM SUGAR There are two mainstays here. First, coconut palm, the ubiquitous and pan-tropical coconut found across Southeast Asia and Polynesia. The Palmyra or Toddy palm, by contrast, is favored for its fruits and is the source of palm sugar desserts. Less known is that toddy syrup is an important ingredient in Myanmar

traditional medicines (a bit like Mary Poppins old explanation "a spoon full of sugar makes the medicine gone down"). If palm sugar is especially hard to grate, it has probably been blended with cheaper cane sugar.

JAGGERY Palm sugar is boiled down and rolled into little balls known by its Indian name. Young jaggery is lighter in color and eaten as a snack with tea, especially after a meal. Dark jaggery, over nine months aged, is firmer and used in cooking.

WHITE & BROWN SUGAR is made from cane, although sugar beet is interchangeable. Slabs of lightly caramelizedd brown cane sugar are sold in village markets for sweet dishes. Although milder in flavor, brown cane sugar can substitute if palm sugar is unavailable.

TAMARIND
There are two sorts of tamarind: sour and sweet, each coming from different trees of the same family; only sour is used in these recipes. Besides the pods, all parts of the tree are used. Its wood produces the finest chopping boards, its tender leaves used in salad and soup. Tamarind fruit pods are variously a souring and sweetening agent, used both to flavor broth as well as a candy base. It is often blended with shallots, onion, chili and garlic, and served as a table dipping sauce.

PASTE AND PUREE are very sour. Sold in block form paste, it requires dilution in water and straining. Ready to use commercial tamarind puree and thinner "water" are both available at supermarkets, plus Indian, Middle Eastern and Southeast Asian grocers. Because there can be a difference in sourness between store bought and home-made puree, quantities required are variable.

=== TECHNIQUE ===
EXTRACTING TAMARIND
PUREE & JUICE
Put a golf ball-sized chunk of tamarind puree in a bowl and cover with an equal quantity water. If the pulp is very soft, you can do this with cool water. If a hard

compressed block, use hot water. Use your fingers to break the pulp apart, and when thoroughly dissolved strain through a coarse mesh, discarding solids and pips.
HINT *If your tamarind paste is brick hard (this depends on your local market) soften it with a little water in the microwave; gently on low to medium in 10 second bursts.*

TAPIOCA & SAGO

STARCH/FLOUR Made from manioc or cassava tuber (also known as yucca). It is first turned into a starchy flour, and used in steamed cake for chewiness and sheen; to thicken sauces; or to coat meat prior to cooking. Substitute with arrowroot or corn starch (corn flour).

TAPIOCA PEARLS are formed from the same flour or starch, then shaped and dried to create pearls. It commonly comes in two sizes: small grain, which resembles "instant" tapioca, and larger pearls of "bubble tea" fame. Commercial Minute(R) or "instant" tapioca is par-boiled or steamed, so cooking time is reduced.

TOFU & BEAN CURD

These terms are not interchangeable in Burmese usage.
BURMESE TO HU/TOFU, is yellow not white, and is made from chickpea, not soy bean. It has an entirely different texture and flavor than soy bean curd, and is relatively fragile, more like a quivering jelly; Shan versions are downright soft like porridge. Substituting soy curd tofu is not an authentic option, although better than nothing.

BEAN CURD Firm white bean curd is made from soy, and is especially popular among Chinese ethnic groups in Myanmar. It is made from coagulated soy milk pressed to create curds.

SOFT OR SILKEN CURD is likewise made from soy bean albeit yellowish. It is now commercially manufactured in Myanmar, but is not traditionally used in local cuisine, although this is beginning to change, especially in eateries frequented by foreigners.

USAGE Burmese to hu/tofu is added to salads, and it is coated with tempura batter then deep fried (but not applicable when set with agar, as it may dissolve when heated.)

It is never stir fried, as it is too fragile. Soy bean curd is invariably mixed with other ingredients, but rarely in salads. It is firm enough to withstand rigorous stir frying, and can also be deep fried, with or without tempura batter. Soft or silken bean curd occasionally makes an appearance in Burmese fusion soups, and is sometimes cut into small rounds, coated with rice flour or tempura batter and pan fried. It's most popular in ethnic Chinese desserts, soups and broths.

STORAGE In Asia tofu and bean curd are eaten very fresh, usually consumed the day of manufacture and have an inherent sweetness. Burmese chickpea tofu is eaten within 1 day of production, if not refrigerated; soy bean curd can be stored longer. Soft or silken bean curd must be refrigerated at all times. Overseas, bean curd usually comes refrigerated packed in water, both in hard and soft varieties. As long storage leads to sourness, this should be countered by soaking in repeated changes of fresh water, or better yet, salted, parboiled then drained.

TOMATO From small cherry-size to medium, firm tomatoes are preferred, often slightly green. While Burmese tomato condiments and sauces are regularly cooked with skin and seeds, some cooks prefer the finer approach. If unseasonably sour, add a pinch of sugar to any savory dish calling for tomato. Adding shrimp paste is also common to tomato dishes.

=== TECHNIQUE ===
PEEL & SEEDING TOMATO
Use a paring knife to core, then score a shallow X on its bottom. Plunge into a pot of boiling water for 10-15 seconds, then immediately drain and refresh in iced water. The skin should easily remove. To seed for salads, cut into quarters and use your finger tip to scoop out seeds. To seed for sauce, halve crosswise and squeeze to extract seeds and excess liquid; strain resulting liquid and cook.

TURMERIC, ALLEPPEY

Throughout East Asia, turmeric is commonly used to counter the smell of fish.

In Myanmar, alleppey turmeric is the variety of choice. If unavailable at your store, order it from a spice merchant. Compared to its pale yellow Madras cousin, alleppey is richer in curcumin, therefore stronger, darker, and cakey textured. Like galangal and ginger, fresh turmeric is a rhizome which grows underground like a root. Pound fresh turmeric, soak in a little water, then strain by pressing through a sieve; use the resulting water and discard the pulp.

VINEGAR Asian vinegars are less acidic than Western counterparts, averaging 5% acid, compared to a French standard of 7%. Consequently, local salads are less astringent. Unless specified otherwise, use white vinegar made from rice, palm or coconut; when using distilled vinegar dilute with a spoonful of water, or more. Locals also use bottled lemon juice in place of vinegar.

WHITEBAIT see Anchovy

WOK A conical Chinese cook pot, especially for stir frying. Even better is the kadhai, or Indian wok, which is made of thicker gauge (and much easier to season, see Technique). Unlike pottery, such as the traditional dae-ooh rounded pot (about half the size of a water jug), metallic pots and pans allow for high heat stir frying. Although flat bottom aluminum pots are typical in the Burmese kitchen, woks and kadhai are increasingly common, especially in commercial kitchens and in Indian- and Chinese- ethnic eateries. As a rule, use conical woks when frying small quantities, especially as it consolidates less oil in a concentrated heat area, while flat bottom pans will disperse. Likewise, woks help contain foods within the vessel during potentially sloppy stir-frying, when ingredients tend to fly.

=== TECHNIQUE ===
SEASONING A NEW WOK,
FRYPAN OR SKILLET
Cast iron and carbon steel pans require "seasoning" with oil prior to first use, lest foods stick. Stainless steel does not require this treatment; in fact, stainless steel woks are not recommended as they stick intolerably. Alternative surfaces such as enamel coating do not require pre-seasoning.

1. Use a paper towel to wipe generously with oil, and place over high heat until smoking. Immediately plunge into hot water, then return to the flame to dry. Wipe again with oil and repeat these steps a total of three times. At no time should you use soap.

2. To keep the wok clean, plunge into hot water immediately after use, scouring with a plastic, natural fiber, or non-metallic brush. Never use soap, as this requires you to season all over again. Do not wipe dry, rather place the wok or pan over a low flame to dry. Wipe or spray lightly with oil and store; this helps prevent rusting.

3. When cooking in cast iron, always preheat the wok or skillet before adding any ingredients, including oil. After adding oil, rotate the pan to spread it to all sides, then heat before adding anything else. Because of a wok's conical shape, gas flame is preferable to electric, as it disperses the heat upward along the sides of the wok. Gas also allows instant regulation of heat.

WINTER MELON see Gourd

YOGURT & DAIRY CURDS
There is a wealth of Indian dairy products that were adopted by the Burmese, pot-set yogurt being the most popular. Source a full fat non-sweetened active enzyme variety from your store. (Buffalo-milk yogurt is richer than cow milk yogurt, so choose accordingly). For thicker curds, tie in a muslin or cheesecloth bag, hang overnight, to remove excess liquid whey. (If unpasteurized, you can do this at room temperature; otherwise, hang refrigerated.) Drained lebne also substitutes, but is more tart. Italian ricotta is another substitute for dairy curds, although sweeter in a non-sugary sense; drain as above before using.

"But the Burmese is not only a large eater, but of very gregarious tastes. Let us note in their order the commodities that are displayed as we proceed; their variety is itself indicative of the tastes of the people. . . radishes, roselle, cucumbers, lemon grass, onions, flowers for ornament, for offerings at the pagodas, and for condiments with or without food. Here are strange soft, unpleasant-looking eggs; they have no calcareous shell, and are decidedly suspicious in appearance; they are those of tortoise and turtle found near and in the neighbouring river, and are said to be highly esteemed as a delicacy by the people. Now we find in close succession tomatoes, tamarinds, French beans, and lemons. Plantains there are in myriads, -- some au naturel, others fried, steeped in oil, and otherwise prepared; for they seem to constitute a principal article of food. Next we come to heaps of cocoanuts divested of the outer husks. Some of them have begun to sprout; and we learn that the enlarged germen found in the interior of such, locally called "the flower," is by the natives esteemed as a particular delicacy. We taste the morsel. It is mawkish and insipid. As if to neutralize this, green and red chillies are spread upon an adjoining table; next to them oranges, pomelos, water-melons, ginger in various forms, preserved fruit and sweets -- the latter by no means bad, and quite free from the peculiar bazaar taste that distinguishes similar preparations in India. And there are yams, the edible arum, sweet potatoes, large jack fruits, -- and finally potatoes, imported from Calcutta, for as yet the tuber is not successfully raised in British Burmah. Elsewhere we see shelves laden with fish of different kinds, obtained from the streams and estuaries in their neighbourhood. Their local names are peculiar, and therefore a few may be enumerated, -- including, as they do, carp, hilsa, prawns, dog fish, cat fish, butter fish, mud fish, cock up, sable, and so on."

-- Charles Alexander Gordon, *Our Trip to Burmah,*
With Notes on that Country (1875)

Measurements

Myanmar retained Britain's Imperial measures well into the 21st century, leaving it the world's last official user of Britain's archaic system. While the US and Liberia were fellow recalcitrants, Britain's (and Myanmar's) system differed from America's in pint and gallon, although linear measurements like miles, feet and inches remained equal. This system is now replaced by metrics almost universally. But there is another holdout. Somewhat like "I love you, a bushel and a peck" ~ the American country song equating love with old harvest measures ~ vis and tical weights remain in local daily use, with pounds and ounces eschewed.

1 vis = $3^{1}/_{2}$ lbs = 1.6 kg

100 tical = 1 vis = 3 lbs 9 oz = 1600 g/1.6 kg

10 tical = $4^{3}/_{4}$ oz = 160 g

1 tical = $^{1}/_{2}$ oz = 16 g

US and metric cup measurements used in this book are similar and generally interchangeable, with the notable exception of baking, when precise measurement equivalents are sought. Use either imperial or metric when preparing each recipe, but do not use both, as equivalents are not exact.

1 teaspoon = 5 ml

1 tablespoon* = 15 ml

1 cup = 250 ml = 8 fl oz

* *1 metric tablespoon is officially 20 ml, not 15, but most countries follow the 15 ml size, which is equivalent to the Imperial original.*

For alcoholic drinks
1 jigger = 1 shot = 3 tablespoons = $1^{1}/_{2}$ oz = 45 ml = 4.5 cl = 0.45 dl

Opium weights For half a millennium, if not longer, traditional Myanmar measurements took the shape of birds, occasionally reptiles and animals, and even rarer, flowers or plants. The actual design varied, depending on the reign of each new king. Commonly ~ albeit inaccurately ~ referred to as "opium weights," they were used at market to gauge the weight of items sold commercially.

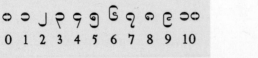

0 1 2 3 4 5 6 7 8 9 10

TEMPERATURE

250^0 F = 120^0C = Gas Mark $1/2$

275^0 F = 140^0 C = GM 1

300^0 F = 150^0 C = GM 2

325^0 F = 160^0 C = GM 3

350^0 F = 180^0 C = GM 4

375^0 F = 190^0 C = GM 5

400^0 F = 200^0 C = GM 6

425^0 F = 220^0 C = GM 7

450^0 F = 230^0 C = GM 8

475^0 F = 250^0 C = GM 9

500^0 F = 260^0 C = GM 10

LENGTH

$1/8$ inch = 3 millimeter

$1/4$ inch = 6 mm

$1/2$ inch = 1.2 centimeter

1 inch = 2.5 cm

$1^{1/4}$ inch = 3 cm

$1^{1/2}$ inch = 3.75 cm

$1^{3/4}$ inch = 4 cm

2 inch = 5cm

4 inch = 10 cm

8 inch = 20 cm

10 inch = 25 cm

12 inch = 30 cm

WEIGHT

$1/2$ oz = 15 gram

1 oz = 30 g (actual 28.34)

2 oz = 60 g (actual 56 g)

$2^{1/2}$ oz = 75 g (actual 70 g)

3 oz = 100 g (actual 85 g)

4 oz = 125 g (actual 113 g)

6 oz = 170 g (actual 170 g)

7 oz = 200 g (actual 198 g)

8 oz = 250 g (actual 225 g)

10 oz = 300 g (actual 310g)

12 oz = 350 g (actual 340g)

14 oz = 400 g (actual 396 g)

1 lb (16 oz) = 500 g (actual 453 g)

$1^{1/4}$ lb = 625 g (actual 566 g)

$1^{1/2}$ lb = 750 g (actual 680 g)

$1^{3/4}$ lb = 875 g (actual 793 g)

2 lb = 1 kg (actual 907 g)

$3^{1/2}$ lb = 1.5 kg (actual 1.58)

TEASPOON / CUPS

$1/8$ teaspoon = pinch

$1/4$ teaspoon = 1 milliliter

$1/2$ teaspoon = 2 ml

1 teaspoon = 5 ml

(3 teaspoons = 1 tablespoon)*

1 tablespoon = 15 ml (not 20 ml)*

(4 tablespoons = $1/4$ cup)*

$1/4$ cup = 60 ml = 2 fluid ounce (actual 59 ml)

$1/3$ cup = 90 ml = 3 fl oz (actual 88 ml)

$1/2$ cup = 125 ml = 4 fl oz (actual 118 ml)

$2/3$ cup = 175 ml = 6 fl oz (actual 177 ml)

$3/4$ cup = 200 ml = 7 fl oz (actual 207 ml)

1 cup = 250 ml = 8 fl oz (actual 236 ml)

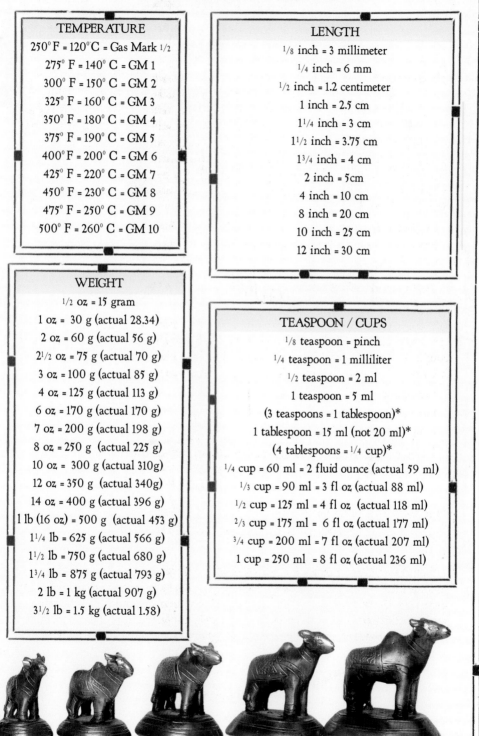

INDEX

INDEX

INDEX

INDEX

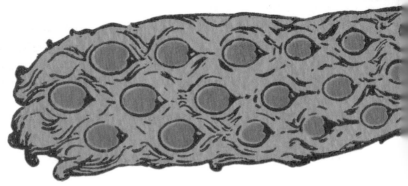

photo insert: Sher-Ali Khan

for updates & apps,
register with us
www.BurmaCookbook.com

ရောဘတ် ကားမက်
ROBERT CARMACK
မောရစ်ဆင် ပေါ်ကင်ဟွန်းနံ
MORRISON POLKINGHORNE

With equal aplomb, Robert Carmack
& Morrison Polkinghorne can arrange
a rare tour of the Japanese emperor's
private soy sauce brewery, sit down to enjoy a multi-course
meal of cobra in a tiny restaurant in rural Vietnam, and prepare a
Burmese style curry with the hill tribes of Myanmar and Thailand. The
duo organize and host Globetrotting Gourmet® culinary tours, uncovering
Southeast Asia's food treasures. www.GlobetrottingGourmet.com

First published and distributed in 2014 by
River Books Co. Limited
396 Maharaj Road, Tatien, Bangkok 10200
Tel (66) 2 225-4963, 2 225-1039, 2 662-1900
E-mail: order@riverbooksbk.com
www.riverbooksbk.com

ISBN: 978 616 7339 38 2

Editor (Text): Narisa Chakrabongse
Editor (Recipes): Di Parks
Design: Morrison Polkinghorne

Printed and bound in Thailand by
Bangkok Printing Co., Ltd

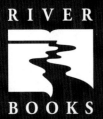

RIVER

BOOKS